DESIGN YOUR HOME for LIVING

DESIGN YOUR HOME for LIVING

Mabel B. Trilling

Florence Williams Nicholas

J. B. LIPPINCOTT COMPANY

Chicago   •   Philadelphia   •   New York

6 45
T 82

About the Authors

MABEL B. TRILLING: formerly Professor of Home Economics Education, Carnegie Institute of Technology.

FLORENCE WILLIAMS NICHOLAS: Lecturer, Division of Education, Carnegie Institute.

Printed in the United States of America

Preface *356 26*

This book was written in the hope that it will bring to young people the pleasurable and profitable experience of creating beautiful and livable homes. Better home life is urged on every hand by those who seek to raise the moral and spiritual standards of modern youth. While the authors do not believe that a formal study of interior and exterior home design will result directly in a higher level of ethical behavior, they do believe that young people who learn how to plan and work for attractive and comfortable homes may find personal fulfillment through a highly advantageous hobby and enjoy the satisfaction of the truly creative art experience. In each of us there springs an instinctive desire to leave our mark upon the world. A definite and organized study of home art projects can help to satisfy this craving for personal expression and can at the same time result in better life for the American family.

Design Your Home for Living has been organized into teaching units which repeatedly have been found effective. Chapter 1 is a short inspirational discussion giving a preview of the whole book. It points out briefly how the student will find the study of beauty in the home pleasant and profitable. Chapter 2 deals with the principles of art and establishes these concepts in the minds of the students. Chapter 3 emphasizes the very close relation between art quality and utility. Chapter 4 deals with color theory and color harmony as it applies to the various problems of home and garden. The remaining chapters in the book point out how the principles of design and color harmony can be applied to specific problems in home furnishings, ranging from accessories for a dinner table to rugs, curtains, and furniture. The design of the house itself is discussed, including wall treatments, floor plans, exterior design, and garden effects.

The method of approach to each of the teaching problems is the one which has proved most effective in the experience of the authors. When interior design was first introduced into the school curriculum, the courses almost always involved much drawing and painting of wall elevations and perspective views. Gradually, teachers have come to realize that few people have need for this technique in planning their homes. They realize, too, that drawing and painting do not necessarily result in good taste. Why, then, require hours of bungling attempts at wall eleva-

v

tions? The old precept that we "learn to do by doing" holds true in this case. We learn to discriminate between good and poor design by practice and experience in selecting the best among many samples of china, silver, furniture, fabrics, and houses. This book suggests many ways in which students can be given this type of experience.

The text also emphasizes the importance of actual materials as part of the learning process. Whenever possible, real curtains, dishes, accessories, wallpaper, and other easily transported objects should be brought into the classroom and discussed regarding their design and color. At other times the class should take trips to see furniture exhibits, model rooms and houses, gardens, and installations of lighting fixtures, bathrooms, and kitchen equipment. Many carefully selected pictures of these things are included in the text, but pictures never can take the place of the real objects. The alert teacher also will find other ways of providing her pupils with opportunities for experiences in discrimination between good and poor design and color of actual house furnishings.

Special attention has been given in *Design Your Home for Living* to beauty of design and color in the less expensive price range. The student is encouraged to look for good design and fine color in the dime store as well as the specialty shop. People should learn that a high price is not a guarantee of beauty. The authors believe that genuine beauty in the home is within the reach of a family with a moderate income. Discriminating taste, not money, produces the charming, livable home.

The illustrations in this text include articles from the ten-cent stores as well as those from the museums. To the sophisticated art critic the simple "art objects" from the dime store may seem trivial, but to the average young person they are important. They may not be great art, but they are the kind of art which young people understand and encounter in their everyday lives. After all, the selection of good design and color in a ten-cent glass tumbler may lead to the better appreciation of priceless glass in the art museum.

Design Your Home for Living is based in part upon the textbook entitled *Art in Home and Dress* by the same authors. Typical of the difference between the two books, however, is the emphasis placed in this text upon the modern or contemporary style in homes and home furnishings. The authors have made provision for the fact that young people are attracted to this style and will select furniture, fabrics, and other accessories in the new twentieth-century style.

Nevertheless impartial attention has been given to both the traditional and the modern styles of home furnishing. Students should learn that there is charm in both historic and contemporary designs of houses and their furnishings. Everyone may have his preference for a certain type of design, but at the same time enjoy good design and color in other forms. Open-mindedness plus discriminating taste provides many opportunities for the enjoyment of beauty wherever we find it.

vi

Contents

DESIGN YOUR HOME for LIVING

Chapter 1

MAKE YOUR HOME BEAUTIFUL

The place in which you live is a matter of circumstance. It may be a six-room house, a twenty-room mansion, or a two-room apartment. It may be located in a great city, far out in the country, on the rolling prairies of the Midwest, near the Atlantic seacoast, or high in the Rocky Mountains of the West. Within a few years the location of your home may change and you will find yourself in entirely new surroundings.

Wherever the spot may be, you naturally wish your home to be as lovely and livable as you can make it. There is something instinctive within each of us that craves beauty in our lives, and most of all within our homes. Remember always that no matter how large or how small your home and no matter where it is situated, you can find a way to make your home more beautiful. A bright flower garden in summer; fresh paint on dingy old furniture; or pretty, new place mats for the dining table can bring a bit of charm to a home that you consider unattractive. Beauty is easy to find when you have learned how to look for it.

YOUR PART IN MAKING YOUR HOME BEAUTIFUL. What role will you play in creating a pleasing home? Even while you are a junior home-maker, you can do much to make your home more pleasant to the eye. A new arrangement of furniture in your own room, providing greater convenience, more comfort, and better effect adds to pleasant living. This and other projects such as a new slip cover for a living-room chair or new color paint for the porch furniture help to make your home more attractive.

When you become chief homemaker in your own home, the main responsibility is yours for creating a livable home. Whether you live in a one-room apartment or a great house with many rooms, the responsibility of planning for beauty is yours. Of course, if you have a great deal of money you can hire architects, interior decorators, and landscape gardeners to plan your home for you.

But even with this help you will wish to know how to select that which is truly beautiful and avoid that which is only ostentatious and ornate. Most people prefer to do their own planning and to do some of the work themselves. Indeed, one of the homemaker's most interesting duties is to become a creative artist. It is she who selects the furniture and the draperies, arranges the rooms, chooses harmonious colors, and creates a beautiful, homelike effect. All this cannot be accomplished in a moment. It takes time to learn how to be a "home artist."

LEARN TO BE A "HOME ARTIST." The homemaker who creates a beautiful home is truly an artist. This does not mean that she paints beautiful pictures. It means that she knows how to hang pictures on her walls so that the effect is good. She need not know how to design interesting drapery fabrics, but she knows how to select the right patterns for her own windows and walls. She may not know how to do "hand-painted china," but she knows how to choose china, silver, table linens, and table accessories which make a delightful table setting. Instead of using brushes and paint to create pretty pictures, she uses furniture, rugs, curtains, wallpaper, and paint to create a room which is "as pretty as a picture." She knows how to select a house design that is good-looking and how to plan a garden that will enhance the house which it surrounds.

Do you not feel that a real artist planned the charming room shown on the opposite page? The soft, lovely colors and the simple, pleasing effect invite one to tarry a while in front of the fireplace. How to create such effects is the kind of art work that you will study to become a "home artist."

GOOD TASTE IS MORE IMPORTANT THAN WEALTH. Our world is full of objects, some of them ugly and some of them beautiful. The purchase of almost any object—a greeting card, a handkerchief, a davenport, an automobile—presents a problem in the choice of good design and color. If you know how to make the right selection, your satisfaction and enjoyment in the article will be much deeper.

It may seem to you that plenty of money is all that is necessary to secure the beautiful things of the world. This is not true. Many of

4

the most expensive selections which you might make for your home would result only in inartistic and gaudy rooms. On the other hand, many less expensive selections can bring genuine beauty into your home. Of course, many expensive things are beautiful and many cheap things are ugly. What makes the difference? How can you select wisely? The answer is: *standards of good taste.*

Unfortunately, we are not born with an instinctive ability to recognize and appreciate beauty. Psychologists tell us that we are born with the *ability* to appreciate, but *what* we appreciate is a matter of training. One person may enjoy raw, crude color combinations which to another are distasteful. One girl may like a desk lamp which she calls "precious" or "cute," but judged by standards of good taste the lamp is ugly.

This book is intended to give you experience in judging home furnishings, house designs, gardens, and many of the numerous articles, large and small, which are found in a home. Do not be discouraged if you cannot learn in a short time to judge these things for good design and color. Good taste is acquired gradually. You cannot memorize it as you do a multiplication table. You must learn some art rules and learn too how to use these rules in each new art problem that you meet. Gradually your art judgment will improve, and then you will be on your way to being an artist—an artist who uses furniture, fabrics, and accessories to create a beautiful home.

THE BIG ART MOMENT IN YOUR LIFE. Have you ever made something which gave you a thrill because it turned out so well? Have you made a model airplane that really was a beauty? Or have you completed a stamp collection with every page of your book in perfect order? If you like to draw, have you produced a picture that was a real gratification? Have you made a dress, a bag, a booklet, or a lampshade that gave you a great feeling of pride and pleasure?

Such thrills come from creative experience. Everyone likes to create something which is beautiful. As you study to become a home artist you will have many creative experiences that bring you satisfaction. Begin now, and work toward the time when you can look at your own home with a great feeling of achievement.

REMEMBER TO BE PRACTICAL. In your enthusiasm for beautifying your home, remember also to be practical. The delicate rose-pink rayon satin bedspread which you select for your room may not long continue to be attractive if you have the habit of sitting on the edge of your bed during the daytime or taking naps without removing the bed cover. It may be that your room is small and that there is not room for a comfortable chair, so that it is necessary to use the bed or couch for relaxing. In this case it is much more economical and generally satisfactory to choose a color and a material which will suit the purpose. This does not mean that you should select a dark, dreary color for the coverlet. Instead of a pastel-pink satin, you might choose a deep dusty-rose corduroy or a lovely blue-denim material. Both of these materials launder nicely and wear well.

There are dozens of such problems as these in the beauty treatment of a home. The selection of such items as draperies, rugs, paint for walls, a piece of furniture, or table china should be considered from the practical point of view before a decision is made. In the following chapters you will find that function or usefulness is always important in creating an attractive and livable effect.

Chapter 2

LAW AND ORDER IN ART

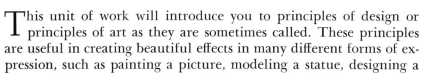

This unit of work will introduce you to principles of design or principles of art as they are sometimes called. These principles are useful in creating beautiful effects in many different forms of expression, such as painting a picture, modeling a statue, designing a dress, making a poster, or planning a room. Familiarity with these principles or laws will often help you to make up your mind in case of doubt. Suppose you are doubtful about the right color to choose for your dressing-table skirt. Your knowledge of the laws of art will help you to make the right decision.

You can think of the principles of design as laws which will help to make the right combinations and to avoid wrong ones. They are guides which help us to achieve *harmony, the aim of all art*. Harmony or unity is the result of law and order. First, we shall try to find out what is meant by harmony, and then to see how it results through the right use of the art principles.

The need for harmony

No effect in color or form is pleasing without harmony. In Christmas cards, houses, or hats it is the same: where there is beauty there is some kind of harmony.

Now let us see what is meant by harmony, and how we know it when we have it. Study the illustrations on the next page. At the top you see two pages from old photograph books showing a wrong and a right way to mount the snapshots. At the left, the pictures seem to be scooting around the page with no intention of settling down. On the

7

Wrong	Right
Wrong	Right
Wrong	Right

The difference between harmonious and inharmonious effects is illustrated here. Top: Pages from two photograph albums. Center: Two teacups. Bottom: Arrangements of articles on two dresser tops. In each case, the second effect is better because there is agreement among the parts of the design.

right, the pictures have found their proper place. Edges and corners conform to the rectangular shape of the page on which the pictures are mounted. The rectangular shapes agree with each other.

Below the two pages are two teacups of the same shape but with differently shaped handles. You will notice at once that the handle to the right seems to belong to the cup, and the effect is much more pleasing than in the design at the left where the handle does everything except echo the lines of the cup. It is all angles and the cup is all curves. The result, of course, is disagreement. In the second cup, there is a nice repetition of curves in the handle and the effect is harmonious.

The diagrams at the bottom show two ways to arrange articles on the top of a dresser or chest. At the left the arrangement is decidedly hit-and-miss. It has no order. Each article seems to have been dropped carelessly by someone in a hurry. In the second arrangement, the effect is orderly and interesting. Lines and shapes seem to agree with the boundary lines of the dresser and the white cover. The brush and comb have been removed to avoid cluttering the dresser top and for the sake of appearance.

> EXPERIMENT. Try this simple experiment to see if you can *feel* the difference between harmonious and inharmonious effects.
>
> 1. Place a piece of white paper so that it covers the row of "Right" arrangements on the right-hand side of the diagrams on page 8. Place another piece of white paper so that it covers the row of "Wrong" arrangements on the left-hand side. The papers should meet in the center of the illustrations.
> 2. Slide the left-hand piece of paper to the left so as to show the "Wrong" arrangements, and let your eye move slowly up and down over them. Cover them again.
> 3. Slide the right-hand piece of paper to the right so as to show the "Right" arrangements. Let your eye move up and down over them. Cover with the paper.
> 4. Do you honestly *feel* or *sense* a more satisfactory and pleasing effect in the "Right" arrangements?

BEAUTY OR UGLINESS AT THE SAME PRICE. The two filet lace doilies shown on the next page were found on the same counter at a bargain sale. Each one cost ten cents. They are equally durable and both launder well, yet one was a waste of money. Why? Because it is very poor and commonplace in design. The other was a real bargain because the design is interesting and unified in all its parts. Before reading further, can you pick out for yourself the doily which has a harmonious and well-related pattern? Try the same experiment that you used with the arrangements on page 8, covering first one doily and then the other. In which case do you feel there is an orderly and harmonious relation of parts?

Obviously you would would choose the upper one. Here the different parts of the design fill the space pleasantly. The center motif and

9

Good taste is essential for the wise shopper. These two doilies were sold at the same price, but only the upper one was worth the money. The lack of pleasing design in the lower one made it a waste of money.

10

the border look as if they belong together in the same pattern. But in the lower doily there is definite lack of unity between the oval shape and the rectangle in the center. The whole effect is unpleasant.

GOOD TASTE NEED NOT BE EXPENSIVE. Harmony need be no special strain upon our pocketbooks. In the case of the lace doilies, the good design cost no more than the ugly one. All that was needed was the good taste to make the right selection. In the case of the pages from two photograph books, it is evident that harmony costs nothing either in time or money. It takes no more time or paste to place snapshots harmoniously than to figure out the odd angles for "different" effects.

It sometimes happens that good taste helps us to *save money*. In the case of the two teacups, the first one cost more than the second. The "odd" handle made it more expensive. Actually, one could save 35 cents per teacup by selecting the good design. The shopper with good taste could also save time by quickly selecting the teacup with nice, harmonious lines. She would not hesitate between the "cute" handle on No. 1 and the harmonious lines of No. 2.

Certainly there is no time or money involved in placing articles on top of a dresser, at least very little time. It might take a wee bit longer to put your mirror and nail file straight with the world instead of just dropping them, but if you care about appearances it is time well spent. Besides, you may save time when you want a certain article because the things do not lie in a jumbled heap on top of your dresser.

ROOM FURNISHINGS SHOULD BE HARMONIOUS. Furnishing a room is a problem in design, and harmonious effect is just as important here as in a lace pattern or any other kind of design. The picture on page 12 shows the corner of a room in which there is a beautiful harmony of line and form. The straight lines of the chairs and bookcase, the geometric pattern of the rug, and the long, horizontal lines of the brick wall combine well with the lines of the ranch plank flooring to create a fine, straight-line harmony.

Notice how the whole design is made up of a series of well-related rectangles in the furniture, bricks, and floor. Even the books echo the rectangular motif. The curves of the plant-holder about the chairs and in the pattern of the draperies contrast pleasantly with the straight-line effect. One cannot help but feel that here is a room that was planned with thought for harmonious effect.

HARMONY IS IMPORTANT. It makes no difference whether we are dealing with teacups, rooms, or gardens, there must be harmony to create a beautiful effect. In other words, there must be *unity*. When harmony or unity is used as an art term, it has the same meaning as

This room has a fine harmony of straight lines and rectangular shapes expressed in the furniture, wall, rug, and floor.

it does when used in other connections. When tones in music are put together harmoniously, the result is pleasing to the ear. When a group of people live together without quarrels, they live harmoniously. Harmony or unity are terms which imply a pleasant relationship among the different elements which are put together to make a whole. In art we are concerned with harmonious relationships for the eye.

Your study to develop good taste and to become a home artist includes some experience in using the four principles of design: balance, proportion, rhythm, and emphasis. This will help you in understanding and creating harmonious relationships.

A PLAN FOR A NOTEBOOK OR PORTFOLIO. You may decide to keep a notebook or portfolio which will contain illustrations of the principles of art. You can find these in magazines and advertising literature. Your aim should be *quality rather than quantity.* It is better to have ten pages of really good illustrations than to have one hundred mediocre pages. It requires no particular intelligence to find *many* things to put in a notebook, but it requires real ability to make one or two selections which are exactly right.

Each page should be thought of as a design and should be well planned according to the principles of design. For example, we have already learned how harmony is secured through the correct use of line, shape, and color. The pages in your notebooks should express this quality. Instead of mounting pictures and writing paragraphs in a careless, haphazard fashion, arrange each page so that the pictures and writing will make one unified whole.

Select for the first page of your portfolio or notebook a picture or design which expresses harmony. Make your selection and show it to the class before putting it into your notebook. If your teacher and class do not approve you must select another illustration. You should take great pains in making your selection because it is through this kind of practice that you will develop better appreciation of good design.

A REPORT. Have you had the opportunity to use what you learned in your study of harmony in art? Perhaps you have rearranged the top of your dresser; perhaps you have made a purchase of a greeting card or a handkerchief or some other article; perhaps you have seen and enjoyed the harmonious lines and shapes in some common article, such as a sugar bowl, a lamp, or a book cover.

Balance: a principle of design

The word *balance* is familiar to all of us. It implies an equal distribution of weights on either side of a central point, and suggests a feeling of rest and stability. We like balanced effects. Good balance is desirable in many things besides artistic arrangements. A balanced diet is best for us. A well-balanced personality is most likable. The well-balanced person is stable, dependable, and interesting. The same thing is true in well-balanced pictures, rooms, costumes, posters, and flower arrangements. We like a feeling of stability and repose. It is more comfortable to look at.

The diagrams on the next page show some varying effects in balance. In the first diagram two little boys of equal weight sit at equal distances from the center of the seesaw. A bigger boy stands in the center with a foot on either side of the fulcrum. Both sides are exactly alike. This bisymmetrical arrangement is called *formal balance*. Notice that the weights are equal on both sides of the center and that they are placed at equal distances from the center. If either little boy should slide in toward the center, or if the big boy should lean to either side, the seesaw would tip. Our sense of balance and stability would be disturbed.

See what happens when the big boy jumps down from the center, runs to one end, and jumps on behind one of the little boys (center diagram). Down comes the board with a bang! The other little boy shoots up in the sky. This effect is decidedly not balanced!

If the big boy insists upon staying on one end of the seesaw, he and the little boy must move in toward the center in order to balance the board. This arrangement, shown in the bottom diagram, produces just as good balance as the arrangement in the first diagram. When the weights are unequal, then the distances from the center also must be unequal. *The heavier weight always moves in toward the center.* Remember this and it will help you in arranging furniture, in placing articles on a mantelpiece, and in planning decoration of many sorts. This kind of balance is called *informal* or *occult balance.* Its use requires more skill than simple formal balance because the unequal weights must each be placed at just the right distance from the center. However, the results are generally more interesting. If you have studied physics, you will remember the principle of the lever, that a lighter weight at the end of a longer lever arm will balance a heavier weight at the end of a shorter arm, and the rule *weight multiplied by distance equals weight multiplied by distance.* So in design a larger or more striking element located nearer the center balances a smaller or less striking element further out from the center.

FORMAL BALANCE HAS MANY USES. Simple bisymmetrical balance has many everyday uses. Most dresses, suits, and coats have formally

This diagram shows how the distribution of weight on a seesaw affects balance. Top: Formal balance. Center: Unequal weights at the same distance from the center destroy balance. Bottom: Unequal weights can be balanced by adjusting their distances from the center.

balanced designs. Many buildings are bisymmetric in plan. Many mantel arrangements are formally balanced. The simple arrangement of a copper plate and two brass candlesticks on page 16 is an example of formal balance. This type of arrangement is frequently used on mantels, bookcases, and dresser tops.

15

A simple arrangement expressing formal balance. The two brass candlesticks of the same weight are placed at equal distances from the copper plate in the center.

The old masters frequently made use of formal balance in their paintings. Fra Angelico's "Madonna and Angels," shown on the opposite page, is an example. The Madonna and child are placed in the center with an architectural canopy over their heads. Six angels are grouped on each side. The picture has an appealing charm partly because of the simple formal arrangement.

The davenport group shown on page 18 is arranged in terms of formal balance. The diagram below the picture shows the exact arrangement when viewed from a point directly in front. The davenport, coffee table, and Japanese print are in the center. Identical

Art Extension Society, New York, N. Y., and Westport, Conn.

In this painting, "Madonna and Angels" by Fra Angelico, formal balance is the basis of the arrangement.

objects, the end tables and lamps, are placed at equal distances from the center. The effect is at once stable and restful.

VARIATIONS IN FORMAL BALANCE. Formally balanced arrangements are sometimes made by using different objects of approximately the same size at equal distances on each side of the center. For example, a pot of ivy and a pottery vase may balance each other on the opposite ends of a mantel. Identical objects are not necessary if they are approximately the same size and have the same attracting power. Formal arrangements are often made more interesting by this method.

17

Good Housekeeping Studio

This group of furniture and decorative accessories illustrates formal balance.

Diagram showing how formal balance is obtained in the grouping shown above.

An arrangement of accessories on the top of a chest which shows a satisfactory informal balance.

THE INTERESTING QUALITIES OF INFORMAL BALANCE. If all pictures, designs, and other arrangements were bisymmetric, the law of balance would be quite simple to understand and use. Although formally balanced effects are nice, we do not want everything in our world arranged bisymmetrically. Pictures would be especially disturbing. Imagine all landscapes and portraits with formal balance! Or imagine all rooms, houses, or hats with both sides exactly alike!

The arrangement of objects in the painting shown on page 21 shows informal balance. The tiny arrows at the top and bottom of the picture indicate the center line. If you wish to understand more clearly how the composition is balanced lay a thread or string from arrow to arrow. (Do *not* draw a line across the picture.) The larger figure, that of the man, is nearer to the center, his shoulder extending over onto the left-hand side. This is balanced by the smaller figure of the woman, which is farther from the center. The pitchfork is mostly on the right-hand side but the house in the background is mostly on the left. This carefully planned balance of forms creates a very satisfactory feeling of stability. Observe that the forms over-

19

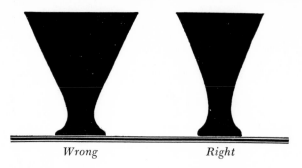

Wrong   Right

Silhouettes of two vases. The second one shows better vertical balance because it is not top-heavy.

lap. The pitchfork is in front of the man, the man is in front of the woman, and both figures are in front of the house. This overlapping of forms helps to create a feeling of unity. It "ties" the composition together. The same idea can be used successfully in arrangement of accessories on tops of chests, mantels, or sideboards.

This painting was done by an Iowa artist, Grant Wood, who liked to put into his pictures the people and the scenes of his native state.

Another arrangement with informal balance is shown on page 19. The larger weight, consisting of the pottery container, lilac branches, and tray, is much nearer the center of the chest than the smaller weight, consisting of the candlestick and little statue. Can you imagine the effect when the tray and container with the lilac branches are moved out to the left to the very edge of the chest? The chest tips up and the candlestick and statue fly into the air! This does not really happen, of course, but it *seems* that way.

BALANCE FROM TOP TO BOTTOM. Good balance from top to bottom as well as from side to side is necessary in order to produce a feeling of stability and repose. In other words, neither the top nor the bottom of a design should be too heavy for a good general effect. A simple illustration of this principle is shown in the two vases silhouetted at the top of this page. The first vase looks as though it would tip over easily, and, even though the bottom is weighted so that it cannot do so, the effect is unpleasant. A vase should look as though it could be depended upon to stay right side up. Now turn the book upside down and compare the vase designs. The one at the right now has a very wide base and a very narrow top. It looks awkward because the base is so much wider than necessary. Flower stems which were put into the narrow neck of the right-hand vase could not possibly need so much room at the bottom.

20

This famous painting, "American Gothic" by Grant Wood, was cleverly planned by the artist in terms of informal balance. The other art principles are also beautifully expressed in this painting.

21

Furniture in the modern style lends itself to arrangements of both formal and informal balance.

PROBLEMS IN BALANCE. Arrange for a class period when you will practice making balanced arrangements of articles on the top of some piece of furniture, such as a table, bookcase, or buffet. Bring candlesticks, vases, pictures, and other objects.

1. Make a formally balanced arrangement using identical objects on both sides.

2. Make a formally balanced arrangement using different objects of the same approximate size on the opposite sides.

3. Make an occult arrangement.

4. Add one or more pages to your notebook which will illustrate formal and informal balance. Label each example, telling what kind of balance is used. You will be able to find examples of balance in magazines and advertising materials.

5. What kinds of balance are expressed in the grouping of furniture shown above? Explain.

Proportion: a principle of design

Surely you have heard someone say about one thing or another, "It is out of proportion." He may have referred to a chimney that was too big for its house, or a lamp shade that was too big for its

22

base, or to something else. We are very sensitive to proportions even when we do not know it. We like harmonious proportions, and when one part of an object seems too large or too small for the other parts, we feel that something is wrong. With a little study we become even more sensitive to harmonious proportions.

On page 24 there are three rectangles. Think of them not as pictures, doors, or Christmas cards, but just as rectangles. One is square, one is long and thin, and one is about a third longer than wide. Which one do you like best? Choose the shape that you like best, not for a door or any other object, but simply the rectangle with proportions which seem most pleasing. When a group of people vote on this problem, the majority usually votes for the second rectangle. Most people may not know the reason for their preference. It is this: The proportions of a rectangle approximately 2 to 3 or 3 to 5 are most interesting.

In a square the length and width are equal. The effect is one of no variety and even of monotony. In a long, thin rectangle there is too much variety. The long sides and the little short ends are not harmonious because they are *too different*. Of course, this does not mean that a square or a long rectangle should never be used. There are places where each is suitable and pleasing. Nevertheless, when we have a choice, as in the shape of a picture or of a building, we prefer a rectangle neither square nor too long and thin but harmonious in proportions.

The aluminum tray and the pottery container which are shown on page 19 are excellent examples of pleasing proportions in house accessories.

The difference between interesting and uninteresting spacing is illustrated on page 25. Each rectangle is divided into three spaces. Which one do you like best? Most people choose the second one. In the first rectangle, the three spaces are equal and the effect is monotonous. In the third rectangle the little black spaces are too small to combine harmoniously with the big gray space. The effect is inharmonious.

In the second rectangle there is a more pleasing relationship between the dark and light spaces. There are many everyday places where this kind of spacing is found. For example, the diagram on page 25 might suggest the best spacing for window drapes. If the drapes are far across the window the spacing is uninteresting, and if they are pushed too far back the effect is inharmonious. Remember that equal spaces are monotonous and very unequal spaces are inharmonious.

23

Three rectangles of different proportions. Which one do you like best?

GOOD PROPORTIONS IN THE HUMAN BODY. Nature as well as man has created some designs in fine and interesting proportions. One good illustration of fine spacing is expressed in the normal human body. The waistline, which divides the body horizontally, is not halfway from the top of the head to the floor, but well above the center. The upper arm, lower arm, and hand are not equal in length; the longest distance is from shoulder to elbow, the forearm is about three-fourths as long as the upper arm, and the hand from wrist to finger tips is about three-fourths the length of the lower arm. Would it not seem strange to see an arm and hand divided into three equal parts?

Interesting proportions are found in other parts of the body. The length from knee to ankle is about three-fourths of the length from hip to knee. Bend your fingers and see if you cannot find the same relative proportions expressed in the length of the finger bones.

The interesting proportions of the human figure can be seen in "The Indian Warrior" shown on page 33. Notice particularly the beautifully gradated proportions of the arms from shoulder to finger tips and in the legs from hips to toes.

GOOD PROPORTIONS IN EVERYDAY THINGS. Most of us do not design great temples or produce bronze statues. However, we *can* use good spacing in many everyday art problems.

The room on page 26 is a good example of pleasing proportions. The coffee table in front of the large davenport is large enough to harmonize well. This is also true of the small tables at each end of the davenport. It often happens that the coffee table or end tables are too small to combine pleasingly with the bulk of the davenport.

Three different space divisions in the same rectangle. Which spacing is most pleasing to you?

The size of the picture above the davenport was well chosen for the wall space and for the group of furniture below. Some home artists might feel that the picture could be larger or that a group of small pictures could fill the space even more desirably.

We shall discuss this problem in more detail in a following chapter. Looking at the room as a whole, we feel that the furnishings are in proportion to each other and to the room. Another way of saying this is that the furnishings are *in scale*.

LEARN TO ENJOY PLEASING PROPORTIONS. You will have many moments of pleasure if you learn to see bits of beauty as you go about your daily activities. For instance, you may discover a beautiful doorway possibly on your own house, across the street, or on your way to school.

American Colonial architects designed some very handsome doorways, and their beauty has great appeal for us now. Contemporary architects have designed many entrances in the Colonial style. You will undoubtedly be able to find some of them in your own community.

Four of these doorways, designed in the Colonial tradition, are shown on page 27. Each of them has its own special charm, and you will like them all, even though one is your favorite. The beauty of a doorway depends considerably on the pleasing proportions of the design, and architects have found many ways to create beauty through arrangement of spacing.

The upper left entrance has simple charm which sets it apart from the commonplace. Notice first the two panels on the door. The two rectangles are in pleasing relation to each other, and each one is a pleasing shape. How ordinary the design would have been if the architect had merely divided the door into two equal panels! The

25

The pleasing quality of this room was produced partly by the selection of furniture which is well related in scale or size.

reeded pilasters (half columns) at each side add interest to the design without being ornate. The caps at the tops of the columns and the top moldings, or architrave, are also without decoration. The whole design depends for its beauty on *fine structural form.*

The entrance shown at the upper right is an adaptation of the fine doorways found on historic homes of Connecticut and Massachusetts. In the design the architect divided the door into four panels and again we find interesting spacing. The pilasters are flat and reeded, and the architrave has a bowed face. Notice that the tops of the upper panels are also bowed. Another interesting bit of fine spacing is shown in the dentil course just below the edge of the cornice. This type of decoration is really a row of small blocks set like a row of teeth. Notice that the space between the dentils is less than the width of the dentils, thus producing a much more interesting effect than if the spacing were even. You will see dentil decoration on many doorways and other parts of buildings.

Curtis Companies Incorporated, Clinton, Iowa

*These doorways, copied from old Colonial homes, are all beautifully propor-
tioned. Their charm lies in their fine spacing and simple, rhythmic lines. The
two upper doorways are severe in their simplicity but are no less beautiful than
the somewhat more elaborate doorways below.*

27

In the entrance shown at the lower left a dentil course extends across the cornice and caps above the columns. The door has been designed in eight panels but they are so spaced that the effect is unified. The transom above the door which admits light into the interior is a practical feature which is often desirable. Notice that it is divided into five small panes, a better spacing than six or four.

The doorway shown at the lower right is a distinguished design which includes glass panes set into the upper door panels. In this case the door has been divided into six panels which are beautifully related in shape and size. The upper part of the entrance is called a pediment. This architectural feature can be traced back through the centuries to the pediments of the Greek temples. As you study the fine spacing of this doorway design do not fail to notice the paneled decoration between the column caps above the door. The proportions between the plain panels and the reeded dividers are especially pleasing.

PROPORTIONS HELP GIVE CHARACTER TO DESIGN. What general effects in design do you prefer? Some people like strong, sturdy qualities; others like more delicate, graceful effects. The two drop-leaf tables on page 29 show these two general types of design. The first table is strong and heavy in appearance. The second table is lighter and more graceful. The difference in effect is created largely by a difference in proportions. In the first the legs are larger and heavier. The crosspieces at the bottom between the legs add to the weight. In the second table the legs are more slender and there are no crosspieces. The proportion of the legs to the table tops makes the difference. Both tables are good design and in good taste. A choice between these two types is a matter of personal preference. If you like strong, sturdy qualities in design you will choose the first table. If you prefer more refined and graceful effects you will select the second. This difference between types of design extends to all forms of art objects. There is no reason why you should not like both types of design as long as you do not use them together. Can you imagine how chairs which match the first table would look placed around the second?

WHAT USES CAN YOU FIND FOR THE PRINCIPLE OF PROPORTION? 1. Add a page to your notebook or portfolio which will illustrate the principle of good proportion. Find a picture of a dress, house, or other object which you wish to use. It should be the best example of good space division which you can find. Write a short paragraph explaining why the space divisions are good. Remember that margins are a problem in proportion and must be considered in planning the

Consider H. Willett, Inc.

These two tables, both of good design, show a difference in effect caused by proportions. Top: Sturdy and strong. The legs are heavier in proportion to the top than those in the bottom picture. Bottom: Also strong, but more graceful than the other table.

Fragment of a palampore (bed cover) from India. This portion of the design shows a series of borders expressing nice rhythmic movement.

page. It is better to have one page that is perfect than to have three pages which are mediocre.

2. Make a list of twenty things in which proportion is a factor in securing beauty.

3. Report to the class any instance in which you have been able to make use of your knowledge of proportion at home or elsewhere.

4. Make some sketches showing good proportion in striped borders for the ends of scarfs, table runners, or towels. Use charcoal, black crayon, brush and ink, or broad lettering pens, so that you can make the stripes easily.

Rhythm: a principle of design

Probably the word *rhythm* suggests music to you. There are march rhythms, waltz rhythms, dance rhythms, slow rhythms, and fast rhythms. These rhythms make us feel certain movements in our bodies. We march, slide, glide, bend, and jump in slow or fast time. Rhythm in art makes us feel movement also. Instead of hearing it we see it, and instead of responding with our muscles we respond with our minds. In both cases we *feel* the rhythms.

30

Rhythmic movement is produced in this shelf paper border by a repetition of similar curves in the scallop and in the little dancing figures. Notice that the eye is not only carried across the border by the scallops and row of figures but it also moves up and down as it follows the tulips and upflung arms.

RHYTHMS IN LINES AND FORMS. Examine the pattern of the palampore from India shown on the opposite page. A palampore is a bed cover. This palampore is a printed cotton. The part of the design shown consists of a series of borders. First, notice the very narrow bands of V-shaped motifs. As your eye follows these little arrow marks it will move from right to left. This is a very simple demonstration of rhythmic movement. Now look at the floral border at the bottom which is between two borders of V-shaped motifs. There is another border just like it near the top.

In these borders there is a strong, wavy line with an easy, undulating movement. The eye follows readily along this curving stem line. Observe how nicely the leaves and blossoms fit into the spaces created by the curves. The widest border is another floral band with a wavelike stem line. In this case the decorative leaves and flowers break the line of the stem somewhat, and, therefore, we do not feel such a strong rhythmic movement. The second border from the top consists of a series of units arranged in a horizontal row. Although there is no line to carry the eye along, the eye does jump from one unit to the next, until it is carried across the page. The repetition of spots creates a rhythmic movement although it is not as forceful as the borders with wavy lines which coax the eye along.

This palampore is so old and rare that it deserves a place in a museum. Not many of us can afford to buy museum pieces, but do not think that rhythm is confined to museums. You can find it in the "five-and-ten."

Notice the rhythmic border on the dime store shelf paper shown above. Your eye skips along from one sprightly little figure to an-

31

Locust trees in winter. The bare branches show delightful swinging rhythms.

other, and from one hill of tulips up and over the next little hill. It is all planned in terms of round little curves. The figures, the tulips, the scallops are all designed in circular forms. Such nice repetition of curving forms creates a pleasing harmony. Thus you see that rhythm can be bought for five cents in the dime store. All you have to do besides pay your nickel is look for rhythmic harmony. You can find it even in a shelf paper.

A SUGGESTION FOR YOUR STUDY OF RHYTHM. Plan a visit to the five-and-ten-cent store for the purpose of finding good examples of rhythmic borders. Look at shelf paper, lace edgings, and china plates. Can you find any examples of rhythmic patterns? Do you find any which you would like better if they were more rhythmic?

32

Monumental statue in Chicago called "Indian Warrior" by Ivan Meštrović. Its rhythmic quality is especially expressive of power and strength.

From the dime store we shall go to the park, where everything is free to all who can see. Here are lovely trees in winter. Their branches makes charming patterns against the sky, and here we shall find more beautiful rhythmic patterns. On the opposite page are branches from some locust trees. See the long, graceful curves of the

Elizabeth Haseltine

A Christmas card made by modeling in clay and then photographing the clay model. The design shows nice rhythmic repeat of forms and pleasing variety of proportions.

bigger branches, and the quick little swirls of the smaller ones. They are like staccato notes in a musical selection. Perhaps you have thought that trees in winter are ugly and uninteresting. After you have studied patterns in tree branches, you may think that winter is when they are most beautiful.

There is powerful rhythmic movement in the statue called "Indian Warrior," by Ivan Meštrovič (page 33). The warrior is portrayed as pulling back the string on his bow, but the sculptor omitted the bow and string as being unnecessary to the effect that he wished to secure. Let your eye wander over the picture at will. Does it not come back to the straight left arm with its powerful thrust? Note that every line, angle, or curve is repeated in another part of the design. The strong vertical of the horse's front leg is repeated in the horse's neck,

34

Diagram showing three types of radiation in rhythmic pattern.

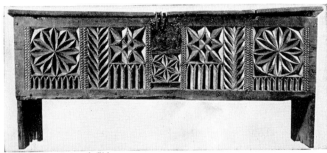

The Art Institute of Chicago

Gothic chest. The rhythmic pattern of the wood carving is based on radiation.

in the body of the Indian, and in part of the horse's uplifted leg. The curve of the horse's neck is echoed in the curve of the tail. The line made by the Indian's left arm is repeated in the right arm, in the horse's head, the open mouth, and upraised leg. It was partly through this arrangement of lines and curves that Meštrović was able to produce this powerful and harmonious work of art.

Rhythm is just as important in small things as in great sculpture. You will find a very charming rhythm in the Christmas card reproduced on page 34. The design was made by a clever sculptress who first modeled it in clay and then photographed the clay model. The curved lines in the cherub heads are repeated in the wings, in the decorative hair treatment, and even in the little mouths caroling Christmas songs. Notice also the gradation of sizes in the heads. It is a charming example of variety in proportions.

RADIATION IS A KIND OF RHYTHM. Both in nature and in art we find an orderly arrangement of lines called radiation, in which lines radiate from a central point. In the diagram at the top of this page there are three types of radiation; in the first and third, lines radiate from a central point, and in the second, from a central axis. It will be a simple problem for you to discover which of these arrangements of lines is used in the decoration of the old Gothic chest shown above.

35

This beautiful Colonial entrance has a charming and beautiful simplicity. Can you see how each of the art principles is expressed?

This lovely spiral staircase is an example of fine rhythmic lines in house design.

and to find the arrangement used in the fanlight over the door shown on page 36. It will be easy for you to find many types of radiation, such as the veins in leaves, snowflakes, rose windows in cathedrals, and rosettes. In historic design this arrangement has been widely used with pleasing effect.

The beautiful Colonial doorway shown on page 36 is an excellent example of the three art principles which we have already studied—formal balance, good proportions, and rhythmic line. The bisymmetric arrangement of the door panels, side lights, and fanlight is stable and satisfying. It suggests dignity and serenity. The panels on the door divide it into interesting spacing, and the division from top to bottom between the side windows and the solid wood panel below is also pleasing. Rhythmic interest is provided in the radial design of the fanlight and in the continuous line of the pilaster, up one side, over the top, and down on the other side.

An unusual example of rhythm in home design is shown in the illustration on page 37. The spiral staircase in front of a floor-to-ceiling window in a modern home is exciting. The great sweep of the lines in the steps and railings cannot help but appeal to our sense of the dramatic.

EXERCISES IN THE STUDY OF RHYTHM. 1. Add a page to your notebook that will illustrate the principle of rhythm. You may find a picture of a piece of sculpture, a painting, a specimen from nature, or a design. Whatever you select should also express harmony and proportion. Write a brief paragraph telling how these principles are used in your illustration.

2. Find a design for a house which you think expresses a good rhythmic flow of line.

3. Trace a design for any object which you think has a rhythmic contour.

4. The following experiment is one that you will enjoy because it will give you experience with delightful rhythmic line arrangements. Use a small plate or shallow pan and cover the bottom with about one-quarter inch of water. Then drop two or three drops of black India ink on the surface of the water. Some of the ink will float on the surface. Blow gently on the surface of the water and swirls of ink will form. Then lay a piece of paper on the surface of the water, leave it a few seconds and remove. You will find that the swirls of ink have printed on the paper, making a delightful pattern. You will find effects which remind you of the grain in wood, clouds of smoke, and other things.

Emphasis: a principle of design

Why is it that of the countless things around us we fail to notice some and our attention is positively seized by others? Why is it that when we turn through the pages of a magazine we stop to read some advertisements and skip others? When we spend a short time in an unfamiliar room, why do we remember one or two things in the room and fail to remember others? It may be because we are more interested in certain things than in others, but more likely because our attention is attracted in spite of our particular interests.

As we observe streetcar or billboard advertisements we may especially notice an advertisement for soap even when we are not interested in buying soap. Our attention was captured by some arrangement of form or color. The artist was clever enough to force our attention to his advertisement. It has some point of interest which stands out so clearly that we cannot miss it. This quality in design is called *emphasis,* or sometimes *subordination.* It means that one part of the pattern is emphasized and other parts are subordinated. The part which is emphasized is called the center of interest. Let us see how it works.

EMPHASIS IN ADVERTISEMENTS, HOUSE DESIGN, AND PICTURES. Emphasis is important in all forms of art productions, but it is particularly important in advertising art. Here the aim is to capture attention, and emphasis on one feature in an advertisement is the way to do it.

The little house on page 40 is the kitchen to one of the mansions of Colonial Williamsburg, Virginia. Without doubt, the chimney is the center of interest. Necessarily there would be a big chimney for the kitchen house. Thus emphasis in the house design grew out of utilitarian requirements. Notice also that the great vertical chimney form is echoed by the very steep line of the roof and the tall dormer windows. Altogether these forms create a nice rhythmic pattern.

The very charming statue standing in the niche of a garden wall (page 41) is a nice example of the principle of emphasis. The plain curved wall behind the statue, the heavy beam above, and the carved border decoration on both sides of the niche make a frame which serves to set off the statue without detracting from it. The curved lines of the fountain basins below also enhance the figure without distracting attention. Imagine the effect if the curved wall of the niche had been covered with a black-and-white tile checkerboard pattern!

This was the kitchen house to an old mansion in Colonial Williamsburg (restored). Notice how the chimney dominates the design and, therefore, serves as the center of interest.

There is a delightful rhythmic feeling in this statue. The lovely curves of the head, the shoulder, the arms, the bowl, and the folds of the robe combine in beautiful harmony.

Emphasis is important in any form of artistic effect, whether in gardens or paintings. In the "Madonna and Angels" by Fra Angelico

A garden statue in the niche of a garden wall. The statue is emphasized by the niche and shrubbery which act as a frame.

(page 17), the mother and child are obviously the center of interest. In "American Gothic" by Grant Wood (page 21), the man and woman are the center of interest. In both these pictures emphasis is secured through size and position.

A decorative arrangement on the top of a small chest. The effect is lost because of the large figured tapestry in the background.

BACKGROUNDS CAN EMPHASIZE THE CENTER OF INTEREST. A comparison of the two pictures on pages 42 and 43 shows very clearly the importance of a plain background. We assume that the bowl filled with bittersweet was meant to be seen as an attractive decoration in the room where it was placed. When we see it in front of the India print it does not stand out clearly and the whole effect is confusing. In front of the plain wallpaper it becomes clear-cut and pleasing in effect. This comparison makes it clear that to secure emphasis for our decorative accessories we need plain backgrounds. The India print shown above is not a good background but is in itself a good center of interest. We cannot expect objects placed in front of it to become a good center of interest.

EVERY ROOM SHOULD HAVE A CENTER OF INTEREST. Upon entering a strange room have you ever immediately noticed a certain feature or part of the room? Or, in some other rooms have you been unaware of anything special? The difference between these two types of rooms is that in one case the room has been planned with a dominant center

The same decorative arrangement as in the illustration on the opposite page. Here it is emphasized, for it is seen against a plain background.

of interest which captures the attention, but the other kind of room lacks anything which catches the eye.

In living rooms it is very often the fireplace which is the predominating feature. When you look at the picture on page 44, your eye is at once drawn to the fireplace and mantel. Other parts of the room are kept subordinate. The plain rug of lovely texture stretches across the floor without interruption, so that the eye travels easily toward the fireplace. The chairs are upholstered in a small check pattern which is interesting but does not pull the eye away from the center of interest. The fireplace is finished in wood paneling which makes a nice surrounding background. The fireplace opening has been filled with greenery for the summer months, but it does not detract from the mantel and its accessories. In the wintertime when a fire blazes on the hearth, our eyes are sure to watch it. A fireplace forms a natural center of interest.

Often a window can provide an interesting focal point. A picture window with a lovely view or a window that has been made into a

The fireplace and mantel form a pleasant center of interest in this room.

window garden is bound to seize our attention. The window on page 45 has been made into a center of interest that would be charming for any room. The green of the plants contrasts pleasantly with the sparkling colors of the glass and china on the glass shelves above. Would you not like to eat breakfast in a room with such a lovely window?

THE IMPORTANCE OF EMPHASIS. The use of emphasis helps to relieve monotony and to prevent a commonplace effect. Every room

Ponderosa Pine Woodwork

This charming window garden always attracts attention as one enters the room

should have a pleasing focal point which attracts the eye as soon as one enters the room. However, let us beware of a dominant feature which is *unpleasant,* and also of *too many* centers of interest. In both cases the effect is disagreeable.

WHAT USES CAN YOU FIND FOR THE PRINCIPLE OF EMPHASIS? 1. Add a page to your notebook that will express the principle of emphasis. You may use a costume, a room interior, a book cover, or an adver-

45

tisement. Write an explanation telling what thing has been made the center of interest and how the emphasis was secured.

2. The two problems included in a study of emphasis are how to secure emphasis, and what to emphasize. Make a list of the things in a room which can be emphasized as a center of interest. For example, a fireplace makes a good center of interest, and the walls would make a poor center of interest and, therefore, should not be included.

3. What architectural features on the exterior of a house may serve as a center of interest?

4. The use of emphasis is essential in window display. Visit a business street. The class should first agree on what street and what portion of the street to visit so that they can compare their observations. Select two windows, one which shows good use of emphasis and one which shows confusion and lack of emphasis. It will be interesting to note how many members of the class select the same windows.

5. Make some diagrams which show how you would arrange articles on a mantel to provide a good center of interest. Use 9″ by 12″ drawing paper or preferably 12″ by 18″ paper. Turn your paper horizontally and draw lines across the bottom which will represent the mantel shelf. Use a soft drawing pencil or crayon for drawing the diagrams. Using your soft pencil or crayon, represent the outlines of the objects which you wish to arrange on the mantel. These objects may include vases, bottles, candles and candle holders, plants, books, and pictures on the wall. Do not try to show the details of these objects such as the decoration on vases or the details in the pictures. Draw the outlines and block in the shapes to make silhouettes with your soft pencil or crayon. It is better to use a soft, medium-gray coloring than to draw heavy, solid-black effects when making the silhouettes.

Remember that this exercise is for practice in making arrangements with a good center of interest. At the same time you should also use the other art principles—proportion, rhythm, and balance. This practice does not require any particular ability in drawing and painting. Anyone can draw a rectangle to represent a picture on the wall and some lines to represent a vase or a candle. Your aim is to select objects of the *right size and shape* and to make a good arrangement with them.

After you have read these directions carefully, make two diagrams:

(a) A mantel showing formal balance with the center of interest in the center.

(b) A mantel showing informal balance with the center of interest *not* in the center.

46

We should consider our present study of design as a mere beginning in developing our ability to select articles that have true art quality. All of us wish to acquire standards of good taste which will enable us to meet our art problems successfully. We wish to plan our clothing and our homes without expensive mistakes that are hard to correct. It is helpful to have in mind definite standards by which we can judge the things we buy and the arrangements we make in our homes. To dislike a certain arrangement without being able to analyze the difficulty, as we sometimes do, shows that we need such standards. The following questions suggest standards which will prove valuable in solving our art problems. We should be as familiar with them as with the multiplication table. It is only by their constant use that we can hope to develop unerring good taste.

1. Is the whole effect unified? Are all the parts harmoniously related or is the effect scattered and disturbing?

2. Are the parts well balanced, producing a feeling of rest and repose? Is it top-heavy, or is it too heavy on either side?

3. Are the space divisions interesting in proportion? Are the proportions of color pleasing?

4. Is there a good rhythmic feeling throughout the whole design? Is the movement smooth and uninterrupted, or is it awkward and spotty?

5. Is there a center of interest, and is it pleasing?

CAN YOU USE THE PRINCIPLES OF DESIGN?

I. One design or picture can express all four art principles. Explain how the designs on pages 36, 75, and 100 express all four principles.

II. Your teacher will hang ten pictures and designs in the classroom. Some of them will be good in design and some will be poor. Write your opinion of each illustration, explaining in one sentence why you think it is good or bad.

III. Can you use the principles of design in your everyday observations of the things about you? Describe something which you have seen lately that is a good example of at least one principle of design. If possible, make a sketch or take a photograph of it.

IV. If you understand the principles of design you should be able to determine which of the following statements are true. Read each statement carefully. Copy the number of the statement on your paper and after it write *true* or *false*.

1. The picture of a house fits better into an oval frame than into a rectangular frame.

2. If five objects, such as a picture, a pair of candlesticks, and a pair of vases, are placed on a bookcase, they must be arranged with the picture in the center and a candlestick and vase on each side, in order to produce formal balance.

3. Napkins folded into a rectangular shape look better on a square table than those folded into a triangular shape.

4. A small medallion used to decorate a book cover should be placed exactly in the center from top to bottom.

5. Rectangular doilies look better than round doilies on a square table.

6. Several small objects grouped together may be made to balance one large object.

7. A picture in an advertisement is *always* a center of interest.

8. There is a fine rhythmic repetition of line in the form of the panther.

9. The upper and lower parts of a window should be made equal in size in order to make a well-proportioned window.

10. The principle of proportion deals with the relationships of space.

Chapter 3

BEAUTY AND UTILITY ARE PARTNERS

Designing and making a rug, chair, kitchen pan, or other article of household furnishing involve the principles of art which we have just studied and an understanding of the *function* or use of the object. A chair which is not comfortable to sit on, cannot be called beautiful no matter how graceful the lines or how valuable the wood used in its construction. Who wants a chair that is pretty to look at but is a pain in the back to sit on? Beauty and use cannot be separated—they go hand in hand.

The art of creating furniture, drapery fabrics, or similar objects is sometimes known as the useful arts or industrial arts. The name distinguishes this kind of art from the fine arts which are concerned with pictorial representation. In a later chapter we shall consider the pictures and sculpture which are suitable for home use. In this chapter we will study the relation of beauty and function in useful articles of home decoration.

Compare the design of the three chairs shown on page 50. The first two chairs are historic pieces now preserved in a museum, and the third is a modern chair on sale in furniture stores at the present time. Each of the three, when first made, was intended for use in a home. Let us see how each one would serve present-day needs. For purposes of comparison, think of them as chairs for the dining-room table or for a game table. What do you require for complete comfort in a chair as you sit at a table? Remember that you do not expect to lounge but to sit comfortably as you eat or play games.

As you consider each of the three designs, think of yourself as fitted into each chair. In the first, the seat is small and the cushion looks

Worcester Art Museum

Sligh Furniture

Compare these three chairs for functional design.

50

as if it would be easy for you to roll off the edge. The back is high and straight up and down. One would have to sit up unnaturally straight to fit this chair back. Probably the moldings around the edge of the cane panel would not be comfortable to lean against. The seat is high and if you are short your feet might not touch the floor.

In the second chair, an eighteenth century Chippendale design, there is much more functional quality. The seat is larger and lower and the back is broader and slants backward slightly so that it would be easier to adjust the body comfortably. The back is also lower than in the first chair. Certainly the extra height is useless and is in the way when one is being served. The structural design is much better adapted to use.

The third chair of contemporary design is excellently adapted to its purpose. The seat is broad and low enough for comfortable sitting. The legs are straight and do not protrude beyond the corners of the seat. In the Chippendale chair, the curved legs sometimes get in the way if one happens to sit cornerwise. The back of the modern chair slants at a good angle and has a slight barrel-like curve which fits the body much more comfortably than the curve of the Chippendale chair.

DECORATION SHOULD ENHANCE STRUCTURE. Structural design refers to the particular shape, size, and construction of an object. Before an object can be made, the designer must decide the dimensions, proportion of the parts, and how it is to be put together. These are problems in structural design and functional quality.

Decorative design refers to ornamentation which is added to the structure. Generally, decoration can be thought of as surface enrichment. A piece of drapery material may be a plain weave of one color, but another piece may be printed with an all-over pattern in several colors. Thus decorative design has been added, and if the pattern is pleasing the plain cloth has gained additional beauty.

The first two chairs on the opposite page show some decorative design. The moldings on the back of the first chair emphasize the shape of the panel but detract from the functional desirability of the chair. The turnings on the legs and crosspieces and the rather queerly shaped feet do not enhance its structure. The effect is heavy and ostentatious. The decoration really *overemphasizes* the structure. The turnings make the under part of the chair much too heavy, and the feet draw too much attention. It is not the *feet* which should attract our attention in a chair design! The real difficulty is that this chair is poor in structural design to begin with, and has too much poor decorative design to end with!

American Cyanamid Company

These plastic dishes rely entirely on structural design (or form), texture, and color for their beauty.

In the second design, the effect is more pleasing. The structure of the chair is better adapted to use, and the small amount of ornamentation serves to enhance the structure. There is a little carving at the tops of the cabriole legs and at the corners of the chair back. The pattern in the brocade seat cover also adds a bit of decorative charm.

In the third chair there is a complete lack of ornamentation. This is a general characteristic of the modern style. The beauty of the chair depends upon the pleasing proportions, the rhythmic line found in the back and legs, and the nice feeling of stability or balance. The chair design is a fine co-ordination of beauty and utility.

BEAUTY IN PLAIN SURFACES. An object with good structural design, fine color, and texture can be most pleasing. The plastic dishes shown above are an excellent example of this kind of beauty. Each dish is designed with the utilitarian quality in mind. Notice the flat plate with an up-turned rim to prevent the food from sliding off the plate. Notice also the interesting design of the cup and saucer, sugar bowl, and creamer. The handles are solid and substantial. The spout of the pitcher is narrow and pours easily without splashing. The cover of the sugar bowl has no handle but is small enough to pick up by placing the hand over the top of it. No handle is needed. The divided serving dish provides an easy way of serving two foods in one dish. How different from the traditional styles of dishes in common use.

Let your eye rove over the whole picture and notice what a satisfactory feeling of harmony is created by the low, broad proportions of the dishes and by the smooth-textured surfaces. Can you imagine these dishes in a delightful chartreuse tone or a deep aqua tint?

The place mat is an excellent example of a textured surface produced by the structure of the weave. The rough, corded effect makes a nice contrast to the smooth surfaces of the dishes. The only bit of decorative design in this place setting is found on the silver. A floral pattern decorates the handles of the knives, forks, and spoons, and emphasizes their shapes.

BEAUTY ENTERS THE BACK DOOR. There was a time when the kitchen was thought of chiefly as a work place, but those days are long past. Kitchens are now planned in terms of beauty as well as functional quality. The utmost care is now taken to plan every detail of kitchen design so as to make cooking quick and easy. Every bit of furnishing from floor to ceiling is planned for efficiency, and equal care is taken to achieve eye appeal. The kitchen illustrated on page 54 is a pleasant place to be. Its structural design resulted in both efficiency and beauty.

The dark-green linoleum floor is smooth and easy to clean and requires a minimum amount of care. Toe room is provided under the edges of the cabinets and stove so that one can stand close to a cabinet or stove with comfort. The range and cabinets are designed with smooth surfaces and very few corners to collect dirt and make difficult cleaning. The range, sink, and counters are the right height for work without stooping. The overhead cabinets provide convenient storage for the numerous things required as one prepares food. Notice the rotating shelf in the corner cabinet which swings out into the room as the door opens. Otherwise the space back in the corner would be very difficult to reach and not readily usable. The overhead cabinet at the right is supported at the free end by two steel chromium pipes allowing a pass-through of food to the dining area (not shown).

All these functional designs and the clean, shining surfaces add up to something of real beauty. There is very little decoration in this kitchen—only enough to add interest to the general effect. The plates over the range, the decorative motifs on the breadbox and

53

Lyon Metal Products, Incorporated

The beauty of a modern kitchen depends chiefly upon structural features and smooth, lovely surfaces.

canisters supply focal points which save the general effect from being blank and monotonous.

MODERN BATHROOMS ARE ATTRACTIVE. New designs in bathrooms have appeared in recent years due partly to the production of new materials. Plastic wall tile, asphalt and rubber floor tile, patterned

The Tile-Tex Division, The Flintkote Company

Beauty in bathrooms as in kitchens depends principally upon structural design and fine surfaces.

glass, fluorescent lighting, and plastic shower curtains give the modern bathroom a new beauty. The bathroom shown above is attractive and easy to keep clean and beautiful. The floor is a dark-green marbleized asphalt tile with cove corners so there are no corners and cracks to catch dust and dirt. The walls are lighter green plastic tile with a wide band of coral pink around the walls and over the shower stall. The upper walls are a light corn yellow, and the shower curtain is a somewhat brighter yellow tone.

Notice the fluorescent lighting tubes at each side of the mirror placed for efficient lighting and the chromium bar for holding to as one steps into the tub. The patterned glass at the end of the tub lets light into the shower stall and adds a pleasing note to the decorative effect. The chief beauty of this bathroom depends upon its structural design. The fish motif in the floor and the flower prints on the wall are the only bits of truly decorative design. The whole effect is mostly one of built-in beauty.

STRUCTURAL DESIGN SHOULD BE FUNCTIONAL. It is not possible to place too much emphasis on the importance of the functional quality in design. Your judgment of any article of home furnishing, large or small, should be based on its usefulness as well as its appearance. Unless it fulfills its function adequately, it is of doubtful value. Fancy decorations, streamlining, or "cute" designs cannot make up for lack of utilitarian quality. Remember always that beauty and utility are partners.

Suppose that you are buying a paring knife for the kitchen. You expect to use it for paring vegetables and fruits. At the kitchen counter in the dime store, you find several knives of different styles and varying prices. One which catches your eye has a red plastic handle, but it costs a little more than the others. However, the red handle will fit in with your color scheme, and you are inclined to buy it, until you pick it up and hold it in your hand. The handle seems small and has a sharp corner at the end which presses into your palm. As you imagine yourself paring potatoes with this knife you know that it would not serve its purpose well. This instance involves only a small amount of money and discomfort for only a few minutes per day. Now we will consider an expenditure of a much larger sum of money.

The windows of a home are very important to comfort, convenience, and appearance. Do they let in enough light? Are they easy to open and shut? Are they convenient for cleaning? Are they interesting in proportions? Is their general appearance attractive?

One of the trends in modern building is to use windows in groups, as shown on the opposite page. This is the result of the demand by modern homeowners for more light and air inside their houses. The windows are wide, extending almost from floor to ceiling, and are called a "window wall." The design for the window

The beauty of this window design depends upon the fine spacing. It is as functional as it is beautiful.

opening is, of course, built into the structure of the house. Notice the pleasing proportions of the opening. It is a beautifully shaped horizontal rectangle. Now notice how the space is divided into three large divisions. The center window is wider than the side windows, creating a much more pleasing effect than equal divisions. Next, notice that the side windows are divided into upper and lower sashes which slide up and down (double-hung windows) and that the division is well above the center. If you count the spaces made by the small square panes, you will see that the division from top to bottom is 2 to 3. Notice also that the division of space horizontally between the center and side window is 3 to 5.

This is an excellent example of the way in which truly functional design is also beautiful. The old-type window would have been made with upper and lower sash the same size. This would have meant less light and air for the interior and less beauty of design.

Rolscreen Company

The functional design of these windows provides for easy cleaning and easy installation of storm and screen windows.

Notice that no ornamentation has been added to the structural design of the windows. Do you know of any old-fashioned houses where tops of windows are decorated with gingerbread trimmings?

EASY CLEANING IS IMPORTANT. Any piece of home furnishing which is difficult to keep clean can hardly be rated as functional. This is true whether it is an upholstered chair, a bedspread, or a window. Before making a selection, one should consider carefully just how much trouble it will be to take care of the article to be selected. The illustrations at the top of this page show how casement windows are now made so as to make their care very easy. In the picture to the left you can see how the window swings from a point a few inches away from the side. This permits easy washing of the outside. Older casements were hinged from the side of the window frame, making it very difficult to get at the outside of the window.

Another feature in easy use of casements is shown in the illustration to the right. Storm windows are made to fit onto the inside of each window and are easily adjusted as shown in the picture. Screens are made which fit into the inside window frame. Some of them are made so that they roll up into a box at the top of the window. This kind of structural design adds considerably to the ease and convenience of home living.

How well do you understand functional design? 1. Add a page to your notebook which will illustrate functional design. Find a picture of some household object which is designed for ease and convenience in use. Write a short statement explaining why you think the design is functional.

2. Find an example of structural design without ornamentation which you consider beautiful. Explain how the principles of art have been expressed in the design.

Good decoration is not pictorial. The true purpose of decorative design is to enrich the surface of an article, and thereby make it more beautiful. The kind of ornamentation which enriches a surface is called *decorative* design. It decorates the surface without changing the quality of the surface.

Consider this idea in relation to a lady's handkerchief. A handkerchief is a square piece of thin cloth frequently carried for decorative purposes, and also quite generally used for a decidedly utilitarian purpose. It is often folded, crumpled, washed, and ironed. Any decoration on it should not interfere with its usefulness as a handkerchief. You would never think of pinning some roses on it for decoration. Neither would you think of painting a fine picture on a handkerchief and hanging it on the wall.

Compare the two handkerchiefs on page 60. The bottom handkerchief is decorated with some beautiful roses fresh from the garden. Someone dropped them on the handkerchief and there they stayed! This kind of decoration is pictorial and should be framed and hung on the wall. Certainly it does not belong on a handkerchief. The idea of wiping your nose with a rose blossom is somewhat disturbing! The decorative design on the top handkerchief is quite different. It is a floral pattern, but here the flowers have been made into decorative forms which seem to belong on a handkerchief. We have no feeling that these are real flowers. They are design flowers. They are flat and made to fit the square structural form of the handkerchief. We call this type of decoration *conventionalized* or *stylized*.

When we paint a picture of a rose, the aim is to make it look as lifelike as possible. This type of decoration is called *naturalistic* or *realistic*. We like realistic pictures of roses on our walls, but on our handkerchiefs is quite another matter. The conventionalized design in the top handkerchief suggests flower forms without giving the impression of realism.

We have used the handkerchiefs as an illustration, but the same idea applies to the decoration of other objects—rugs, wallpaper, sofa

Good and poor design in five-cent handkerchiefs. Top: Conventionalized floral forms which fill the space. Left: Naturalistic floral forms not well adapted for decoration.

pillows, and dress materials. Conventionalized decoration can enrich a surface without changing the character of an object. A handkerchief remains a handkerchief and does not become a picture.

A CLASS DISCUSSION. Collect a group of decorated articles from home and school. Decide which decorations are realistic and which are conventionalized.

FINE DECORATIVE DESIGN IN HISTORIC ART. Historic art furnishes us with many interesting and beautiful examples of decorative design. The portfolio called "Folk Art of Rural Pennsylvania" supplies us with some charming examples of stylized bird and flower forms. (See page 62.) Two of these show bisymmetric balance and the other occult balance. They show nice rhythmic repeats of curves and forms, and each has a definite center of interest. These motifs were used mostly as painted decorations on chests, baptismal certificates, hymn books, dishes, and other everyday articles. This type of decorative design is quaint and charming. It is also a bit crude and very simple, but it is honest and unpretentious.

In contrast to this simple decorative quality, we have the more elaborate and sophisticated type of decoration found in the palampore from India (page 63). Here, too, are floral forms, but treated in a much more complex and intricate pattern. The tree form is the center of interest, and the border pattern is charmingly subordinated. There are lovely, graceful rhythms throughout the design, pleasing proportions, and a splendid informal balance in the tree form. Altogether, it is a most beautiful and satisfactory example of decorative pattern.

In comparing these two types of historic decorative design, do not feel that one is better than the other. Both are good design, but they differ in character. One kind of decoration may appeal to you more than the other, but there is no reason why you cannot enjoy both kinds. As you study design in rugs, dishes, furniture, and fabrics, you will find other examples of these two types of decorative pattern. The important thing is to know good design no matter what its character.

SUGGESTIONS FOR FURTHER STUDY. 1. Make a collection of conventionalized designs. If you find these in objects that you cannot bring to school, make a simple sketch of the units used. You may find it interesting to take some one form, such as a bird, an animal, or a flower, and see how many different conventionalized treatments you can find for it.

2. Choose a topic and make a report on decorative design of some historic period. You will find a list of reference books at the end of this book which will be helpful.

3. If there are art galleries or museums in your town, visit them and study the decorative designs used on various articles.

FROM A BOOK PLATE IN MENNONITE HYMNAL 1829

FROM A DOWER CHEST C. 1790

FROM A BAPTISMAL CERTIFICATE 1841

Index of American Design; Pennsylvania Art Program

Design motifs from the portfolio called "Folk Art of Rural Pennsylvania."

STANDARDS FOR JUDGING FUNCTIONAL DESIGN

The study of this unit of work has given us additional standards for judging the design of objects used in home furnishing. The following questions contain points to consider in judging a design for utility and beauty.

1. Does the structural design fulfill its purpose in the best possible way?

A palampore from India. This type of decorative design is characterized by grace-ful forms, delicacy, and refinement of curves.

2. Is the structural design beautiful? Is it well proportioned? Well balanced? Unified?

3. Does the decorative design interfere with the usefulness of the object?

4. Has the right amount of ornamentation been used? Is it too elaborate, or is there a reserve of ornament that gives a pleasing simplicity?

5. Is the ornamentation an integral part of the structure, empha-sizing the main lines of construction?

6. Is the design realistic or conventionalized?

7. Is the color and finish of the object practical as well as beautiful? Will it soil easily and lose some of its beauty in the process of washing or cleaning?

8. Is the color and design of the article harmonious with the sur-roundings in which it is to be used?

The Art Institute of Chicago

Which design expresses the principles of art in the most pleasing way?

64

A TEST ON STRUCTURAL AND DECORATIVE DESIGN

I. Compare the two platters on the opposite page for structural and decorative design.

1. Which has better structural design? Why?

2. In which one does the decoration harmonize better with the shape of the plaque?

3. Which one shows better rhythmic movement?

4. Which plaque shows a definite center of interest?

5. Is the decoration on both plaques thoroughly conventionalized? Explain.

II. This is a test of your ability to discriminate between pictorial and conventionalized design. Ten designs will be hung on the wall, numbered from 1 to 10. Write on your paper the numbers of the designs, and after each number write the word *pictorial* or *conventionalized* to describe each design.

III. Have a committee select one article showing decorative as well as structural design which is to be judged according to the standards on pages 62 and 63. Write sentences concerning the quality of the article with respect to each standard. Exchange papers with someone in the class and correct any mistakes which you find. In case of disagreement, refer the question to the class for discussion.

IV. Report an instance of how you have recognized good or poor design in some article in your home, your clothing, or at school. This should be something you failed to notice before your study of the chapter.

Chapter 4

USING AND ENJOYING COLOR

What a dull world this would be if there were no color! Would you not feel depressed if everywhere you looked you saw only black, white, and gray? Even though you do not think about it much, you cannot help but respond to the sparkling yellow sunlight and the soft green of young leaves and grass on a lovely spring morning or feel exhilarated by the brilliant autumn coloring on a fine October day. It is hard to feel depressed in such surroundings. Would you not rather live in a room that is gay and pretty in color than spend your hours in one that is dark and drab?

What do you know about color? Have you learned how to choose colors which are in harmony with each other? Can you choose colors which are suitable for their purpose? Most of all, have you learned to notice and enjoy beautiful color anywhere that you see it—at home, at school, or in a shop window? Using and enjoying color properly requires study. In this chapter we will begin our study of color, and in later chapters you will use what you learned in this chapter. Color is a big topic, and although you will learn much about it in this course you can learn still more in the future. Color in the home is a never ending source of pleasure and a challenging problem.

The characteristics of a color

To understand and enjoy color, it is necessary really to see all the qualities of a color when you look at it. Perhaps you think you can already do this, without further study. Here is a test to see how well you observe colors. Think of something that you know is blue. Is the blue a true blue, or is it slightly greenish or slightly purplish? Is it midway between light and dark, above or below the middle? How much gray is in it? What is its texture?

There are three characteristics of color which help us to recognize and identify colors accurately. These are *hue, value,* and *intensity.* As you study these color characteristics you will see how much they add to one's understanding and enjoyment of color.

HUE GIVES A COLOR ITS NAME. When you say that the sky is blue, you are naming its hue. When you are asked to describe the color of an object, your first thought is its hue. Color names such as blue, pink, brown, yellow, and lavender indicate the color characteristic called hue. The first thing we learn about color is to recognize hue. Kindergarten children learn to distinguish the six color families, yellow, orange, red, purple, blue, and green. Each of these families has a particular hue which gives it a name.

Everyone, unless color-blind, learns to recognize these hues. That is about as far as some people get with their recognition of colors. As far as they are concerned, all yellows are just yellow, and all blues are merely blue. To understand and enjoy color you must see far more than this. You must be able to see when a hue is not a standard color but has borrowed a little color from its neighbor. For example, an orange may not be plain orange; it may be a little reddish or a little yellowish. The very first requirement in the enjoyment of color is to *recognize hue.*

HUES ON THE COLOR CIRCLE. The small circle A opposite page 68 shows you three familiar colors, red, yellow, and blue. Sometimes these three are called the primary colors. Notice that they are equally spaced on the circle at three equally distant points. In circle B you will see three more colors fitted into the spaces between each two primary colors. Orange fits in between yellow and red. This is easy to remember because when red and yellow are mixed the result is orange. For the same reason purple fits in between red and blue, and green belongs between blue and yellow. This should help you to remember the order of colors on the circle. It is also true that red can be made by mixing the two hues on either side, orange and purple. This is not easy to do with paints, and perhaps you cannot manage it. Do not expect to produce a bright red, for it will be dull. It is easy to do, however, when mixing colored lights. Blue can be made by mixing green and purple, and yellow can be made by mixing orange and green. Thus, as you see from the illustration, any hue on the color circle can be made by mixing its two neighbors.

MORE HUES ON THE COLOR CIRCLE. So far our study of hues on the color circle has been simple. Now it begins to get more complicated. The outer circle of C shows you how each hue blends with its neighbor. Between yellow and orange you see a new hue, yellow-orange. In fact, there are several shades of yellow-orange (or orange-yellow— whichever you want to call it). Between orange and red there are several shades of orange-red or red-orange. As you go on around the circle you will find red-violet, blue-violet, blue-green, and yellow-green, each sandwiched in between two of the six colors shown on circle B.

Altogether there are twelve easily distinguished hues. Besides these twelve, there are many more gradations of hue. For example, starting with yellow and moving toward orange there is a gradation of hues. The yellow becomes slightly orange, then more and more orange, then the orange becomes slightly reddish, then more and more reddish until the hue is pure red. It would not be possible to name all these gradations of hue, but at least we can say that a color is yellow slightly orange, or that it is a straight yellow-orange, or that it is a slightly orange-red.

Now you see why this matter of hue is quite complicated. We must learn to recognize hues accurately. It helps in matching colors and in remembering colors. It is also fun to be able to see the difference between orange, yellow-orange, and red-orange hues, or between blue, blue-green, and yellow-green. *To recognize hue accurately is the first step in the use and enjoyment of color.*

EXPERIMENT WITH HUE. If you have not had much experience in mixing colors you will enjoy this experiment. Use water colors or soft chalk.

1. Mix orange, green, or purple. Remember the two colors which make each of these hues.
2. Try mixing red, blue, and yellow. Remember that the results will be dull if you are able to secure them at all.
3. Mix each of the intermediate colors, yellow-orange, red-orange, red-violet, blue-violet, blue-green, and yellow-green. *Note:* It is not worth while spending a long time making a perfect color circle. Experiment with making spots of color until you remember how each hue is related to its neighbors.

SPECTRUM COLORS AND NEUTRALS. Undoubtedly you have seen the rainbow with its lovely colors—in the sky, in the spray from a waterfall, or when sunlight passed through a glass prism and broke into a

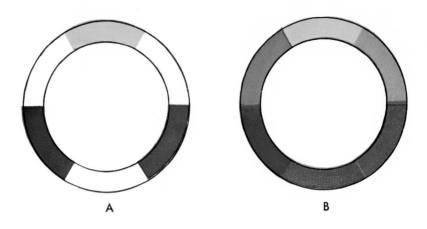

A B

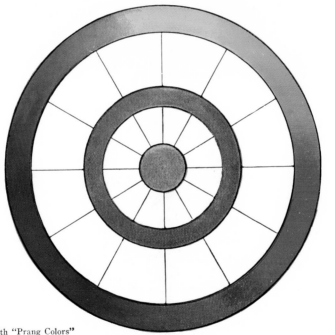

Made with "Prang Colors"
by courtesy of the American
Crayon Company

C

A: Color circle showing the location of the three primary colors—red, yellow, and blue.

B: Color circle showing the addition of the three secondary colors—orange, green, and violet.

C: Color circle showing a gradation of hues. Outer circle shows spectrum hues. Inner circle shows neutralized hues. Center spot shows neutral.

many-hued display. But perhaps you have never noticed the exact hues of the rainbow or how they are related. Now that you have learned the colors on the color circle, you know the rainbow colors. If you cut the circle between red and violet, and straighten the circle into a vertical strip, you will have a slice from the rainbow. Beginning with red at the top, it will gradate downward to violet at the bottom. There may be hints of red-violet at each end.

These rainbow colors are called *spectrum colors*. As you know, rainbow colors are very bright. We say they are *spectrum hues*. Rainbow hues are always brighter than colors painted on paper, because they are produced with colored lights. However, we refer to the brightest possible painted colors as spectrum hues.

In contrast to the hues on the color circle there are black, white, and gray. These do not belong to any of the color families. They do not "take sides" with any hue; therefore we call them *neutrals*. In fact, they lack hue or color. They are colorless, or neutral.

What happens when a spectrum color and a neutral are mixed? You can see for yourself on the inner circle of C. Each color is grayed or *neutralized*. They are no longer spectrum hues. Most of the colors in the world about us are neutralized. No one lives surrounded by spectrum hues. Since there are so many neutralized hues in our world, it is worth while to study them a bit. Notice what happens to each spectrum color when it is neutralized. Red, violet, blue, and green, each becomes duller. Orange changes character and becomes brownish. (The browns and tans all belong to the orange family.) Yellow becomes greenish. Dark yellow is the kind of green known as olive green.

EXPERIMENTS IN NEUTRALIZING COLORS. Using soft crayons or water colors, try neutralizing each color with black, white, and gray. How does the effect differ when you use white and when you use black? What colors neutralized will produce tan, pink, brown, cream, and lavender?

EXERCISES TO AID IN THE RECOGNITION OF COLOR. 1. Collect examples of color, such as in pieces of cloth, paper, yarn, glass, stones, feathers, leaves, and leather. Try to have at least fifty different samples. Arrange these in groups according to the twelve hues shown on the color circle. Have someone examine your groups to see if you have identified the colors correctly. Can you distinguish green from yellow-green, yellow-brown from red-brown, and so on? Perhaps a contest can be arranged where different colors are shown to the class while the class writes down the names of the colors. If you are uncertain about the hue of some of the colors, try mixing paints to match them. In this way you can discover the true hue.

2. To what hue on the color circle do the following colors belong?

crimson	salmon	purple	sand
taupe	cerise	pink	gold
mustard	lemon	cedar	beige
lavender	rust	jade	mauve
coral	plum	cream	russet
mulberry	mahogany	terra cotta	ecru
aqua	chartreuse	bronze	raspberry

3. Make a list of as many color names as you can for each of the hues on the color circle.

4. Discuss in class the "new colors" that are popular this season. In your opinion are the *colors* new or are the *names* new?

5. Experiment with dyeing pieces of cloth. Use small pieces of white cloth and any commercial dye. Can you dye a piece of white cloth yellow by using orange and green dye? Brown by using orange and black? Olive green by using yellow and black?

WARM AND COOL HUES. Some colors are much warmer than others. Of course, you cannot heat your house with them, but they certainly can make it *seem* more comfortable. You can find out for yourself which are the warm colors by trying the following experiment. Hang on the wall six pieces of paper showing the six spectrum hues, red, orange, yellow, green, blue, and violet. They should be of equal size and at least six inches square, and the brightest that you can secure. Place them against a neutral background. Now view them from across the room and decide which ones seem warm to you and which ones seem cool. People invariably agree that red, orange, and yellow are the warm colors, and that blue and green are the cool colors. There may be some disagreement about violet. Naturally, a blue-violet suggests coolness and a red-violet suggests warmth.

Probably the reason red, orange, and yellow suggest warmth is that we see these colors in fire, burning coals, molten metal, sunrises, and sunsets. We see the cool colors in sky, shady trees, lakes, and streams.

Repeat the experiment with neutralized shades of the six spectrum hues. Choose light, delicate tones of pink, tan, yellow, green, blue, and lavender. Can you not feel the same suggestions of warmth and coolness? Imagine that each of the colors is a sample of wallpaper for your room. Which one would give the most agreeable effect to you?

We are all sensitive to this quality of color, even when we are not really aware of it. Here is another true story about color. The owner of a prosperous, well-patronized little restaurant decided that he would have his dining room redecorated in a very modern, up-to-date style. In the old room, the walls were cream, and the furnishings were soft green with bright orange trimmings. In the new room the walls and all furnishings were painted a brilliant blue, almost a spectrum blue. There were also mirrors and chromium fixtures, but these served only to reflect the violent blue color. To anyone the least bit sensitive to color, the effect was positively alarming. It was cold and forbidding. Soon business began to drop off, and in six months the restaurant closed its doors. Perhaps the unhappy color was not the only reason for this catastrophe, but it undoubtedly helped. One woman who knew nothing about color said, "I don't know why it is, but I don't feel comfortable in here any more."

SOME PROBLEMS IN THE USE OF WARM AND COOL HUES. 1. Name some colors that will help you to appear cool on a hot summer day.

2. Describe a room in which you think gray woodwork and light blue walls could be used successfully.

3. Do you think warm or cool hues better for most rooms in your own climate? Why?

AGGRESSIVE HUES. Hang the six spectrum hues on the wall and again view them from across the room. Which ones seem to have more carrying power? Or, in other words, which ones seem more aggressive and more forceful? The aggressive colors seem to be nearer or to advance beyond the other colors. If possible, hang the colors at the end of a corridor where you can look at them from an even greater distance, and again compare them as to their aggressiveness and carrying qualities.

The majority of people agree that the warm colors, red, orange, and yellow, are aggressive and advancing colors, while the cool colors, green, blue, and violet, are retreating and quieter colors. This contrast is more marked when comparing spectrum colors of full intensity, but neutralized reds, oranges, and yellows are more advancing than neutralized blues, greens, and violets.

PROBLEMS IN THE SELECTION OF COLORS. 1. Will a small room seem smaller or larger if the walls are painted a strong pink color?

2. If a girl is too stout, should she choose to wear bright yellow or a neutralized green? Why?

71

White

Light

Middle

Dark

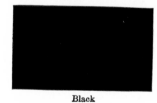
Black

Neutral value scale with five values.

3. Will an advertisement to be read from across the street be more effective in blue and white or black and yellow?

4. Can the red or the green signal-light at the street crossing be seen farther? Why?

5. Compare spectrum and neutralized colors for aggressiveness. Which is more advancing, spectrum or neutralized green?

THE VALUE OF A COLOR. This sounds as though we might place a financial value upon color, but it really has nothing to do with dollars and cents. Value is a quality of color which depends on the amount of light and dark in the color.

Take all the color samples which you used in practicing recognition of hue and sort them into three piles, the lightest, the darkest, and the in-betweens. You have now sorted them into three values, light value, middle value, and dark value. Sometimes the light values are called tints and the dark values are called tones.

This diagram, with five steps ranging from white through light gray, middle gray, and dark gray to black, shows what is called a neutral value scale. You can test your grouping of the color samples with this value scale. Hold each sample of color close to the scale and look at it with your eyes partly closed. The hue becomes less prominent and if you close your eyes enough seems neutral. Then you can judge its value. To give yourself practice is distinguishing values accurately, look about the room at the colors you see and try to decide the true value of each. Then hold your value scale near the color and test it by looking through partly closed eyes.

An understanding of values will help us to use colors to the best advantage. As we look at the value scale it seems natural that we should hold it so that the black comes at the bottom. Try turning your book upside down; the value scale seems wrong side up. This

72

The Tile-Tex Division, The Flintkote Company

The colors in this bathroom are planned to give a pleasing effect of color values.

little experiment offers a suggestion for the arrangement of color values in interior decoration. Some decorators believe that floors should be the darkest value in a room, the walls should be lighter, and the ceiling should be lightest of all. This corresponds to nature's arrangement of values, in which the earth, grass, and trees near at hand are darkest, the distance is lighter, and the sky is lightest.

A second point to remember in our use of color values is that sharp contrasts of black against white or light against dark are more conspicuous than slight contrasts of value, such as light against middle value or middle value against dark. If you wished to be inconspicuously dressed, would you choose a bold black-and-yellow striped sweater or one with light-value tan stripes and middle-value brown stripes? Since sharp contrasts of values are forceful in their general effect, it is best to avoid them for backgrounds. For example, if one is choosing a blue-and-white striped wall for a bathroom, as shown above, it is much better to select a light or medium blue than a

73

dark navy blue. Notice that the asphalt tile floor is darker than the blue of the walls and the ceiling is slightly lighter. This blue-and-white bathroom has accents of color in red, which was used for the Venetian blinds, the cover on the dressing-table bench, the door, and the circle in the floor design.

SHARP VALUE CONTRASTS ARE DRAMATIC. Sharp contrasts of black and white or very light against very dark are striking and can be used to create a dramatic effect. The dining-room setting shown on page 75 achieves its theatrical quality in this way. The large painting in tones of deep browns against the white brick wall catches the eye at once. The bottle-green dishes contrasted with the pale, blond wood of the table top, and the dark forest-green upholstering of the chair seats with the pale wood of the chairs contribute to the dramatic quality. The group of bare branches against the light wall, and the figure with black hair in a white robe are especially dramatic.

> EXPERIMENTS IN STUDYING VALUE. 1. Make a sample of dark value for each of the spectrum colors. Be sure to add enough black to yellow and orange so they are really *dark* value. It requires much more black than color. What seems to happen to each of these colors? Compare your samples with the neutral value scale. Are they as dark as the dark value neutral?
>
> 2. While outdoors look off into the distance with your eyelids almost closed. What value are the objects near at hand? The distant objects?
>
> 3. Can you give the correct value for the different objects in the room?
>
> 4. Experiment with commercial dyes and cloth. How can you dye orange cloth dark brown without using brown dye? Dye it a light value, a middle value, and a dark value of red, yellow, blue. Can you mix dyes to secure these results?

INTENSITY OR CHROMA GIVES A COLOR STRENGTH. Here is another color quality which you must understand to enjoy color fully. Compare a dull pink and a bright red. They are both reds, but which is a stronger color? Which is more intense? Obviously the answer is red. A spectrum color is full intensity or chroma. A tint or tone is weaker in intensity. Any color to which neutral has been added is less intense than a spectrum hue. The more black, white, or gray that is added, the weaker the intensity.

Spectrum red is a little below the middle on the value scale. Gray can be added to a spectrum red without making it either lighter or darker, or in other words without changing the value. Spread out

The Widdicomb Furniture Company

Sharp contrasts of color values help to create the dramatic effect in this dining-room area.

75

your color samples and try to find two reds of the *same value but different chroma*. Remember that intensity or chroma means the *strength* of a color.

Intense colors attract a great deal of attention. Sometimes they scream and yell for attention. If not used properly they are great nuisances. Weaker colors can be used in larger doses without becoming objectionable. This is a good rule to remember in house furnishings. Spectrum blue walls and ceiling are not very restful. This is another reason why the restaurant owner who painted his dining room spectrum blue soon found himself with no customers. If he liked bright blue, it would have been better if he had used it in smaller bits of decoration, such as the dishes, the chair backs, or the window curtains.

SUGGESTIONS FOR THE STUDY OF INTENSITY. 1. Make a sample of color that is full intensity, choosing any hue that you like. Then make a less intense sample of the same color, keeping it at the same value.

2. Can you describe any color in the room in terms of hue, value, and intensity? For example, the color of a dress might be described as blue in hue, middle in value, and about three-fourths intensity. Sometimes it is interesting to make a game of this in class. One member of the class describes the color and the other members of the class try to guess what article she is describing.

3. Is your schoolroom properly decorated as to intensity and value of the colors used? How would you change it if you think it should be changed?

4. Try mixing red, yellow, blue, orange, green, and violet together in equal quantities. What is the result?

5. Experiment with dyes in neutralizing bright colors. What happens when you dip bright yellow cloth in gray dye? Can you neutralize bright red dye by adding black dye? By weakening the solution?

COLOR NAMES ARE PRETTY. Each season there are new color names for fashionable colors. Quite often we hear these referred to as "new colors," but, of course, it is the names which are new, not the colors. Because a color is newly fashionable one year does not mean that it is a *new* color.

The names which are invented each year for the colors of fashion are fascinating, and we like to use them for the old colors which we have known before. After our study of the color circle and the variations of each hue, you know that there are no *new colors*.

New color *names* often call up the most delightful color pictures.

Pacific blue brings us visions of the deep, clear blue of that great ocean; forest green makes us feel the cool depth of the pines; and pansy violet reminds us of the soft petal color of the garden flower. Brick red, Spanish brown, hyacinth blue, gardenia white, and rusty red are intriguing names. Of course, each of these colors could be described in terms of hue, value, and intensity, but new color names are much more interesting. As long as we understand the variations of color qualities, we can enjoy both the lovely colors and their pretty names.

QUALITY OF TEXTURE AFFECTS BEAUTY. Probably there are millions of rooms in the United States with cream ivory walls. All might be the same hue, the same color value, and the same intensity, but some are sure to be much more beautiful than others. Why? Because some are much more pleasing in texture. Many walls are painted with thick enamel paint which has an extremely shiny texture. This kind of surface is easy to wash and seems suitable in bathrooms and kitchens where the wall is splashed frequently, but it is very unpleasant in the living portion of the house where a quieter texture seems more desirable. Other walls are painted with a dull-finish paint which has a softer and more agreeable texture. Still other walls are papered with smooth, flat-colored papers which are not objectionable in texture but lack interest. Other papers have delightful textures produced by mottled or stippled effects and by very small patterns which at a slight distance from the wall have the effect of texture rather than of an all-over pattern.

There is no hard-and-fast rule to tell us when a texture is beautiful and when it is ugly. We learn by experience and by comparison which textures are most agreeable. Often our preference for a texture depends on the use to which the surface is put. We do not like hard, shiny walls in the living room, but in the kitchen we are delighted with smooth, gleaming surfaces. We do not like oilcloth for a bedspread, but on the kitchen shelves it is fine.

Now let us think about textures in color without reference to a particular use. Think of a piece of red velvet, a piece of red canvas, a piece of red satin, and a piece of red patent leather. Practically everyone will say that the red velvet and the red satin are most beautiful. Of course, we cannot use them on the kitchen shelves—but that is another matter! Suppose you are buying material for a blue wool dress. You will find that some materials have a much nicer *texture* than others. Suppose you are buying a desk. You will find that the finish on some desks is much more pleasing than on others. Some are

Kentile, Inc.

The interesting texture of the tile floor in this room contrasts pleasantly with the white brick wall.

varnished with a high-gloss varnish that is very ugly. Others are finished with a rubbed polish that is lovely.

The only way you can learn to appreciate differences in textures is through experience in seeing and feeling them. Make it your business to collect several samples of dress materials, all the same color. Study the differences in texture. Watch for differences in the finish of furniture, in walls, draperies, rugs, hats, and the dozens of other places where texture is important. Soon you will see how texture can add beauty to a color.

The room shown above has an interesting combination of textures which can be seen easily in the black-and-white reproduction without any color. Notice first the tile floor with its pleasing stippled effect. The contrast with the white brick wall is particularly nice. The luster of the plastic-covered chair at the right and the ribbed texture of the chair at the left add further interest to the general effect.

Suggestions for the study of texture. 1. Collect samples of color, the same in hue, value, and intensity but differing in texture. You may find pieces of paper, cloth, glass, feathers, and similar articles. Explain why you think some of the textures are more beautiful than than others.

2. Try describing the most beautiful example of finely graded color and texture which you have seen recently.

3. Collect as many samples as possible of one kind of material—for example, silk crepe dress material or cretonne for curtains. Study these for their texture to determine which are most pleasing.

Related color harmonies

Monochromatic—a self-tone harmony. As you may guess from its name, the monochromatic or self-tone harmony is made up of several tones of one hue. For instance, a cretonne pattern may include orange, tan, brown, and other tones from the orange family, and it may also contain black, white, and gray. Remember that the neutrals belong to no family group. Therefore, they can be added to a self-tone harmony without changing the type of color combination.

Monochromatic harmonies are used quite frequently in dress. A beige dress with brown belt, hat, and gloves, or a dark blue suit and hat with light blue blouse, purse, and gloves are examples of this type of color combination.

Self-tone harmonies are not used so frequently in interior decoration as are other types of harmonies. However, most pleasing effects can be secured with self-tone combinations. Suppose you have a set of maple bedroom furniture with a soft yellow-brown finish. With this you would perhaps use ivory woodwork, cream-colored walls, brown rug, brown-and-orange cretonne drapes, and a dull orange-and-tan bedspread. Bathrooms and kitchens are particularly well suited to monochromatic combinations. A bathroom with jade-green tile walls, a black-and-white tile floor, white fixtures, and a green shower curtain with a black-and-white pattern is most attractive. A kitchen in black and white and red is equally nice in color.

Monochromatic harmonies are the simplest and easiest to use. If you use different values and intensities of the same hue, you are practically sure to achieve a good harmony. The reason for this is obvious. Harmonious colors seem to belong together. They do not fight with each other. They do not argue or even suggest a disagreement. Different tones of the same hue all have something in common, so it is easy for them to agree. But do not think that *any* tones of the

79

same hue will combine harmoniously. You know that different members of the same family sometimes disagree most violently! Perhaps this is more likely to be true with a human family than with a color family, but nevertheless you must use care in combining various tones of one hue if you expect to secure a real harmony.

There is no rule which will tell you when two colors harmonize. You must be able to see it and feel it. The best way to acquire a good sense of color harmony is to keep "trying it on your eye." Combine different colors. Always ask yourself, "Do these colors seem to belong together?" Soon you will feel that certain colors harmonize much better than others. It is best to begin with monochromatic combinations because the colors are more likely to blend.

ADJACENTS—A NEIGHBORING HARMONY. In this type of color combination two or three neighboring hues on the color circle are used together. For example, tones of green, yellow, and orange can produce a most delightful harmony. Let us consider again the bedroom with maple furniture in a soft yellow-brown finish. To carry out an adjacent harmony we might use yellow-and-white striped wallpaper, yellow-orange linen covers for the dresser and table, a corn-yellow chenille bedspread, green-and-yellow cretonne drapes, and a dull green rug for the floor. Remember that you cannot take just any tones of green, yellow, and orange and expect to produce a harmony. They are neighboring colors, but sometimes neighbors do not get along with each other! They must have something in common. Green, yellow, and orange do have something in common because there is yellow in both green and orange. For this reason yellow-orange and yellow-green are more easily blended with yellow than blue-green and red-orange. When you try to create an adjacent harmony of green, yellow, and orange for your bedroom with the maple furniture, you are more likely to be successful if you choose yellow-greens and yellow-oranges.

An attractive living room can be planned to be finished in a yellow, green, and orange combination. Light pouring through sheer yellow window curtains creates the keynote to the whole color effect. Colored window curtains always cast a faint color tone over the whole room. In this case the yellow tint serves to draw the colors closer together, and creates a pleasant, warm effect.

Nature gives us many examples of adjacent color harmonies. The yellow jonquil has a yellow-orange center and yellow-green stem and leaves. Autumn landscapes are full of reds, red-oranges, yellows, and browns. The sky often shows a gradation of hue from blue-violet at the zenith down through blue to blue-green at the horizon.

Some neighboring colors get along with each other better than others. Red, red-orange, and red-violet are very difficult to harmonize successfully. They are all warm colors and all aggressive. It is difficult for aggressive people to get along with each other, especially if they are hot-headed! This is equally true of colors. Blue, blue-violet, and blue-green are also difficult to combine happily. They are all cool and receding colors. Such a combination is likely to be monotonous and uninteresting unless there is a variety of value and intensity. Dark value blue with light value blue-lavender and jade green may make a good harmony. This combination is not generally desirable in interior decoration because the colors are all cool. Red with its adjacents is also a poor color scheme for a room. In this case all the colors are warm. Generally it is better to have a balance of warm and cool colors in a room. Yellow with its adjacents provides this contrast. Of course, there are other uses for blue with its adjacents and red with its adjacents. A dark blue dress with an orchid collar and jade costume jewelry is very attractive. A bouquet of gladioli in tones of rosy lavender, maroon red, and salmon pink is a fine combination.

Good adjacent harmonies can be produced by using other groups of neighboring colors. Orange and its neighbors, red and yellow, often make a particularly exciting harmony. Imagine a scarlet coat with gold buttons and trimmings, white trousers, and a tall black and orange hat. It is just the thing for a band uniform. Green with its adjacents blue and yellow, and purple with its adjacents red and blue, can be used to make equally interesting and pleasing harmonies.

Study of related color combinations. 1. Collect samples of wallpaper, plastics, drapery and upholstering materials, and any other available materials that will serve to show color. Work in small groups or committees. Each committee is to make the best possible monochromatic harmony and the best adjacent harmony with the materials at hand. The harmonies are to be discussed by the class.

2. Collect colored pictures from magazines in which the predominating colors form a related harmony.

3. Be prepared to describe a monochromatic and an adjacent harmony which you have seen in nature. If possible, bring the specimen to class.

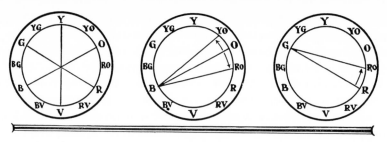

Diagram showing three types of contrasting color combinations. Left: Comple-
ments. Center: Split-complements. Right: Near-complements.

Contrasted color harmonies

COMPLEMENTARY COLORS—A BUSINESS PARTNERSHIP. Colors which
lie directly opposite each other on the circle are not related. They do
not belong to the same family, and they certainly are not neighbors.
However, they are business partners. The first circle in the diagram
above shows three pairs of these opposite colors, blue and orange,
red and green, and yellow and violet. These pairs of colors have
nothing in common, but they can be united very agreeably in a
business partnership.

Let us see how we can persuade a pair of opposite colors, blue and
orange, to form a harmonious partnership. Take some blue paint
and add a little orange. You will notice that the blue is grayed or neutralized. Now take some orange and add a little blue paint. It also becomes gray or neutralized. Neutralized orange is called brown or tan.
If we mix the orange and blue so that they balance perfectly the result is a neutral. In this sense, we can say that the two colors need
each other or complete each other in order to produce neutrality.
Thus we get the term *color complements,* and we can think of this
type of color combination as a business partnership.

Since complementary colors contrast with each other so strongly,
they are more difficult to use harmoniously than are the related color
combinations. However, when properly harmonized they give very
interesting and beautiful effects.

Look at the color illustration opposite page 4 and you will see at
once that the basic color scheme is complementary. Blue and orange
tones dominate this delightful color effect. The soft blue of the wall
forms a perfect background for the orange-red of the sofa, the copper
tones of the accessories, and the bright flame in the fireplace. The

wood tones of the furniture belong to the orange family. The red-orange sofa and the yellow-orange wall introduce the split-complements of orange, adding a delightful color variation. Split-complements are described in the following paragraph.

SPLIT-COMPLEMENTS AND NEAR-COMPLEMENTS. True complementary colors are always directly across the color circle from each other and when properly mixed make a perfect neutral gray. A variation of complementary color harmony is indicated in the second diagram on page 82. The lines show a combination of blue with orange, yellow-orange, and red-orange. Instead of using the one color, orange, as a complement to blue, the orange has been split so as to include yellow-orange and red-orange. This adds variety and interest to the color scheme.

The second variation of the complementary color combination is called near-complementary. In this case only one of the split-complements is used—for example, blue and yellow-orange. The lines on the third diagram show green and its near-complement, red-orange. Green and red-orange is a particularly usable scheme for the colors in a room. Rust (dark red-orange) may be used for the plain floor covering, a lighter tone for the draperies, and brighter bits of red-orange in pieces of pottery, copper bowls or plates, and in small decorative tapestries.

The Swedish tapestry in the illustration opposite page 84 shows an interesting use of near-complements—red-orange and blue-green, plus tones of orange and yellow-orange. The browns and tans, of course, belong to the orange family. Notice how well balanced and satisfactory the harmony seems.

SUGGESTIONS FOR PRACTICE IN HARMONIZING COMPLEMENTARY COLORS. Complementary colors in spectrum intensity offer the most violent contrast that can be obtained with color, a contrast too violent to be agreeable. We can learn some helpful things about combining complementary colors by a simple experiment. Collect many samples of blue paper and cloth, including light blues, middle-value blues, dark blues, neutralized blues, and intense blues. Collect also many samples of orange, tan, brown, cream, and ecru. Lay these out on a table in two groups and combine samples from each group according to the following suggestions.

1. Select the most intense blue and the most intense orange and put them together. If both the colors are intense they will not harmonize. Then take the intense orange and try it with different

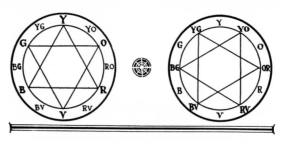

Diagram showing the four triad color combinations.

samples of neutralized blue until you find the one which seems most harmonious. Do you find it better to have a large spot of dull blue with a small spot of bright orange, or a large spot of bright blue with a small spot of dull orange?

Make the best combination of two dark tones: blue and brown. Make the best combination of light, delicate tones: pale blue with cream or light tan.

Find the best combination of blue and orange, one light and the other dark value.

2. Try the same experiments with red and green, and with yellow and violet. Which pair of complements do you find most difficult to combine harmoniously?

3. Try the same experiments with a pair of near-complements. Blue and yellow-orange, green and red-orange, or orange and blue-green are good combinations to try.

TRIADS—ANOTHER BUSINESS PARTNERSHIP. The triad combination is composed of strongly contrasting hues. As you can see in the above diagram, three colors located at equal distances around the circle are combined. The red, yellow, and blue combination is sometimes spoken of as the major or primary triad. Certainly these three hues do not belong to the same family, nor are they neighbors. Again three hues are combined in a business partnership. These three when mixed in the right proportions will produce a perfect gray. When used properly they can be combined in very interesting and beautiful harmonies. The same thing is true of each of the other triads indicated on the above circles. Of course, it is necessary to use neutralized tones in order to secure good harmonies. Spectrum red, yellow, and blue used together produce a most glaring and discordant effect. A room done in such tones would be truly terrible! But the room shown opposite page 186, with light blond (yellow) furniture, dull blue walls and a rose-red rug, is most charming.

84

*A Swedish tapestry showing the use of a complementary and near-comple-
mentary scheme—blue-green and red-orange plus near-complementary tones
of brown and tan (the orange family).*

The orange, green, and violet triad also offers a suggestion for a pleasant room. Brown walnut furniture, pale green walls, mulberry upholstering, a moss-green rug, homespun drapes striped with orange and green, and bright orange vases on the mantel make a delightful effect. This is the secondary triad.

The tertiary triads shown in the second circle on page 84 also offer good suggestions for interior color schemes. It is not so easy to use three colors in a costume. Present fashion uses only one or two hues for most costumes. However, we frequently find a triad combination used in the print materials which are so popular. Even men occasionally wear triad color harmonies. For example, a dark blue suit, red socks, black shoes, white shirt, and red-and-yellow figured tie make a triad harmony.

> PRACTICE IN MAKING TRIAD HARMONIES. 1. Experiment in making triad harmonies just as you did in making complementary harmonies. Secure as many samples of color as possible. It is not possible to make really good color combinations unless you have the right colors from which to choose. As you make the combinations, constantly ask yourself this question: "Do the colors blend perfectly?"
>
> 2. Cut pictures from magazines and collect specimens from nature that you think are good examples of contrasted harmonies. Select your examples carefully. It is better to have one good example than ten poor ones.

Color and the principles of design

Color effects are most successful when planned in acordance with the principles of design. Some of the rules about design which you have already learned will help you to use color wisely.

BALANCED ARRANGEMENTS OF COLOR. We cannot have truly balanced arrangements unless we take color into consideration. Color can change the apparent weight and size of an object. This implies that in a formally balanced arrangement the colors on each side of the central point will be alike in hue, value, and intensity. But in the informally balanced arrangements we must take into account the weight and attracting power of colors.

> AN EXPERIMENT IN BALANCING COLORS. Experiment with intense and neutralized colors in making informally balanced arrangements. Choose an intense orange-colored paper and a dull well-neutralized orange, or what we generally call tan. Cut three squares from each

paper—a half-inch square, an inch square, and a two-inch square. Make a diagram representing such a seesaw as that shown on page 15, with a board about eight inches long. Experiment with the different-sized squares of intense orange and neutralized orange (tan or brown), placing them on opposite sides of the center until you find a balanced arrangement. Can you use the same size squares of bright orange and tan at equal distances from the center and secure a balanced feeling? Does the intense color or the neutralized color seem to be heavier and have more attracting power? You should be able to find at least three different balanced arrangements.

In performing this experiment you will discover that intensity of color must be taken into account when making balanced arrangements. You have used two different intensities of the same color, but the problem is the same in using different colors. For example, an intense orange and a dull blue can be balanced against each other. Do you always find that a small amount of intense color will balance a large area of neutralized color?

BALANCE OF COLORS ABOVE AND BELOW THE CENTER. Color plays an important part in creating a balanced effect above and below the center of a design. We have already mentioned that rooms generally appear better balanced if the darker and heavier colors are on the floor and the lighter colors are above. Can you imagine the effect in a room with a white floor and black ceiling? You probably feel as though the ceiling was about to come down on your head! This is an exaggerated arrangement of colors which you will probably never see. It is quite likely, however, that you will see other color arrangements where the colors seem upside down in a room.

We have found that a small amount of intense color will balance a larger amount of neutralized color. This must be taken into consideration when balancing from top to bottom. Suppose that you are making a flower arrangement using some brilliantly colored gaillardia blossoms and some smaller yellow and white flowers. You will want to use the bright gaillardias near the bottom of the arrangement and the smaller, less intense flowers at the higher points in the arrangement. (See the arrangement on page 282.)

In concluding our study of balanced color let us emphasize its importance as a means of securing a feeling of rest and repose. Any picture or design, no matter how simple or how complicated, must satisfy this requirement in order to be truly artistic. Shapes, lines, and colors must be arranged on each side of a central point so as to produce a feeling of stability and balance. When formal balance is used, shapes of equal size and weight are placed on each side, equally distant from the center. When informal balance is used, the larger shapes are placed near the center and the smaller ones farther away. The feeling of stability and repose which we secure through balance and arrangement also depends on balance above and below a central point.

A SUGGESTION FOR YOUR NOTEBOOK. Add colored illustrations of the following to your notebook: (1) formal balance; (2) informal balance; (3) balance from top to bottom.

Write a short explanation under each illustration telling what kind of balance it has and why. Remember to follow the rule about margins when you are arranging these pages in your notebook.

OTHER PROBLEMS IN THE BALANCE OF COLOR. 1. Experiment in balancing warm and cool colors either side of a central point. Any combination of complementary colors furnishes a contrast of warm and cool colors. Does it require a larger or smaller amount of warm color to balance a cool one?

2. Experiment in balancing values. Cut some squares of black and of middle gray and try balancing them on a white background. Is the black or the gray heavier? Try the same experiment with a light-value blue and very dark blue. If you were balancing two vases approximately the same size, one a dark green and the other a light green, on top of a bookcase, which would you place nearer the center? Why?

GOOD PROPORTIONS IN COLOR COMBINATIONS. The principle of proportion is helpful in combining colors successfully. We found that exactly equal spacing is monotonous. Here is a hint for combining colors. Exactly equal amounts in a combination makes an uninteresting effect. There should be more of one color than of the other to make the most pleasing harmony. Let us see how this works out in combining black and white. In a checkerboard pattern there are equal amounts of light and dark. A quilt with a plain checkerboard pattern is not so attractive as the quilt shown on page 88. In this pattern there is definitely more light than dark. The quilt is an old one made about 1850. The pattern was worked out in Turkey red on a white background. Although it is a simple pattern, it is very effective.

An old quilt made about 1850. It shows an interesting proportion of light and dark with more light than dark. This is much more pleasing than equal amounts as in a checkerboard pattern.

Nice proportions between light and dark are also found in the old Colonial coverlet from Virginia shown on the opposite page. If the reverse side of the coverlet were shown you could see the opposite effect of light and dark. This is because the coverlet was made by weaving the light and dark threads together to form the pattern. Instead of thinking of the coverlet in black and white as shown here, think of it in blue and white, or blue and tan, or rose and blue.

Remember this rule when combining colors: *Combine colors in pleasing proportions.* Avoid equal amounts of two or more colors. Also avoid a great deal of one color and only a tiny bit of another.

OTHER PROPORTION PROBLEMS IN COLOR COMBINATIONS. Another problem is the relation of warm to cool color. One must decide whether the predominating effect is to be warm or cool. For example, we may wish to give a room an effect of warmth, yet we need small areas of cool color for pleasing contrast. A room finished entirely in

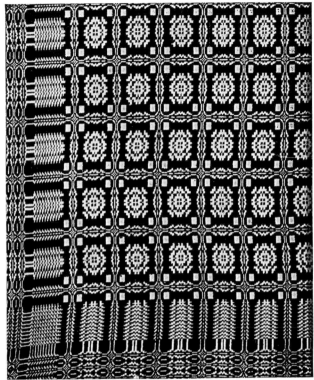

Laura S. Copenhaver, Director of "Rosemont Workers"

An old Colonial coverlet from Virginia. In this pattern the dark predominates.

warm color probably would seem unpleasant. Not all color schemes require a contrast of warm and cool color. For example, a costume may be carried out successfully in either warm or cool color. A red dress needs no contrast of cool color. It is interesting to study paintings for contrasts of warm and cool tones. Generally you will find that the artist chooses a dominant effect of either warm or cool tones and uses small areas of opposite tones for contrast.

Still another problem in color proportions is the relation of intense and neutralized hues. Here is a rule to remember: *Small areas of intense color and larger areas of neutralized color combine most successfully.* A gray wall with bright orange vases on the mantel is all right, but a bright orange wall with some tan vases is terrible! A navy blue dress with a brilliant blue tie is all right, but a brilliant blue dress with a navy blue tie may look queer. In general, it is best to use small areas of intense color with larger areas of neutralized color.

A SUGGESTION FOR YOUR NOTEBOOK. Find illustrations which show colors used in pleasing proportions. These may be room interiors, costumes, magazine advertisements, or posters.

RHYTHM IN COLOR. Spots of color in a design can carry the eye across a mantelpiece or around a room as well as can black and white spots or lines. To accomplish this, there must be a repetition, or echoing, of the color on each side of the mantelpiece and in the different parts of the room. This is particularly evident when bright colors are used, because the eye is so easily attracted to them. In a room where vivid yellows are used for the small areas, care should be taken to repeat the yellow color notes in different parts of the room. If a yellow bowl is used on the mantelpiece, its color should be repeated in other parts of the room, perhaps through yellow accents in figured curtain materials or yellow objects placed on tables or tops of bookcases. Then the eye is drawn naturally about the room from one yellow spot to another.

Repetition, or rhythmic repeat, of the neutralized colors is also important, because they, too, help the eye to travel about the room in a restful manner. Sometimes the color for a curtain or table runner is best decided by thinking out what color should be repeated. Care must be taken in repeating the colors not to make equal areas, as this would violate the principle of good proportion. One helpful way to think is in terms of small repeats or echoes. Each large mass of color should be echoed by smaller masses of the same color in other parts of the room.

FOR YOUR NOTEBOOK. Find a colored illustration which shows the rhythmic use of color. This may be an advertisement, a reproduction of a painting, or room interior.

HOW COLOR IS USED TO SECURE EMPHASIS. Another means of securing a center of interest is contrast of color. This may be a contrast of values, such as black against white, which makes a striking contrast, or a contrast of intense color against neutralized color. A bright orange tie worn on a dark blue dress always attracts attention. The same tie worn on an orange-colored dress would not be noticed. Since intense color is bound to force our attention, it behooves us to use it only in those places where we want a center of interest. If we color our walls a bright canary yellow, they cease to be a good background and attract far too much attention.

Enjoying and using color in your world

Color more than anything else can help our homes and our wardrobes to be attractive. Our rooms can just as well be full of delightful colors as dull and drab. Our clothing can just as well be right for our faces and figures as wrong. *It costs no more.* A can of lovely yellow paint costs no more than one of dismal gray. A pretty blue coat costs no more than an ugly blue. All it requires is understanding of color qualities and harmonies. You will not learn everything there is to know about color in this unit of work. But it should give you a start toward the better use and enjoyment of color. The more often you notice colors, the more often you try to harmonize colors, the better your taste will become.

SOME REMINDERS ABOUT COLOR

Ask yourself these questions when you are choosing colors. Consider them as standards for the use of color.

1. Is the hue right? Does it lean too much toward its neighbor? Is it the exact hue you want?
2. Are the color values right? Is the contrast of light and dark too striking or too slight?
3. Does the color give the effect of coolness or warmth which is needed?
4. Are the colors too aggressive?
5. Is the color too intense or too weak?
6. Is the texture pleasing and suitable for its use?
7. Are the colors blended into a harmonious whole?
8. Is the combination of colors haphazard or consistently related? Is the general effect monochromatic, adjacent, complementary, or triadic?

To TEST WHAT YOU HAVE LEARNED ABOUT COLOR

I. List some of your own personal color problems that have occurred to you since you began your color study. Discuss solutions for your problems.
II. Report any instance of how you have enjoyed beauty in color since your study of this chapter.
III. Plan the ideal color scheme for your own room that you would like to carry out if it were possible for you to do so. Collect as many

samples of wallpaper, rugs, and curtains as you can. Make drawings of the walls if you can and color them. Be prepared to report to the class, telling them your plan and showing your samples. When each member of the class reports, the other members of the class should ask questions as to why certain colors have been combined and should criticize the general scheme.

IV. Choose the word in each of the following exercises which you think gives the correct answer.

1. What quality of color prevents spectrum blue and orange from being harmonious? *Hue, value, intensity.*

2. What is wrong with a sand-colored wallpaper for a living room having a very shiny surface? *Hue, value, texture, coolness.*

3. What is wrong in the arrangement of colors in a room in which the walls are paneled in brown oak, the ceiling is cream color, and the floor is light yellow maple? *Hue, value, intensity, warmth, coolness.*

4. What is wrong in a room in which the furniture is red mahogany, the rugs are dark blue, and the walls are bright Chinese red? *Hue, value, advancing color, texture.*

5. What is wrong in a room in which the walls and ceiling are white and there are heavy, dark brown beams across the ceiling? *Hue, value, intensity, coolness.*

6. What color name would you use for a color that can be described as red in hue, dark in value, and about one-half full strength in intensity? *Pink, maroon, scarlet, crimson, rose.*

7. What color name would you use for a color that can be described as orange in hue, light in value, and about one-fourth color strength or intensity? *Brown, flame, sand, gold, mustard, coral.*

8. What type of color harmony is produced when tones of lavender, jade, peach, orchid, tan, gray, and white are blended together? *Monochromatic, complementary, self-tone, analogous, triad.*

9. If you wished to make a small room appear larger, what color would you paint the walls? *Light green, pink, yellow, buff.*

10. What makes rough plaster walls generally produce a more pleasing effect than the smooth plaster walls when painted the same color? *Hue, value, intensity, texture.*

V. Some questions to answer:

1. Why are there many more color names than appear on the color circle?

2. If blue and orange make a complementary combination, how does it happen that blue and brown are also complementary?

3. Since red and green are complementary colors, will all combinations of red and green produce *harmonious* results? Explain.

4. List the things that you have learned in this chapter that would help you in planning the color scheme for a room.

5. What have you learned about color that will help you to match colors more accurately?

6. Can you detect differences in shades of color when you are trying to match them? What causes the differences? Give an illustration.

7. Give an example of proper use of warm colors; of cool colors.

8. What is the correct distribution of color values in a room?

9. How does texture contribute to fine color quality?

10. What are monochromatic and triad harmonies?

11. Of what value is it to know which colors are advancing and which are receding? Give an illustration.

VI. Your teacher will hang ten examples of color combinations around your classroom. These may be textiles, pictures, or advertisements. Some of them will show real color harmony and some will not. Each example of color will be numbered. Make two rows of numbers from one to ten on your paper. Opposite the first row of numbers record whether you think each example of color is harmonious or inharmonious. Opposite the other row of numbers write down the type of color combination which you think is predominant in each example.

Chapter 5

MAKE THE MOST OF WHAT
YOU HAVE

B egin your study of beauty and comfort in your own home by considering the arrangement of the furnishings which you already
possess. Perhaps the beauty of what you have is lost because it is
not shown off properly. Possibly your rooms would be more livable
if the furniture were rearranged for comfort and convenience. It is
not always a new chair or new drapes that adds beauty and livable
quality to a room. Often, a new arrangement of old furnishings with
an eye for harmony and convenience is better than the most expensive purchase.

GOOD ARRANGEMENT HELPS TO PRODUCE HARMONY. We have already
learned that there must be an agreement of lines, shapes, and colors
to produce an effect of harmony. This is just as true in the placing
of furniture and rugs in a room as in placing a picture on the page
of a snapshot book. Good arrangement of the furniture and rugs in a
room implies that they must be placed so that they are in harmony
with its structural lines. Most rooms and most pieces of furniture
are rectangular in structure. This makes it necessary to place the
larger pieces of furniture and rugs parallel with the walls of the
room in order to secure a harmonious effect.

Compare the two arrangements of the same furniture in the same
room on the opposite page. The quiet, comfortable effect in the top
picture is due in part to the arrangement of the davenport, chairs,
and tables. The davenport and Duncan Phyfe table are parallel with
the wall. The two chairs are not parallel with the walls but are set at

94

A contrast in effects produced chiefly by arrangement. Top: Dignified, harmonious, and comfortable. Bottom: Restless, fussy, and uncomfortable.

angles which seem harmonious with the shape of the room. In the bottom picture these same pieces of furniture are arranged so as to make a decidedly inharmonious effect. The cornerwise arrangement of the rugs, the "tidies," the picture wires, and the stairstep arrangement of the pictures all contribute to the feeling of unrest and confusion. Observe that one rug, the three small pictures, and several small articles on the mantel and tables have been eliminated in the top arrangement, thus adding greatly to the effect of restful comfort.

Too many decorations give a room a cluttered, restless appearance. If we have more possessions than can be used successfully at one time, we should store them away until ready for a change.

In the attempt to make our rooms quiet and restful, we should not go to the extreme of having them bare of decorative accessories, or arrange the furniture and rugs in too severe and formal a fashion. It is not necessary that *every piece of furniture* and *every rug* be placed with absolute geometrical accuracy to coincide with the structural lines of the room. Often it is desirable to place the smaller pieces of furniture, such as chairs and small tables, at slight angles to the walls. This relieves the stiff and formal effect, and is often more convenient.

> SUGGESTIONS FOR FURTHER STUDY. 1. Find two pictures of room interiors in magazines which illustrate the following: (1) harmony, unity, and convenience; and (2) confusion, disorganization, and lack of comfort. List the special points which you think important about each room. If the pictures are in color, give your opinion of the effect in each one.
>
> 2. Can you suggest a better arrangement of furnishings for any room in your own house? Describe what you would do to accomplish it.

CONVENIENT ARRANGEMENTS ARE IMPORTANT. Room arrangements that are convenient and comfortable for living are far more pleasing than awkward and inconvenient arrangements. The diagrams on page 98 show two plans of arrangement for the same furniture in the same living room. These floor plans are like maps. The large outside rectangles show the shape of the room and the location of doors, windows, and fireplace.

In the top arrangement, little thought has been given to convenience and comfort. The davenport has been placed in front of the windows, making it difficult to reach them for opening or closing, and also making it impossible to place a chair so as to get the best light for reading. The fireplace, which is a natural center of interest in a room even when there is no fire in it, has been disregarded. The desk has been placed so as to prevent having a chair at the left of the fireplace. One chair has been placed so as to interfere with easy entrance from the hall. Two of the tables are not placed so as to be within convenient reach from any chair. This arrangement of the tables is bad, since often we wish to lay some object, such as a book or a letter, on a table without rising from a chair.

Now study the arrangement of the same furniture in the bottom diagram. Chairs have been arranged on each side of the fireplace, and tables and lights are convenient to these chairs. The chairs to the right of the fireplace have good daylight from the windows. The davenport is against the opposite wall, with a floor lamp at one end and a small table at the other. The desk has a corner to itself where one could work without being located in the center of other activities. Passage to and from the hall is not obstructed by a chair, as in the top diagram.

SUGGESTIONS FOR FURTHER STUDY. The idea of convenient arrangement of furniture applies to other rooms in the house as well as to the living room. The best arrangements for the dining room and bedrooms are problems to be thought out. A study of the following questions and diagrams will suggest points to be considered in arranging the bedroom and the dining room.

1. Examination of the floor plans on page 99 will show that in one plan the furniture has been placed in the room without regard to convenience or harmonious effect. In the other plan the furniture has been placed in the room in a convenient and harmonious way. Answer the following questions:

In which plan is the bed well placed with respect to light from the windows? Is it pleasant to have the light shine in one's eyes in the morning?

In which plan is the bed well placed with respect to general appearance when one enters from the hall? Which position of the bed will make the room seem larger and less filled with furniture?

Should the dresser be placed near the closet? Why?

In which plan is the rule about harmonious placing of furniture violated? Why?

Which position of the dresser is better for the light?

2. Draw a floor plan of a room at home showing the present arrangement of furniture. Then draw another floor plan showing how you would improve the arrangement. It will be best to draw the plan to scale, as otherwise the drawing may show a plan that cannot be used with the real furniture. A scale of one inch to one foot on large paper is easy to work with.

THE ART PRINCIPLES HELP IN ARRANGEMENT. Good arrangement of home furnishings requires placing for both beauty and utility. As pointed out in Chapter 2, pleasing effect and practical considerations go hand in hand. This partnership has been further explained in the discussion and illustrations given on the last three pages.

For further study of good arrangement, we shall consider the ways in which the principles of design are helpful in making satisfactory and attractive arrangements.

97

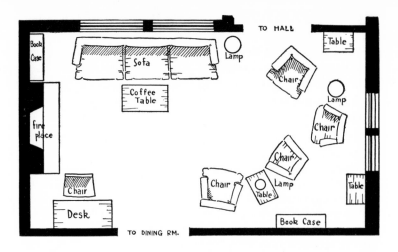

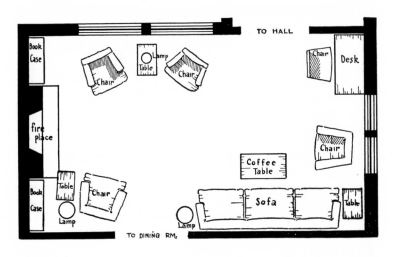

Two plans of arrangement for the same furniture in the same living room. Top: Inconvenient for use. Bottom: A more comfortable and convenient arrangement.

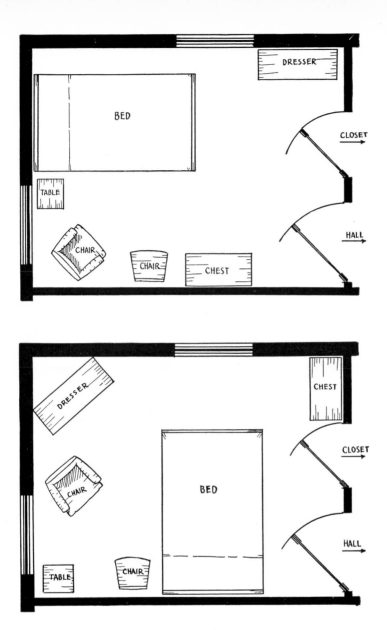

Two arrangements of the same furniture in the same bedroom. Which is more convenient for use?

This formally balanced arrangement of a bedroom grouping is very satisfactory for beauty and convenience.

BALANCE YOUR ARRANGEMENTS. We know that a picture or design with good balance gives a sense of stability and repose. Certainly we desire this quality in our rooms. It is not restful to sit in a room which lacks stability and repose. Balanced effects in rooms are secured by the right arrangement of both large and small furnishings. Each small arrangement of decorative accessories on the tops of mantels, bookcases, desks, and dressers should be well balanced. Earlier in the book we discussed both formal and informal balance as expressed in such small arrangements. (See pages 16 and 19.) Each large arrangement of furniture and accessories should also show good balance. Here too either formal or informal balance may be successfully used.

In planning arrangements it is advisable to think of the balance as seen on each wall. A good example of formally balanced furniture is seen in the davenport group shown on page 26. Another formally balanced group is shown above, with a bed, headboard, bedside

*This television–sitting room is a good example of balance, proportion, rhythm,
and emphasis in arrangement.*

cabinets, lamps, and pictures. This is an especially nice use of the
contemporary style in furniture.

An interesting fireplace wall arrangement is shown in the room
on this page. Again the arrangement is simple. A large piece of driftwood, a group of books, and two pictures are arranged to give an
unusual but pleasing effect. The group of books is just off center
toward the right. The piece of driftwood at the extreme right is balanced by the two pictures which are a little closer to the center on
the left-hand side. The fireplace and sofa provide an interesting base
for the whole design. A feeling of repose and stability is well estab-
lished.

The room is used as a combination television-sitting room. The
sectional furniture can be moved as desired and made to form a
long couch for an overnight guest. The folding wall at the right
leads into a modern type bedroom.

BALANCE YOUR ROOMS FROM SIDE TO SIDE. Each room as a whole, as well as each small arrangement and each wall, should have a balanced effect. When you stand in the center of a room and look about, you should feel an equal distribution of weight. Not all of the heavy pieces should be crowded into one half of the room. Of course, we are not thinking of weight in terms of pounds but weight in terms of power to capture attention.

Observe the balance of weight on the three walls shown in the television-sitting room on page 101. In this case we feel that there is an equitable distribution. The television cabinet on the right is balanced by the davenport with the group of four pictures above, and the fireplace wall holds its own in interest and power to attract the eye.

SUGGESTIONS FOR FURTHER STUDY. 1. Since it is difficult and often impossible to use full-sized furniture in experimenting with different arrangements, it is a good plan to use toy furniture that can easily be moved about. It is wise to select toy furniture of fair size in order to approximate actual conditions. This makes easy the experimenting with arrangement which is generally impossible when we have to shift heavy furniture and climb on stepladders to rehang pictures. Use your small furniture to see how many good balanced arrangements you can secure. This will enable you to carry out your ideas of arrangement without the inconvenience and fatigue of shifting large pieces of furniture.

2. What type of balance is shown on page 180? Do you consider the balance good? Why? Be sure of your reasons and be prepared to present them to the class.

3. Make a sketch showing a wall arrangement in your home that you think shows good balance.

GOOD ARRANGEMENTS DEPEND ON GOOD PROPORTIONS. We have learned that proportion is the relationship of spaces to one another. When we arrange articles on a mantelpiece or furniture in a room, we produce spacing that is either interesting or uninteresting. The placing of the furniture against the wall in the illustration on the opposite page is managed so as to secure interesting proportions. Observe that the chairs are not placed exactly in the center of the space on each side of the chest, but that they are nearer to the chest. Notice, too, that the candles are not so tall that they are level with the picture. All these relationships of space make for pleasing variety. If you wish to see how much more uninteresting the spacing might be,

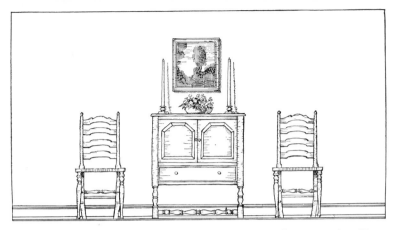

A dining-room wall arrangement that shows formal balance. It also illustrates especially nice proportions in the placing of the chairs, the height of the candles in relation to the picture, and the size of the picture in respect to the chest.

make a tracing of the wall, sliding the paper so as to place the chairs in the center of each wall space and the candlesticks level with the picture.

A comparison of pleasing and of monotonous spacing is illustrated on pages 104 and 105. The effect in the first picture is monotonous because the table is in the exact center of the wall space, the vase and statue are just the same height, and the picture is hung too high. In the second arrangement the table has been moved to the left, and the picture has been lowered. The vase has been eliminated. Remember, it is not necessary to use *all* your decorative accessories at once. You will observe that better balance has been secured in the last arrangement. The principles of art co-operate with each other. When the spacing in this arrangement was improved, balance was also improved.

The drawings on page 106 show six treatments of the wall space above a davenport. In number 1 there are four pictures exactly the same size, and the width of the space between each two pictures equals the width of the pictures. The result is monotonous and uninteresting. In 2 one small picture has been hung above the davenport, but this also violates the principle of proportion. The picture is much too small for the space and seems lost. The difference in size is too great. In 3 a large picture is hung above the davenport, fitting

103

Uninteresting arrangement of table and decorative accessories in a small wall space. The effect is haphazard.

into the space much more harmoniously. In 4 the principle of proportion is again violated. Things which vary too greatly in size cannot be successfully combined, and the two tiny pictures are out of scale with the larger one. In 5 the three pictures of equal size are arranged to produce a unified effect, or we might say a panel effect, which is in nice proportion to the davenport below. In 6 the five pictures of unequal size have also been arranged to give the effect of a unified panel. The separate pictures are in good proportion to one another, and the whole panel of pictures is in good proportion to the davenport.

The principle of proportion is a most helpful guide in the arrangement of furniture and decorative accessories. It helps to make a whole wall more interesting and a small group of decorative accessories more pleasing, and is an aid in selecting the right accessories for various uses. As one student of interior decoration remarked, "It

A more interesting arrangement than the one shown on the opposite page chiefly because of better spacing.

is astonishing how much it helps to move a chair a little to the right or left, or to hang a picture a little lower, or to take away one vase."

SUGGESTIONS FOR FURTHER STUDY. Many problems in proportion confront the person who arranges the furnishings of a room. It is helpful to remember that spaces which are too much alike are monotonous and that spaces which vary too greatly will not give a unified effect. But in addition to this we need experience in "feeling" fine proportions. The following problems suggest some ways that will help develop your sense of good proportions.

1. Draw a rectangle to represent a wall, not less than 6 by 10 inches in size. Cut rectangles of the correct size and shape to represent a table, chairs, pictures, or whatever you wish to use. Move these rectangles about on the paper until the spacing seems most pleasing to you. Then draw the furniture in more detail and ask the other members of your class to criticize it for spacing.

In which of these arrangements is the picture not in harmony with the size of the davenport? In which one does the size of the picture harmonize with the davenport? Which arrangement has monotonous spacing? In which one are the pictures not harmonious in size? In which two arrangements is the spacing pleasing?

2. Study the arrangement on the mantel shown on page 107. Explain how balance is achieved. Why not push the clock in toward the center? Why not place one small object on the other side of the framed picture?

How is the principle of proportion used in the placing of the articles on the mantel? Why are the proportions of the mantel itself pleasing?

The Donley Brothers Company

A simple and pleasing arrangement on a simple but dignified mantel.

RHYTHM HELPS IN MAKING ARRANGEMENTS. Our earlier study of rhythm was concerned mostly with the movement of the eye carried along by lines. Rhythmic movement can also be produced by spots as shown in the diagram below. In the first part of the diagram our eyes naturally follow along the curve of the line. In the second

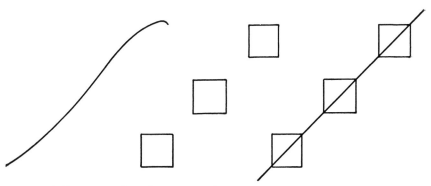

A diagram to show how the eye is carried along by lines or spots.

This arrangement lacks a good center of interest. The whole effect is confused and cluttered.

part, our eyes jump from spot to spot. The line drawn through the spots in the third part of the diagram helps the eye to move a little faster. However, the feeling of movement from spot to spot is just as definite as when the eye follows a line.

A good example of rhythmic room decoration created by the use of both lines and spots is shown on page 101. Attention is likely to be caught first by the unusual decoration at the right of the mantel— the gnarled and twisted piece of driftwood. Your eye will wander up and down the main branch, then travel out over the lines of the arms which reach across the mantel, then jump to the spot created by the group of books, and then make a bigger jump to the pictures at the right. Next your eye may possibly travel back under the cornice to the driftwood or it may drop down to the dark sofa silhouetted against the light wall and over to the fireplace. Thus your eye tours around the whole wall, stopping here and there at points of interest.

Compare the arrangements on these two pages. In which one does the eye get around more easily from spot to spot? What effect does this have on the feeling of unity in the whole arrangement?

Mrs. Allan Masser

In this arrangement the mirror has become a pleasing center of interest. The improvement was achieved by removing several articles shown on the opposite page and placing the remaining articles advantageously.

The rhythmic effect in the grouping of modern bedroom furniture (page 100) is one of low horizontal lines. This is one of the important characteristics of the contemporary style. Your eye is caught first by the gooseneck lamps with their crossed lines, then your eye probably will jump to one of the pictures with its horizontal rectangle, then down to the top of the bookshelf, on down to the cabinet, across the bolster, around the other cabinet, and back to the lights.

You will find it interesting to look through the illustrations in the other chapters of this book to find pleasing rhythms. Notice particularly the types of rhythms expressed in the Pennsylvania Dutch designs on page 62 and the rhythmic forms in the house exterior on page 365.

SUGGESTIONS FOR FURTHER STUDY. 1. Make a sketch showing an arrangement for the top of a bookcase or sideboard with good balance, pleasing proportions, and interesting rhythm.

2. It is an interesting experiment to try making rhythmic color arrangements, using toy furniture and a box with one side open for the room. It is easy to paint the furniture, walls, and floors different colors, using opaque water colors or poster paint. If the first combination of colors does not seem satisfactory, wash off the color that is wrong and try another color. It is possible to try several colors in a small amount of time because the objects are small and it does not take long to repaint them. Use pieces of colored cloth and paper for rugs, curtains, and wallpaper. We can think of this small room and its furniture as a miniature stage setting. You will remember that the aim of this experiment is not to play with doll furniture but to produce a color arrangement that expresses good rhythm, good balance, and good proportion.

A CENTER OF INTEREST IS IMPORTANT. In our study of the principles of art we learned that it is important for every design to have a center of interest. Arrangements large or small, a mantel, a dining table, or a whole room, should be thought of as designs, and each needs a center of interest. Some feature should be emphasized so that it dominates the design. In the television-sitting room on page 101 the driftwood dominates the fireplace wall. This emphasis is secured partly by its large size, partly by the sharp contrast of dark against light, and also by the use of an unusual feature.

Do you ever think of a table setting as a design? This is another instance where beauty and utility are close partners. Certainly tables are set for a practical purpose, and at the same time we enjoy having them attractive. Do you not enjoy feasting your eyes on beauty while you feed the inner man?

The table setting on the opposite page was carefully planned to give a very pleasing effect. Can you see it in your mind's eye with deep-green china on a lemon-yellow cloth, and the centerpiece with orange-yellow or flame-colored blossoms and dark glossy green leaves? Notice how well the principles of design have been expressed. The design is nicely balanced with a place at either end and the large centerpiece balancing the two place settings on the opposite side. The proportion of light and dark is interesting and gives a pleasing effect. Lovely rhythmic patterns are found in the contours of the dishes, the silver, in the green leaves, and in the flower petals. The centerpiece dominates the design in a very satisfactory way. It seems just the right size, neither too large nor too small. In planning a center of interest, be careful not to make it so large that it overwhelms the rest of the design or so small that it lacks emphasis.

110

The principles of design are well expressed in this beautiful table setting.

EACH SMALL ARRANGEMENT NEEDS A CENTER OF INTEREST. The principle of emphasis is just as important in small arrangements as in the arrangement of the whole room. When all the objects in an arrangement are equally important, the effect is confusing. In the mantel arrangement on page 108 there are several articles fighting for attention. The mirror may seem a trifle more important than any other object, but it is hardly a good center of interest. In the illustration on page 109 a transformation has been effected, and the mirror has become a real center of interest. The improved effect has been produced by removing several objects, especially those close to the mirror. This helps the mirror to stand out as a center of interest. The tall candles close to the mirror echo the vertical movement, thus emphasizing the mirror itself. The smaller objects at each side are subordinated to the mirror, both in size and in position.

THE CENTER OF INTEREST IN A ROOM. A room, like each small arrangement, should have a center of interest. In a living room with a fireplace, the fireplace is quite likely to dominate the room. Lacking a fireplace, the emphasis may be placed on a picture window, a davenport group, or a piano. In the dining room, the table is the natural center of interest, although other features such as a window garden may be made more important. In the bedroom, a window, the bed, a dressing table, or a chest and mirror may be chosen for the center of interest. The bed is a large piece of furniture and can easily be emphasized by using a figured spread or one with bright color. If you do not wish to make it a center of interest, use a spread which echoes the color of the walls and it tends to retire into the background.

In the bedroom shown on the opposite page, the bed group has been made the center of interest. The cabinets and lamps at each side of the bed, the group of pictures above, and the dark rug at the foot of the bed are arranged to create a very nice center of interest.

SUGGESTIONS FOR FURTHER STUDY. 1. Find a magazine picture of room furnishings which illustrates the principle of emphasis.

2. What is the center of interest in the picture on page 180? Opposite page 186?

3. Describe the center of interest that you would like to have in your own room.

COLORS NEED ARRANGEMENT. Perfect arrangement in your rooms will include a good distribution of colors. Again the principles of art guide us in producing pleasing arrangements.

Balance your colors in both large and small arrangements. For example, if your living room has a green davenport, a green chair, and two rust chairs, you should not put the green davenport and chair on one side of the room and the two rust chairs on the other. It is better to have some of each color on each side of the room. If you have rust-colored draperies at the window on one side and pale green walls on the other side of a room, it is better to put a green chair in front of the window and a rust chair in front of the green wall. This keeps a better balance of color.

The same principle applies in smaller arrangements. Suppose you have several yellow decorative accessories and several green ones to use in a mantel arrangement. No one would put all the yellow ones on one side and all the green ones on the other, but you will get a better arrangement if you think about it in terms of balanced color.

A pleasant bedroom furnished in traditional-style furniture. The grouping of bed, cabinets, pictures, and rug creates a center of interest.

It is not necessary to have exactly equal amounts of the same color on both sides of the center. You will remember from the study of balance in Chapter 4 that a small amount of intense color will balance a larger amount of neutralized color. The best thing to do in balancing colors is to "try it on the eye." As you look at your arrangement, think, "Is it too heavy on either side?"

The principle of proportion also guides us in the arrangement of colors. If you are arranging six candlesticks with red candles on the top of some bookshelves, do not make a picket fence out of them. Group them in twos or threes. The effect will be much more pleasing. The same rule applies to the grouping of colors as seen in other objects.

Rhythmic movement in the color scheme of a room also helps to create a pleasing effect. There should be a repetition or echoing in different parts of the room of each color that forms a basic part of the color scheme.

Let us imagine a room in which the red, yellow, and blue triad is used as the basis of the color scheme. Dull reds will appear in the color of the mahogany furniture, and since several pieces of furniture are used there will be a rhythmic repetition of this color in different parts of the room. The dull red may also be echoed in the figured rugs or draperies. Dull, rich blue is used in the upholstering of the chairs and is echoed in the pattern of the rugs and curtains. If a bright yellow bowl is used on the mantelpiece, its color should be repeated in other parts of the room, perhaps through yellow accents in figured curtain materials or yellow objects placed on tables or tops of bookcases. Then, as the eye travels about the room, it passes easily from one yellow spot to another.

Repetition or rhythmic repeat of the neutralized colors is also important because they, too, help the eye to travel about the room in a restful manner. Sometimes the color for a curtain or table cover is best decided by thinking out what color should be repeated. If one side of the room described in the preceding paragraph seemed lacking in dull red, a curtain, table runner, or sofa pillow might supply the necessary color note. Care should be taken in repeating the colors that equal areas are not made. This would violate the principle of good proportion. One helpful way to think of it is in terms of small repeats or echoes. Each large mass of color should be echoed by smaller masses of the same color in other parts of the room.

Color arrangement is especially important in securing emphasis. Bright color always attracts attention. If a bright orange bowl is placed on a mantel with other objects of duller browns and greens, the orange bowl is sure to attract attention first. If it is placed far to one end of the mantel, attention is pulled to that end. If you want emphasis in the center of the mantel, then place the bright orange color near the center.

Practical arrangements can be beautiful

Practical considerations, convenience for everyday use, comfort, and ease in cleaning are no hindrances to attractive effects. After your eye becomes skilled in judging rooms, you will see immediately when an arrangement is not convenient, although at first glance it seems very pretty. Remember there is no quarrel between usefulness and beauty. Never sacrifice the utilitarian quality in favor of artistic arrangement, because in real beauty there is harmony with the useful requirements.

SOME SPECIAL ARRANGEMENTS. In many modern homes there is no longer the traditional separate dining room and living room. In

114

Consider H. Willett, Inc.

An attractive and convenient arrangement of furniture for a small, informal combination living-dining room. The warm, mellow tones of solid maple drop-leaf table, chairs, and Colonial cupboard combine delightfully with the green and brown tones of the braided rug.

order to save space, to eliminate work, and to reduce expense a combination living-dining room replaces the two separate rooms. This creates a special problem in arrangement. If the traditional furniture for these two rooms were arranged as usual at opposite ends of the combination room, not much would be gained. The arrangement in the above illustration shows an interesting and practical way of saving space, and the general effect is very attractive. In this room one would expect to find informal happy living. It is easy

115

Bigelow-Sanford Carpet Company, Inc.

This simple and pleasing arrangement of modern-style furniture provides a divider between living and dining areas. Notice the effective texture of the carpet as contrasted with the smoother texture of the davenport.

to imagine the family lingering over a meal amid these pleasant surroundings, talking over the events of the day or planning for coming events.

> A CLASS DISCUSSION. Do you think that meals in a room such as this might have an effect on family life? If so, in what way?

Modern furniture design makes possible new styles in arrangement. In the above illustration you can see the round-the-corner davenport which has become very popular in recent years. This is sectional furniture and the pieces can be used to fit into a corner, in a straight row, or as separate chairs.

The group forms a corner by making an ell which extends into the room. The ell is backed by a low bookcase, and together they form a divider between living and dining parts of the combination

116

Convenience, comfort, and space-saving are provided in this arrangement of bedroom furniture.

room. This is a very simple arrangement, and gives the impression of well-organized, harmonious forms and shapes.

The grouping of bedroom furniture shown above includes a space-saving arrangement for twin beds. When the room is small, the beds can be pushed together for daytime, even though they are separated at night for bedmaking operations. The storage headboard is also a space-saver and most convenient.

The comfortable arrangement for lounging and reading at the left has eye appeal as well as utilitarian value. Notice the convenient location of the lamp, high enough for good light, and the step table, large enough to hold reading material within easy reach.

STANDARDS FOR JUDGING ROOM ARRANGEMENTS

After our study of making artistic arrangements, we should be able to apply what we have learned to new problems which will confront us from time to time. Sometimes when we are trying to find the best arrangement for a room, we feel that there is something wrong without being able to analyze the difficulty. There are certain definite standards we can use that will help us to discover our mis-

117

takes. Try judging the arrangement in any room which you may choose according to the following standards. These standards should not be thought of as belonging only between the covers of a book but as being helpful to us in our everyday life.

1. Is the placing of the furniture and rugs in harmony with the structural lines of the room?

2. Is the arrangement thoroughly convenient and comfortable?

3. Is there a feeling of rest and repose in the room? Or is it unbalanced because there is too much weight at one side?

4. Is interesting spacing produced by the placing of furniture against each wall?

5. Is the combination of objects such as to produce interesting proportion of sizes?

6. Is there good rhythmic arrangement in each group and in the room as a whole, so that the eye travels about easily and pleasantly?

7. Is there a pleasing center of interest in the room?

8. Are the pictures hung correctly?

9. Do the arrangements of smaller objects, such as are found on the tops of bookcases and mantelpieces, express the principles of design?

A TEST ON ARRANGEMENT

I. The arrangement of furniture and decorative accessories on page 180 is very good. You should be able to give at least four reasons why it is pleasing. State your reasons in terms of art principles.

II. Criticize the arrangement on the chest shown on page 227. Remember that criticism includes both good and bad points. Criticize this arrangement for harmony and unified effect. If you could change anything in this arrangement, what would you change? What are the best points?

III. Criticize the arrangement of the furnishings in the room shown on page 167. Remember always that criticism includes *good* points. Include reference to all four principles of art in your comments.

Chapter 6

ON THE DINING TABLE

Let us have a test for taste! This test has nothing to do with your taste for roast beef or apple pie! It is a test for good taste in design as applied to the things you use every day on your dining table —china, glass, linens, and table settings. The same rules for design and color that we have studied in earlier chapters can be used for the breakfast table. Do you see and enjoy the bits of good design and color which appear on the table with your dinner? When you select glassware for a gift do you think of proportion, rhythm, or emphasis? When you set the table do you think about design? Can you score 100 per cent on the problems that follow?

1. When you select your silver pattern will you think about practical considerations as well as beauty? What points should be considered from the standpoint of utility?

2. When you choose a breakfast set, how can the principles of design and color help you?

3. If your dishes are decorated with a strong, floral pattern in bright colors, will you choose a plain tablecloth, lace doilies with a floral pattern, or a plaid luncheon cloth? Why?

4. How do rules for setting the table create a harmonious effect?

5. Why should you have an over-all plan for selecting your china, glassware, silver, and table linens before buying any separate items?

Art three times a day

No household articles are used more frequently than the silver, china, glass, and table linens which we put on our tables at mealtimes. Why not give ourselves a treat for the eyes as well as our ap-

Three water goblets showing varying degrees of beauty in contour. Left: Delicacy and refinement of curves. Center: Broken curves with slightly clumsy effect. Right: Good strong curves though with less delicacy than in the first goblet.

petites? Beautiful design and color in table equipment costs no more than ugliness. Your own good taste can guide you in picking out inexpensive tablecloths of lovely color and texture instead of linen damask, and pretty earthenware instead of bone china or porcelain. Eating utensils of stainless steel or other low-cost metals are made in pleasing patterns and make excellent substitutes for plated or sterling silver. The important thing which only *you* can provide is *good taste*. It is more important than plenty of money in your purse if you wish to enjoy beauty on your table three times a day.

Good design in glassware

Contour is important. The shape of a china or glass article, such as a plain glass goblet, is a most important element in design. Contour or shape can give it distinction. Rhythmic, harmonious lines delight the eye in a water glass, plate, or bowl. Contour depends on the structural design of glass or china, so once again we find that beauty begins with structure.

Duncan & Miller Glass Company

The charm of light shining on lovely, clear glass.

Now let us compare the three goblets on page 120. They are somewhat similar in shape, and at first glance we notice no great difference
in contour. Closer study shows that the first goblet is most lovely.
It has a refinement and subtlety of curve not found in the other
two. The eye can slide around its graceful curves with the greatest
satisfaction. Can you not feel this delicate and graceful water glass in
your hand? The contour of the second goblet is least pleasing. The
curves are less rhythmic and the twisted stem gives a somewhat
clumsy effect. The curves in the third goblet are strong and graceful.
There is no fussiness or clumsiness. The contour shows less refine-

The Imperial Glass Corporation

Crackle ware has a delightful textural quality.

ment of curves than in the first goblet, but it is a satisfactory design. A comparison of prices here is astonishing. The least pleasing design is the most expensive—one dollar each. Goblet A cost eighty cents, and C cost fifty cents. This is another case where price is not the guide to beauty.

BEAUTY IN TEXTURAL QUALITY. There is no need to point out the marvelous beauty of clear, gleaming glass. As light shines through this wondrous substance millions of sparkling, light rays catch the eye with the brilliance of sunbeams. Elusive shadows and dancing reflections mingle in fascinating array. The illustration on page 121 shows a photographic study of light shining on beautiful glass. Here you feel the clear, lucent quality of the glass as light shines on its smooth, lustrous surface. The tiny spheres which enhance this "Tear Drop" pattern emphasize the lovely contours of the plate and goblets.

Modern glassmakers are producing glass with quite a different

Fostoria Glass Company

This pattern is designed with beautiful simplicity. Notice that the decoration is built in.

textural quality from the clear, smooth type which we have just discussed. Crackleware gives the impression of cracked ice molded into drinking glasses, as shown on page 122. The irregularities in the glass create a very nice texture which is particularly pleasing in colors. Would you not like the tumblers in frosty green, rich brown, or heather blue? Surely the reds of the radishes and tomatoes and the greens of the lettuce and cucumbers in the salad bowl would be enhanced by an icy blue-green crackle-glass bowl.

WATCH FOR BEAUTY IN GLASS. Do you notice and enjoy the beauty in glassware that you see on your own table, in shop windows, or in other places? It is fun to find a glass goblet with beautiful contours or a glass dish with lovely, clear-crystal texture or gorgeous crackle effect. Report verbally in class on this type of beauty which you have seen.

DECORATION CAN MAKE OR MAR. Decoration added to the structural design of glassware may add emphasis to its beauty or may destroy some of it. Either too much or the wrong decoration can ruin a pleasing effect in glass just as in any other article.

Decoration in glass dishes may be "built in," etched onto the glass, or cut into its surface. The glass in the illustration above

123

has decoration which is really part of the structure. The decorative effect in the pattern is made as the glass is formed. The stems of the goblets are made by pressing the molten glass into molds, thus creating the ornamentation as the glass is constructed. Therefore, we can say that the decoration is built in.

Another type of decoration is produced by a process called etching. In this case the ornamentation is etched on the glass by the use of acid, and has its own characteristic effect. The parts of the pattern which are "eaten" by the acid have a dull velvety texture which forms a pleasant contrast to the smooth, shining surface of the glass. Etched glass is very popular with homemakers and is made in a variety of patterns. You will find it interesting to study these patterns and compare them for the manner in which they enhance the structural design of the glass. (See center goblet, page 120.)

Still another type of decoration on glassware, shown in the illustration on page 125, is known as cut glass. In this style of decoration the pattern is cut with a revolving stone wheel. When first cut, it leaves the surface a soft gray or frosted. The design may be left as it is and called a gray cutting, or it can be polished until diamond bright and transparent. This is a polished cutting. In some cut glass, part of the design is polished and some is left frosty gray.

Cut glass was very popular during the early part of the twentieth century, and during recent years has again become popular with many people. The illustration on the opposite page shows some hand-fashioned tumblers made in yesterday's styles. It may seem to those of you with modern tastes that some of these designs are over-elaborate. However, you will surely like the first one with its sun-ray pattern which so nicely emphasizes the flaring structural form of the tumbler. You will also like the center one in the bottom row with its straight sides and the decoration which so nicely echoes the perpendicular movement. The decoration on the tumbler in the lower-right-hand corner emphasizes the cylindrical shape in an interesting manner. Notice the star-shaped design cut in the base of the glass which shows through the crystal-clear glass.

TABLE SERVICE IN GLASS. If you like the sparkle and brilliance of clear glass or the glowing richness of colored glass, you might like to plan for a complete glass table service for your own table. Many glass patterns are now available in pieces ranging from soup cups to dessert plates. Breakfast sets, luncheon sets, and tea service are particularly attractive for informal living. The picture on page 126 shows a very attractive and inviting buffet service for luncheon on

Imperial Glass Corporation

Polished cut glass has a brilliant, flashing effect which brings sparkle and life to the dining table.

a hot day or perhaps a Sunday night supper. Iced tea, a mixed vegetable salad, and rolls combine with the sparkling glass to appeal to the most critical eye.

The type of glass used in this buffet setting is the type known as pressed glass. This means that each piece is made by pressing molten glass into a metal mold, instead of by the blown glass method. Pressed glass is an American invention first introduced about 1825. There are many steps in the process requiring great skill. Diamond-shaped patterns such as these are characteristic of historic designs in pressed glass.

Sparkling glass helps to make a delightful buffet table.

The other general method of shaping molten glass is known as blown glass. Nothing is more exciting to watch than the moment when the glass blower picks up some molten glass on the end of his blowpipe and, raising it like a trumpet, breathes gently until a bubble is formed. The blower lowers the bubble into a cork-lined mold and blows gently until the goblet or bowl is formed. Many other steps follow in completing a piece of blown glass.

Blown glass was produced in Europe for hundreds of years before it was introduced into America, so it happens that this method of glassmaking came to the New World from the Old World. With the other process it was just the opposite. Pressed glass was first produced in the New World and has spread to all parts of the Old World. Fine glass in beautiful patterns is made by both processes.

CONTRASTS IN CONTOUR. After our discussion of decoration and processes of glassmaking, let us return again to a consideration of contour because this is the foundation of beauty in every piece. There are many good designs in contour, each with fine rhythmic lines. However, one particular style may appeal to you personally more than others. You will find it interesting to compare the different types of contours found in goblets.

Look at the goblets shown on the last few pages. Which contour do you like best?

The pattern shown on page 128 is characterized chiefly by straight lines and practically no decoration. This style is a good example of modern design. In comparison with the patterns we have just examined, this one is perhaps less graceful but has more forceful and dramatic quality.

If you were to choose one of these patterns for your own glassware, which one would you select? Why?

HINTS ON BUYING GLASSWARE. When you go shopping for glassware you should look for signs of quality in manufacture as well as in design. Think of these things:

1. Will the pattern harmonize with the china and other glassware with which it will be used?
2. Is it too delicate and fragile for the use to which it will be put?
3. Avoid "cute" or fantastic shapes. Look for real art quality.
4. Hold stemware by the stem and tap with the knuckle or fingernail. Good blown glass, containing lead, has a clear, fine, musical tone. Good pressed glass does not have the same resonant tone, but this is not a sign of inferiority.

Fostoria Glass Company

Clear-cut lines and simplicity of form characterize contemporary design.

5. Feel the edges of the glass for smoothness. Poor-quality glass often has scratchy edges.

6. Examine the glass for clearness and luster. Good glass is sparkling clear. Remember that some fine glass is spoken of as crystal, but poor quality is indicated by cloudiness and often bluish or greenish tinge. Remember that in the trade the term "crystal" is used to mean clear glass as distinguished from colored glass. The term "rock crystal" means a fine-quality glass made with quartz as one of the ingredients but is not the same as natural rock crystal taken from the earth.

7. Look for defects. No glassware is entirely free from such defects as waves, specks, or bubbles, but there are very few in good-quality glass. Look also for mold marks or ridges on pressed glass. Good-quality glass is free from these defects.

SUGGESTIONS FOR STUDY OF GLASS. 1. Cut silhouettes of goblets, tumblers, and cups from paper. Use folded paper so that both sides will

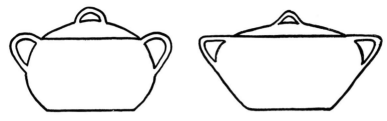

Contrast of contours in two sugar bowls. Left: Uninteresting curves in bowl and inharmonious curves in handles. Right: Pleasing curves in bowl and harmonizing handles.

Marshall Field & Company

China designed by the famous contemporary designer, Russel Wright.

129

These historic pieces of Sèvres porcelain are richly decorated in dark blue and gold pattern.

be alike. Each member of the class will place her very best contour silhouette on the exhibition board. Give each silhouette a number and let the class vote for the one which the members think most beautiful.

2. From the designs of glassware shown in this chapter, select the one which you think is most dignified. The one which is most graceful. The most formal and elegant. The one you would like to use every day.

3. Assign committees to report on the following topics:
Pressed glass including manufacture and historic patterns
Blown glass: its history in Venice and in ancient civilizations
Current prices on glassware

Good design in china

RHYTHMIC CONTOURS FOR GOOD DESIGN. In china as in glassware good contour is essential for pleasing design. The two sugar bowls illustrated on page 129 show a contrast in this quality. The curves of the first sugar bowl are so nearly circular that they are not very interesting, and the handles look like ears which stand straight out from a billiard-ball head! In the second sugar bowl the curves are more pleasing and the handles grow naturally from these curves.

This style of pitcher, popular in the eighteenth century in England and America, is known as a Toby jug.

Here the rhythmic movement is smooth and agreeable. The eye slips easily around the contour without interruption.

The dishes shown at the bottom of page 129 were designed by a famous contemporary designer, and are excellent examples of rhythmic form. Observe how the contour of the cup blends with the curve of the saucer and how the handle grows naturally from the side of the cup. Notice also the interesting shapes of the pitcher, teapot, and vegetable dish. Notice, too, the complete lack of ornamentation. Beauty in these dishes depends entirely upon color and form. They are made in such delightful colors as seafoam, chartreuse, coral, granite gray, brown, and white.

WHEN CHINA IS DECORATED. There is great beauty in plain china when contours and color are fine. It has been only in the modern era that this type has been popular. For centuries some form of decoration has generally been applied to the surfaces of plates, cups, saucers, and other pieces. This decoration has varied considerably in character from time to time, but much of it is still popular and china patterns in historic styles are available in our stores today.

Whether china decoration is modern or historic is not the criterion by which we should make our selections. Standards of good taste and our own personal preferences are the important considerations.

131

First we shall consider decorative versus naturalistic types of ornamentation. The two handkerchiefs and the discussion on pages 59 and 60 point out the desirability of conventionalized or stylized design when used for decoration. The principle is the same for the decoration of dinnerware. The illustrations on pages 130 and 131 give two historic examples which are extreme opposites in design. The plate, sugar bowl, and cream pitcher are museum pieces of Sèvres porcelain. This china was first made about two hundred years ago in France. It is named for the town, Sèvres, where it is still made. Its design is characterized by elegance and luxury. The pieces shown in the illustration have gold borders on a dark blue background. The floral pattern is completely conventionalized. The curves of the contours are highly refined and delicate. From the standpoint of functional design, one might wish that the handles on the sugar bowl were somewhat larger, but the whole effect is rich and beautiful.

The cream pitcher illustrated on page 131 is very different from the Sèvres pitcher. It is highly naturalistic, being made to represent a man's head and fashioned so that the cream pours from a corner of his three-cornered hat. It is called a Toby jug and is named after the character in the popular song of the eighteenth century, "The Little Brown Jug." These pieces were made both in England and America and are now highly prized as collector's items.

You may find the idea of a man's head used for a pitcher amusing or "quaint," but you can hardly describe the pitcher as beautiful. The old fellow is not exactly a handsome man, and even if he were, a pitcher made in the form of a man's head hardly meets our modern standards of design.

Toby jugs were made in England at the same time Sèvres ware was being made in France, and both were popular. Of course, other china was being made in both countries, and much of it was decorated with stylized patterns.

Patterns today vary from very realistic representations of flowers or other motifs to highly stylized and decorative effects. Judge each pattern according to design principles and *your own preferences*. Do not make a selection which you do not really like because you think it is the thing to do. Be honest in your choices. Study the principles of art, make comparisons, and then after consideration select the patterns which you really prefer.

COMPARISONS IN DECORATIVE DESIGN. Compare the four china patterns on the opposite page. These are modern designs and vary in degrees of conventionalization. In the upper right design the floral

These four china patterns show varying treatments of floral motifs. Which one seems to you most pleasing?

forms are stylized and the whole decoration fits the shape of the plate in such a way that it truly enhances the structure.

The pattern at the left is conventionalized in character. The flowers are "pleasing design flowers." The decoration does not fit the shape of the plate very well because the sprays of flowers appear to have been dropped there carelessly. The whole effect however, is gay and informal.

133

The design at the lower left is planned to conform nicely to the circular shape of the plate but does not harmonize too well with the shape of the cup. The flowers and leaves are very realistic, giving the impression that one could pick a spray off the plate quite easily.

The pattern in the lower right-hand corner has an interesting arrangement of spots within the circle. One large spray is balanced by two smaller ones. The proportions are pleasing. This design is rather realistic, however, and you may prefer the one above.

Here are some questions to answer for further study of these designs:

1. Notice that the structural design is the same in all four plates. In what way does structure add to the decorative effect?
2. In which pattern do you feel that the effect is most unified and harmonious?
3. In which pattern do you feel the decoration fits the teacup most successfully?
4. Do you feel that the design of the handle on the teacup is good? Why?
5. Which type of decoration is most pleasing to you?

GOOD DESIGN NEED NOT BE EXPENSIVE. In china, as in other articles of house furnishing, good design does not mean high prices. Can you tell which patterns on the opposite page are most expensive? Two of the patterns are priced a little more than twice as much as the other two. There is no way in which you can tell the price by looking at the pictures. The difference in price depends upon the quality of the china: the two at the right are bone china and the two at the left are dinnerware. Now compare the designs. The two upper patterns each have a medallion in the center and borders around the outside. Both are good design, and need not depend on the price tag as far as art quality is concerned. In the following paragraphs we will learn more about qualities in the chinaware itself.

The two lower patterns have floral motifs in what is sometimes called *free design*. Which one seems more interesting? Which one seems better organized? Which one is more realistic? Again your choice will depend on your personal preferences, not on the price tag.

HINTS ON BUYING CHINA. When you select your china, you should consider the kind of ware which you wish to have, its costs, and its design and color.

Doulton and Co., Inc.

Can you guess which two patterns are most expensive?

1. Decide what colors you desire. Remember that your dinnerware must harmonize with your glass and table linens.

2. Decide whether you want plain china or decorated.

3. Learn to know the types of dinnerware, which can be divided into three general classifications.

Pottery or earthenware is the least expensive and the least durable. It is made of unmixed clay and is fired at a lower temperature than other dinnerware. It breaks easily, chips, and crazes which means that a network of surface cracks may appear.

135

Fine earthenware or semiporcelain is moderately priced and much more durable than common pottery. This is fired at a higher temperature than common pottery and is much less inclined to chip or craze. Semiporcelain will take colored glazes and has a rich, velvety feel. In the trade this type is often called dinnerware.

Porcelain or china is the most expensive tableware and is truly vitreous, which means that it is melted all the way through as it is fired. The firing temperature is at least 150 degrees higher than that for semiporcelain. It can always be identified by two characteristics. It is translucent when held to the light, and it has a clear, ringing tone when tapped with a fingernail.

Porcelain, china, and bone china are all terms used for vitreous ware. It is customary to use china as the term which includes all kinds of tableware, but properly used it means porcelain or other vitreous ware. The name was given to the porcelain which was first brought to the Western world from China.

4. Examine dishes for defects such as cracks, crazing, marks which look like pinholes, and for evenness of colors.

5. Be sure that the pattern which you choose is open stock. You will wish to replace any that are broken, and you may wish to add additional pieces.

SUGGESTIONS FOR FURTHER STUDY. 1. Arrange for a day when every member of the class will bring a piece of pottery or china to class. No one is to tell whether he or she likes it or not. In class discussion let each piece be criticized for structural and decorative design according to the principles of art.

2. Using a compass, make a drawing of a plate with plain bands for decoration around the edge. Plan interesting spacing for the bands.

3. Appoint committees to report on the following topics:
History of porcelain
Prices and names of patterns in semiporcelain and bone china
English china

Good design in silver

When you select your silver pattern you will again meet problems in structural and decorative design. There are dozens of silver patterns on the market, many of them of very fine design, others not so good. In addition to the selection of a good pattern, you must also decide whether you wish to buy sterling or plated ware. Excellent designs are obtainable in either kind of silver, so the problem is a

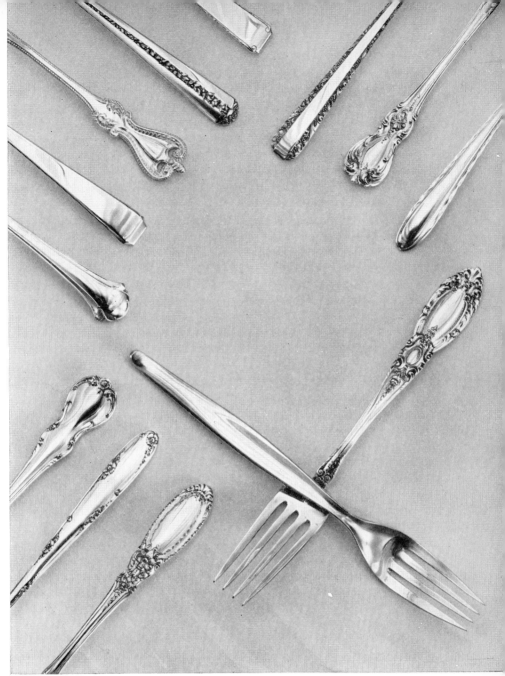

Designs in silver flatware ranging from old traditional to the latest modern pattern.

practical one. Sterling costs much more than plated silver, but its appearance may be no more attractive. Sterling is solid silver and will wear forever. On the other hand, plated silver will wear for a very long time before the plate wears off along the edges of the knives and other points of contact. If your funds are limited, you might wish to buy a complete set of plated ware, rather than a partial set of sterling which does not meet your needs. Then at a later time you may buy replacements, if necessary.

WHAT TYPE OF DESIGN DO YOU PREFER? Now that you have had some practice in comparing different types of design effects, you can select your pattern with greater assurance of making a wise choice. Whatever the pattern, your silverware is something which you are likely to have all your life, so try to pick a pattern which will give you *lasting satisfaction*.

What type of design effect do you prefer? Graceful elegance? Richness of ornamentation? Simplicity and restraint in decoration? Clean-cut modern lines? Delicacy? Strength? Extreme elaborateness? Now study the flatware patterns on page 137, and try to select each of the effects just mentioned. You may find more than one pattern which answers the same description. For example, there are at least three patterns which have graceful elegance.

Next, study these flatware designs for beautiful, rhythmic lines throughout the whole pattern. In which pattern do you see the most beautiful harmony between the handle and the service end of the tool? In which spoons do you find the most satisfactory harmonies between the two parts? In which designs are the lines of the handles least pleasing to you? Which pattern do you think would give you the most lasting satisfaction?

FUNCTIONAL DESIGN IN SILVER FLATWARE. All knives, forks, and spoons which serve as eating utensils are functional in some degree. Emphasis on functional quality in modern design has inspired some designers to create new patterns which are functional in ways unthought of by designers of past eras. The silver flatware shown on the opposite page is in a new and modern style. It has a suitable name, "Contour," because the whole design has been created in terms of shapes or contours.

A study of these contours in some detail will point out how functional quality has been secured. For example, the handle of the knife is longer than in most flatware and the blade is shorter. This gives a more comfortable grip as one uses the knife. The blade is quite long enough for any cutting action required of a dinner knife. Notice

A modern design in silver flatware which emphasizes functional quality.

also the shape of the handle, which is somewhat like the handles of old-fashioned pistols. The curve at the end increases the ease of one's grip and balances the curve at the end of the knife blade. The diagonal joint between blade and handle makes an interesting line and adds to the structural strength of the knife.

The function of the fork today is more nearly like that of a spoon. In this modern pattern, the fork has been shaped somewhat like the bowl of a spoon. The bowls of the spoons have been made wider and more shallow for easier use. The shapes of the bowls are also less pointed than in many traditional patterns.

The salad fork has three wide tines instead of four narrower ones. This gives extra strength for cutting such food materials as lettuce and fruits. The butter spreader, like the dinner fork, has a diagonal joint which helps to create a pleasing effect. The wide curve at the end of the blade is an extra help in spreading butter or jam.

Another special feature in the design of this silver pattern is the rounded smoothness of the handles. There are no sharp corners or projections caused by raised ornamentation to press uncomfortably into the palm of the hand. Each handle is large enough and thick enough to be grasped with ease. You will find it interesting to imagine how each handle shown on page 137 would feel in your hand.

SOME POINTERS ON BUYING SILVER FLATWARE. Keep the following points in mind when you buy your silver.

1. Make a buying plan which fits your purse and your needs. Will you buy a set of sterling or plated ware or both? Some people keep their sterling put away in tarnish-proof chests or containers and use plated ware for everyday meals. Others believe that it is more intelligent to have only sterling and use it every day because it cannot wear out. The plated ware does show wear after long and continued use. Still others believe that it is best to have stainless steel for everyday use because it is much cheaper and does not tarnish. Other people use flatware called "Dirilyte," made from a gold-colored alloy which is much less expensive than sterling, does not tarnish, and is guaranteed not to wear out.

2. Choose a design which will give you lasting satisfaction. It is well to consider this matter for several weeks before you make up your mind. First impressions do not always seem so attractive after a time.

3. Always ask about guarantees on any kind of flatware which you consider buying.

4. Before deciding on a pattern, hold a knife in your hand to see how it feels. Is it a comfortable handle? Does the knife seem too small or too large? Do the same with a spoon and a fork.

Good design in table linens

The term *table linens* no longer means exactly what it says. There was a time when it was considered proper to use only linen for tablecloths, but this idea has long since gone out-of-date. In place of the big snowy linens of long ago, modern tables are clothed with cotton and rayons, very often in color. Instead of an over-all cloth, doilies or place mats are used for most meals.

This brings us to another art problem in planning the dining-room accessories. If the color of your doilies does not blend with the color of your china you cannot expect to have a pleasing table. Orange plates on pink doilies will not help you to enjoy your lunch. The problem of harmonizing colors on the dining table is much the

140

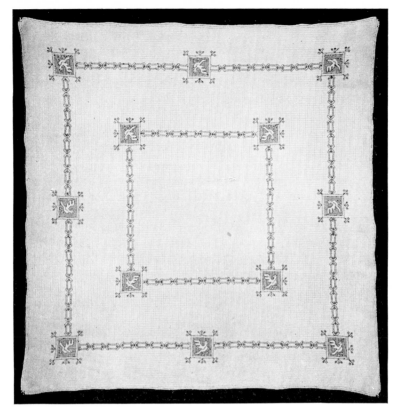

Square cloth for a bridge table or a small dining table. The embroidered pattern, worked out in outline stitch and cross-stitch, is interesting and attractive.

same as that of harmonizing colors in other parts of the house. There is no place in the house where you can have more fun creating beautiful color effects. Can you picture in your mind the lovely color effect produced by yellow linen place mats and napkins on a cherry table (deep orange-red), orange dishes, and yellow daffodils for a centerpiece?

Plain mats are good backgrounds for dishes and silver, but sometimes we want to use decorated doilies and tablecloths. Some of them are good decorative design and some are bad. Look again at the two filet lace doilies shown on page 10 in Chapter 2. Decorative design in table linens should not prevent them from serving as good backgrounds. This means that the pattern should not be overelaborate or so forceful that it attracts too much attention to itself.

Discriminating taste is more necessary than an unlimited pocket-book. Expensive lace tablecloths are not always in good taste. Some of them have bold designs which make very poor backgrounds. This type of tablecloth should be selected with special regard to its effectiveness as a background. There are many simple, attractive luncheon sets in our stores which are suitable for almost any informal occasion. On special occasions we may feel the need of something less simple. Let us then buy beautiful material and secure beauty in our table linen through color and good decorative design rather than overornamentation with lace and embroidery.

The square cloth shown on page 141 belongs to a bridge set, but, of course, it can be used for a small dining table. It is natural linen embroidered in blue. The decorative pattern is satisfactory in every respect. The little stylized bird forms are charming. The whole pattern is well related and harmonizes very interestingly with the square shape of the cloth. This attractive cloth is a hint to those who like to embroider. Beautiful embroidery patterns do not require difficult stitches; the whole pattern is worked out in outline stitch and cross-stitch.

VARIETY OF MATERIALS FOR TABLECLOTHS. In recent years many new and novel materials have been adapted for tablecloths and place mats. Colors and patterns strange to the dining table have proved most attractive as backgrounds for dishes and silver. The tables shown on pages 144 and 145 have unusual table coverings. In the table setting on the left, a drapery cretonne with a bold modern design forms an effective background for plain-colored plastic dishes. How much more interesting than if a plain background had been used. In the picture on the right, a bamboo screen forms an enchanting background for the dark-brown dishes.

Instead of the traditional white of our ancestors' tables, we now may choose colors: jade or forest green, pastel pink or maroon, beige or autumn brown.

All sorts of materials are used for place mats. Plastics—transparent and printed with lace patterns or thick and opaque made to represent fabrics—are available. Here again, knowledge of design and color harmony is helpful for a wise selection. Place mats or tablecloths of such materials as Indian head, linen toweling, burlap (fine quality), or homespun can be used most successfully. These are easy to make, especially if you choose to fringe the edges as shown on page 146.

SUGGESTIONS FOR FURTHER STUDY. 1. The class should collect as many table runners, luncheon sets, dresser scarfs, and place mats as possible for a lesson in design. Each piece should be discussed according to the following:

Is it overornamented?

Are the principal lines of the decoration in harmony with the structure of the piece?

Is the color harmonious?

Into what kind of room will it fit harmoniously?

Is the decoration conventionalized or pictorial?

2. Make a list of materials suitable for doilies. Your list will include linen and cotton fabrics, of course, and several others which make interesting doilies.

3. Plan and make a set of place mats and napkins. For your first set you should use inexpensive material that is easy to work with. Plan to use two colors, one for the doilies and a harmonizing color for the napkins.

Harmony when you eat

Doctors tell us that we should feel pleasant and happy when we eat our meals. It is not good to shout, argue, or sulk at mealtimes. We should be at harmony with the world. Surely it will help us to feel more agreeable if the table is attractive and inviting. A great deal depends on the combinations of china, silver, and linens that we use. For example, if your china has a pronounced pattern it will not look well on a background with much pattern.

Probably you know the rules for setting a table. Knives, forks, and spoons should be placed at right angles to the edge of the table, water glass at the tip of the knife, bread and butter plate at the end of the fork, and so on. The many lines created by the silver harmonize with the rectangular shape of the table. The smaller circles of the glass and bread and butter plate are placed so as to be related to the straight lines of the knives and forks and to the larger circle of the main plate. The dishes and silver at each place form an orderly and well-related design.

Every table needs a center of interest, and there should be a centerpiece which meets this requirement. To achieve this, one does not require fresh flowers from the florist every week. A glass bowl of ivy cuttings, a pottery bowl with bittersweet, a small fern, a bowl of fruit, or a basket of gourds will make a good center of interest. There are dozens of other things which also can be used, but *not artificial flowers!* Imitations do not help to create beauty. Besides, the imitation flowers soon get dusty and soiled.

The decorative material used for a tablecloth in this table setting makes an effective background for the plain plastic dishes. Can you imagine this setting with dull blues in the cloth and coral pink for the dishes?

Richards Morgenthau Company, New York City

The bamboo screen makes a very effective background for this interesting buffet table.

An inexpensive table setting that has beauty of design and color.

The table shown above has an attractive centerpiece of iris and garden heliotrope. Iris and heliotrope both grow on very long stems, stems, but in this arrangement the stems were cut in order to make a suitable arrangement for a dining table.

The table setting in this illustration is interesting and attractive. The family that ate at this table enjoyed both good design and color at very moderate cost. The dishes are corn yellow, the doilies and napkins are green with yellow, orange, and dark blue stripes. The flower container is dark blue, and the flowers were yellow, blue-purple, and white. The table is cherry with an orange-red tone. Here is an itemized list of the prices paid for each article on the table.

Dinner plates	10 cts.	Doilies	15 cts.
Bread-and-butter plates	15 cts.	Napkins	10 cts.
Water glasses	20 cts.	Center doily	20 cts.
Salt and pepper shakers	15 cts.	Flower container	25 cts.
Sugar bowl	25 cts.	Flowers from the garden	
Knives, forks, and spoons	19 cts.		

TABLE SETTINGS ARE DESIGN PROBLEMS. When you plan a party table you are a designer. Instead of using paints and brushes, you will use place mats, china, silver, glassware, and a decorative centerpiece. Your design will depend not only upon the kind of dining-table accessories which you use, but also on your placement of these articles.

146

This luncheon table is nicely arranged for three.

In the picture above you will see a party table for three. In this case, the hostess-designer moved the centerpiece, a bowl of fruit to one side of the table and used the other three sides of the table for the three place settings. The large glass plate in the center of the table will hold some of the foods from which the guests will fill their plates. How much better balanced is this table than if the centerpiece had been left in the center and one side had been left empty. Can you see how this same scheme could be used for seating any odd number of guests, for example, five or seven?

Now turn to the buffet table shown on page 145 and observe the arrangement. Here the setting has been arranged in diagonally crossing lines. Notice that the handle of the casserole, the handles of the teacups, the sugar bowl, cream pitcher, and teapot are turned so as to emphasize the diagonal arrangement. The very attractive centerpiece of fruits and vegetables is located at the corner of the table, again emphasizing the diagonal pattern.

Even an everyday setting for family meals can be fun if you spend

Which of the combinations do you like best?

a little time planning a pleasing arrangement. Harmony with your meals can do much to provide for better living.

> SUGGESTIONS FOR FURTHER STUDY. 1. Collect pictures of table settings. Select one which you think is harmonious and explain why you think so. Select one which you think could be improved and tell how you would change it.
>
> 2. Arrange an exhibition of attractive table settings. Plan to have at least two tables for family meals and one for a buffet party.

A TEST ON THE DINING TABLE

I. Answer the questions at the beginning of this chapter and compare with your answers before studying the topic.

II. Your teacher will exhibit three dinner or luncheon plates. Criticize each for the following points: harmony, pictorial or decorative quality, rhythmic lines, proportion.

III. Study the four groups of dining-table accessories shown above. Which group would you like for your own? Why do you make this choice? Is there any article which you would like to change? Why?

Chapter 7

WHAT WILL YOUR WINDOWS WEAR?

There is no problem in interior design which occurs more frequently than the window problem. Curtains must be replaced more often than rugs, furniture, or other furnishings, and each replacement is a fresh problem. Appearance, usefulness, and cost are the chief factors which must be considered. Once again beauty cannot be planned without taking into consideration utility and function.

Study each window problem. Not all windows can be treated alike. The best treatment depends on many things. The amount of light, the size of the room, the shape of the window, and the color and character of the other furnishings make a difference in planning the window curtains.

First, we must decide whether to use glass curtains, drapes, or both. Sheer glass curtains hang close to the window and soften the glare of light. They also secure privacy from passers-by. However, if the window does not face on the public street and if there is a good view, you will prefer no glass curtains. For windows with a pleasant outlook, drapes with no window curtains is a good answer to the window problem. This treatment permits a great deal of light to enter. If it is necessary to shut out some of the light, you may use glass curtains, roller shades, or Venetian blinds.

Many people use roller curtains at their windows, and keep them halfway down regardless of the amount of light. Interior decorators feel that roller shades are ugly, and avoid their use whenever possible. A roller shade drawn down halfway cuts a window into two parts

The small windows at the end of this large, comfortable room are attractively curtained. These curtains can be drawn to secure privacy from the outside.

which have no relation to each other. In place of the roller shade, some people prefer drapes which draw across the window or Venetian blinds. (See page 167.) Some people do not like Venetian blinds because in a dusty, smoky city a great deal of time and care is required to keep them clean. Other people do not like them because their effect is rather severe.

The average-sized window can be treated to both glass curtains and drapes if you desire. Small windows generally look better if they have only glass curtains or only drapes. Too much on a small window is likely to make it look overdressed. Casement windows and small windows like those pictured above are most attractive when only one set of curtains is used. These curtains have plenty of fullness so that they can be drawn across the windows to shut out the view. Every curtain should be wide enough so that when it is pulled shut the fabric still falls in folds. Skimpy curtains are not attractive.

Sometimes an ordinary window can successfully be made into a real feature in the room. The window garden shown on the next page is a pleasing center of interest in a dining room. Small plants combined with colored glass accessories create a nice effect. The cretonne drapes hang in straight folds, and serve to soften the rectangle of the window frame. The glass shelves which hold the plants are supported

A window garden that is made more attractive by decorative accessories of colored glass.

by wooden brackets screwed to the window frames. These brackets are stained the color of the woodwork and are not conspicuous. In summer when the window garden is planted outdoors the brackets are hidden by the drapes.

The first problem that must be settled in window treatment is the type of curtains to use. Decide first whether it will be best to have glass curtains, drapes, Venetian blinds, or roller shades. Then you are ready to consider other problems.

THE CHOICE OF COLOR IN CURTAINS. If the curtains are to form a part of the background, they should not offer too bold a contrast in hue, value, and intensity with the color of the walls. All the rules for a good background apply to curtains. If we have sand-colored walls and use bright gold-colored curtains, they will not remain in the background. Although the hue and value may be near to that of the wall, the intensity is much too strong for a background color. But if a grayish-tan homespun is used, the curtains will harmonize with the walls and make a good background. Another example of curtains which do not form a part of the background occurs when the walls and woodwork are ivory and the curtains are dull rose color, a hue which makes them dominant. The dull rose curtains may give a pleasing effect, however, if the other furnishings in the room de-

151

mand that the curtains used give a decorative note. Choice of color depends upon the effect desired.

In some cases where there is no other strong center of interest in a room, a pleasing effect is obtained when the window is curtained so as to make it dominant. In other cases where there is already a point of emphasis in the room and where the room contains numerous articles of furniture and decorative accessories, it is best to keep the curtains entirely in the background. This means the selection of a light-value neutral color which will blend with the walls. It is not necessary to make the curtains either a center of interest or entirely subordinate as a part of the background. They may stand out in pleasing color contrast to the walls, for example, rust-colored draperies with sand-colored walls, not as a dominating center of interest, but as articles of furnishing which occasionally catch our attention.

Our first problem, then, is to decide whether the curtains should remain entirely in the background, be the dominant center of interest, or stand out slightly from the background without attracting too much attention. It is chiefly through color that we can achieve this effect. The cretonne drapes shown on page 151 create a slight contrast with the wallpaper. This contrast is produced by the pattern in the cretonne in contrast with the plain walls and by the dull tones of rust and green against the pale green walls.

If thin glass curtains are to be hung across the window, we must choose the color which is right. For example, light entering a room through lavender or pale blue curtains will be cool; this is certainly not desirable in a room with a north exposure and little sunshine. Such a room should be curtained in shades of cream, yellow, tan, or tints of pink and rose. It is not necessary that the color in curtains be very intense in order to effect the quality of warm or cool light in the room. Quite neutralized shades and delicate tints will color the light that is transmitted through the curtains and pervades the room. It is an excellent plan when buying curtains to hold them up to the light and study the color which comes through them. Some interior decorators think that only yellow tints and white are suitable for glass curtains.

Other tints, however, are used with success in many rooms. Can you imagine the sheer curtains in the room on the opposite page a pale sea-green? Perhaps in your mind's eye you can see how the delicate greens, which shine through from the outside, fall on the duller green of the carpet and give it a more lively color. You can imagine, too, the trees outside that throw their shadows on the sheer curtains.

152

Alexander Smith & Sons Carpet Co.

The sheer curtains at the floor-to-ceiling windows cast a lovely light over the carpet and other furnishings.

153

Another point to be considered in choosing the color of our curtains is to make sure that they harmonize with the general color scheme of the room. It is safe to follow the rule of making the color of the curtains echo one of the large color areas in the room, the walls, the rugs, or the upholstering on the furniture. This creates a rhythmic and balanced arrangement of color that is pleasing. However, it is best not to repeat the vivid color found in a piece of pottery or picture by using plain, bright-colored draperies, as vivid color should be used only in small areas. Curtains form one of the large color areas in the room. Even when curtains form a center of interest, the color should not be too bright, as intense color in large areas is fatiguing. Can you think of any other reason why intense color in large areas should not be used?

The white curtain is a particular problem which must be considered in harmonizing the color of the curtains to the rest of the room. In a living room where the color scheme is built around the triad combination of red, yellow, and blue and is kept dark and rich in tone, a white curtain fails to harmonize. It seems staring, out of place, and obviously bad. Even in a room which is lighter and more delicate in its coloring the white curtain may be out of place. For example, a room with ivory woodwork, cream walls, a violet, tan, and green rug in light tones, and light gray-green furniture cannot be correctly curtained with white. Even though the walls are light in value, the absolute whiteness of the curtain is not in key with the cream and ivory tint.

The white curtain can be used successfully only in rooms where there are other areas of white or very light color. In the bedroom where the walls are covered with a light figured paper having a white background, or where a light bedspread and light dresser covers are used, the white curtains may be most attractive.

The size of the room must also be taken into consideration in selecting the color of the curtains. If the room is small and an increase in the effect of space is desired, the curtains must be kept as a part of the background. If the curtains are contrasting in color so as to make a decorative note, they will divide the background into smaller areas and make the room seem smaller.

SOME EXPERIMENTS IN THE CHOICE OF COLOR FOR CURTAINS. 1. Experiment with large pieces of thin, colored materials, such as cheesecloth or voile. Hold each piece up to a window through which the light shines strongly and note the color and quality of light which falls on the objects near the window.

154

2. Experiment by combining pieces of curtain material and wall-paper. How many combinations can you find where the curtains help to form a part of a pleasing background? How many combinations are there where the curtains form a decorative note without offering too vivid a contrast? How many combinations can you find where the curtains would make a room look smaller?

PLAIN OR FIGURED MATERIAL. The next important decision to be made is whether to use plain or figured materials. This depends mostly upon the other furnishings in the room. If the wallpaper is figured, the curtains should be plain. Otherwise the two patterns will compete with each other, and the result will be a confused effect. This does not hold true, however, when the figure in the paper is an inconspicuous, small pattern. Indistinct patterns generally have the effect of texture rather than the effect of pattern. Several strong, bold patterns in the same room always produce a feeling of unrest and confusion. A figured rug, large floral cretonnes for slip covers, a strong pattern in the wallpaper, and a bold pattern in the curtains are sure to create a most disagreeable effect.

Several patterns can be used in the same room if selected with care. The rooms shown on pages 156 and 157 show pleasing combinations of patterned and plain materials. In the room on the left the mantel is light ivory against a knotty pine paneled wall. The other wall is deep green and the curtains are natural homespun with a deep-green band across the valance. The cretonne slip cover on the davenport is printed in greens and browns against an ivory background. The braided rug has tones of green, and the chair at the left is covered in a brown, tan, and green plaid. The plaid chair, the oval rug, and the floral pattern of the slip cover are in harmony because the patterns vary enough in character so that they do not "fight." They are also held together by the harmony of color. The plain surfaces create rest spaces as the eye moves about the room, so that the effect is not confusing.

The room shown on page 157 also has a successful combination of figured materials. The draperies are figured cretonne and the upholstering is plain. A plaid lamp shade contrasts pleasantly with the plain areas, the braided rug, and the floral pattern at the window.

A good recipe to follow in making such combinations is this: Use one large floral pattern; add a plaid or striped pattern; if desired add a small, quiet pattern; and always use plenty of plain surfaces.

INTERESTING TEXTURES ADD BEAUTY. A plain-colored, textured curtain material can bring interest and beauty into a room. A wide

155

Consider H. Willett, Inc.

Here is a successful combination of a floral pattern, a plaid, stripes, and plain surfaces.

variety of textures is available, ranging from fine, delicate voile to coarse fish nets, and from smooth linens and brocades to rough homespuns and corduroys. In some fabrics, the effect of texture is produced by a small pattern. This is demonstrated in the curtains shown on page 158. The little diagonal lines create a pleasant variety of surface that contrasts pleasantly with the wood-paneled walls. In this case the curtains remain part of the background, but at the same time they provide interesting variety or effect.

The fish-net curtains in the dining room shown on page 159 are well chosen for contrast in texture with the brick wall and the patterned carpet. The coarseness of the net blends nicely with the brick wall. This is a good example of the type of curtain material which

A pleasing effect is created by combining a braided rug, a plaid lampshade, cretonne curtains, and plenty of plain surfaces.

softens the glare of light and partially obscures the view when looking in from the outside.

Texture is a tremendously important factor in creating the right effect. When you are planning to buy new curtains, it is a good idea to sit down in the room where the curtains will hang and try to imagine the effect of different textured materials at the window.

GOOD DESIGN IN FIGURED MATERIALS. If you decide to use a figured material for your curtains, you must be sure to select a good pattern. We have found that good design costs no more, and sometimes less, than poor design. Our ability to select well-designed curtain materials depends more upon our knowledge and understanding of art principles than upon the amount of money which we spend. The

The small diagonal pattern in these curtains creates a texture which blends beautifully with the wood-paneled walls.

three pieces of cretonne shown on page 160 show this point very clearly. The first cretonne cost fifty cents a yard, the second cost ninety cents, and the third cost thirty-nine cents. Now let us see how they compare in art quality.

The first is little more than a picture of roses, pinks, and larkspur with tangled stems sprawling in great confusion across the width of the fabric. There is no feeling of rhythmic quality, nicely related proportions, or stability anywhere in the pattern. The second cretonne is what we might call semidecorative in character. The blossoms are realistic, but they are made to fit into an orderly, rhythmic pattern. We feel that the pattern is organized and therefore much more pleasing than that of the first cretonne. The third cretonne is still more pleasing than either of the others. The design is thoroughly decorative. We have no feeling that the flowers are pictures

The fish-net curtains at the window of this dining room harmonize beautifully with the brick wall and the floral pattern of the carpet.

which accidentally were painted upon our curtains. They are "design flowers" and charming. Each cluster of flowers is a center of interest to which the stems and leaves are subordinated. Altogether, the pattern is entirely satisfactory judged according to the principles of design. Here is one case in which the least money bought the most pleasing curtain materials.

CRETONNES IN MANY PATTERNS. Counters in drapery departments are loaded with cretonnes and other materials with a great variety of patterns. Like the three patterns shown on page 160, some are beautiful, some are poor design and color, and others are mediocre. Once again your own good taste must come to your aid.

Among the cretonnes of good design and color there are different types, those inspired by historic styles in design and many moderns.

159

Three cretonne patterns varying in qualities of design. Top: A naturalistic pattern which rambles in a most disorderly fashion. Center: A semirealistic pattern which conforms to orderly arrangement. Bottom: A completely decorative pattern with pleasing organization.

A cretonne pattern copied from a French historic style.

The textile shown above is copied from a historic French style called toile du Juoy. These patterns are generally available in one-tone prints of blue, red, green, or brown on white or cream background. They can be used at many windows with great success.

The design of the fabric shown on page 162 is in the modern abstract style. It is printed in tones of chartreuse, yellow, brown, and black outlines on a white ground. This pattern was selected by a group of modern designers as "characteristically modern" for use at an exhibition of modern furnishings.

Curtains generally hang in folds at the windows, and it is well to consider this point in selecting the pattern. Always try the effect of the pattern as it hangs in folds before making a purchase.

SUGGESTIONS FOR FURTHER STUDY. 1. Describe a room that you know and tell whether you would use plain or figured curtain material. Give the reasons for your choice.

2. Collect samples of curtain material with patterns. Criticize each pattern according to art principles.

The design of this cretonne is in the modern abstract style and is printed in tones of chartreuse, yellow, and brown, with black outlines on a white ground.

SCALE OF PATTERN. One factor that should influence our selection of figured curtain material is the size of the pattern. If the pattern is very large it should not be used at small windows because it is out of proportion. Another way of expressing this is to say that it is *out of scale*, or that the scale is too large for the window. When we speak of objects or the parts of objects as being well proportioned to each other, we say that they are *in scale*. If they are not well proportioned we say that they are not in scale. When we are selecting figured curtain material the scale of the pattern is a consideration to keep in mind. The pattern should be small enough to repeat several times in order to give a unified effect or to be in scale with the window.

SUGGESTIONS FOR FURTHER STUDY. 1. Criticize three pieces of figured curtain material which your teacher will hang on the wall for study. Make your criticism according to the principles enumerated in the preceding paragraph.

2. Many sheer materials used for glass curtains are figured. Collect samples of these materials and discuss them for pleasing pattern.

3. Try draping your samples of curtain materials in folds. Which ones hang in good folds? Are any of the materials too stiff to hang well? Which of the sheer materials would be more suitable for use in a bathroom or kitchen? Why do we like a certain crispness or stiffness in the texture of the curtains which we put in bathrooms and kitchens?

WHEN CURTAINS ARE TIED BACK. Most curtains are allowed to hang straight in long, natural folds, but sometimes it is desirable to drape them back against the window frame. Thin, ruffled glass curtains, like those in the illustrations on pages 45 and 57, are more attractive when drawn back, but the draping must be done carefully in order to secure a pleasing effect. Study the lines of the draped curtains on these pages, and you will see that they are tied back so as to allow the curtains to hang in graceful curves. Avoid pulling your curtains back in straight, tight lines which form diamond-shaped lines. Rhythm of line is just as important in the draping of a curtain as in a spiral stairway.

HOW LONG AND HOW WIDE? Practical questions, which have to be settled when you plan your curtains, are length and width. These questions, as well as the type of heading, must be settled before you can estimate how much material to buy.

The length of a curtain is determined by the height of the window. It is a good general rule to make all curtains, especially draperies, floor length, unless there is some special reason for making them window length. Curtains which hang to the floor seem to make the window appear more an integral part of the room than the shorter ones. Some thin glass curtains are very attractive when made window length, but draperies should be floor length if possible.

Never allow a curtain to stop anywhere between the bottom of the window frame and the floor. Remember that a curtain is really a kind of dress for the window and should *fit the window*. A curtain which fits its window perfectly covers the window to the top edge and falls just to the sill, to the bottom of the window frame, or to the floor. The curtains in the room shown on page 158 just reach the window sills—a perfect fit. In this room, the curtains could not hang to the floor because of the built-in bookshelves across one wall. The designer naturally took this into account, and was successful in planning curtains which seem tailor-made for the room. This sort of beauty does not happen by accident.

Measurements for length must allow for hems, headings, shrinkage, and clearance at the sill or floor. A curtain should not actually touch the floor or sill. A clearance of about 1 inch at the floor and $\frac{1}{2}$ inch at the sill helps the curtain to hang more gracefully. The hem at the bottom of a glass curtain should be about $1\frac{1}{2}$ to 3 inches wide, and for heavier materials 2 to 4 inches wide. If the material is preshrunk, no allowance need be made. If the fabric has not been tested and is not guaranteed preshrunk, allow about 2 inches per yard. The extra allowance will have to be turned up in the hem, and let out after laundering.

When making curtains, it is a good idea to hang them at the windows for a few days after they are finished except for the hems. Some materials, especially the homespuns, stretch considerably, and this will alter the hem line. Pin the hems up before taking the curtains down. Check each one with a yardstick before sewing so as to correct inaccurate pinning.

The type of heading on the curtain affects the amount required for its length. If the curtain is to have a casing for a rod, allow about 3 inches, and be sure to make the casing wide enough so that the rod slips through easily. If the curtain hangs on rings allow 1 to 2 inches for a hem, and remember when measuring the length that the top of the curtain will come just below the rod on which the rings slide.

If the curtain is to have a heading like those shown on page 151, allow about 4 or 5 inches to turn down over the buckram used for stiffening.

Every new set of curtains has special problems in measurements which will have to be worked out. Remember that all this should be done *before* you buy your material so that you will not purchase too much nor too little.

The width of the curtains should be about 2 to $2\frac{1}{2}$ times the width of the window. A perfect fit in this case means generous allow-

Kentile, Inc.

An illusion of space is created in this room by the horizontal lines in the pattern of the curtain fabric, the lines of the bookshelves, and the spreading pattern of the tile floor.

ance for fullness. When curtains are pulled across the window they should still look as though they could do the job easily and gracefully. It is pleasant to sit in a cozy room on a wintry night with the drapes pulled shut and enjoy the lights and shadows on the long, full folds of the fabric.

CURTAINS CREATE ILLUSIONS. Just as the design of a costume can make you appear taller and thinner or shorter and wider, so can the dress you choose for your windows make them appear wider and lower or just the opposite. The pattern of the material has considerable effect on the proportions of a window opening. In the room shown above you will see at once that the horizontal lines of the curtain fabric tend to make the eye travel horizontally and thus create an illusion of width. In this case the lines of the bookshelves and the square tiles of the lovely floor help give the feeling of breadth and space.

Another way of creating an effect of width is to let the curtain rod

E. L. Bruce Company

A wall curtain used for a background sets off the figured upholstery and contrasts pleasantly with the plank flooring.

Draperies hung in the space beside a window create the impression of a wider window and form a center of interest.

extend out past the edges of the window frame. Then when the curtains are pushed back, they extend beyond the actual window but expose only the window opening, thus making a wider window.

Still another way of creating an illusion of a lower, wider window is by the use of a valance which contrasts with the curtains. This stops the eye from traveling upward and causes it to move horizontally. Note this effect in the windows on page 165.

CURTAINS COVER WALLS. In the twentieth-century style of furnishing, floor-to-ceiling curtains are often used to cover an entire wall even though there are no windows in the wall. The folds of the curtain form an interesting background, as shown in the picture on the opposite page. Notice the interesting combination of patterned upholstery and textured surfaces in the curtain wall, shaggy rug, and oak-plank flooring.

A curtain wall may cover a window as shown the above picture. There are endless possibilities for lovely effects with the use of a curtain wall. A curtain may provide an interesting covering for an uninteresting wall, or conceal undesirable features such as an ugly, imitation fireplace.

Libbey-Owens-Ford Glass Company

Good curtaining for a picture window requires generous width which allows the curtains to be pulled completely across the window opening. There are times when it is desirable to shut out glaring light or to secure privacy.

PICTURE WINDOWS NEED CURTAINS. The modern style in architecture has given us some new problems in curtaining—picture windows and window walls. Large areas of glass, which let in plenty of light and bring the outdoors within easy view, are characteristic of the style. While it is pleasant to have plenty of light and view, there are times when it is equally desirable to shut them out. There are days when light can be too strong and glaring, and hours when privacy for those within is required. The only answer, of course, is curtaining. The picture window illustrated above has a delightful view, but when occasion requires it to be shut out, the cretonne curtains can be drawn. This means that plenty of width must be allowed for correct curtaining. A window wall presents the same problem. When the glass extends from floor to ceiling, the curtains must extend from top to bottom of the wall. Here again, plenty of fullness and width are required so that the curtains when drawn will hang gracefully.

SOME POINTERS ON BUYING CURTAINS. Here are some points to remember when you plan to purchase new curtains:

168

1. Do you need glass curtains, draperies, or both? Choose the curtains that will answer the needs. Glass curtains soften the light and provide partial privacy, but if the window is opened for air they may soil quickly from dust which blows through them. The laundry problem should be considered. Heavier fabrics used in draperies can be vacuumed or brushed and require only periodical washing. Do not overdress your windows.

2. Do you wish the window to become part of the background or to be an accent of interest? Plan the color and pattern (if any) accordingly.

3. Will you use plain or figured material? This will depend chiefly on patterns used in other fabrics. Avoid a confused effect.

4. Bring home samples for matching and harmonizing colors. If possible, take samples of slip covers, upholstery, and wallpaper with you when you shop. Do not try to carry the color tones in your eye. There are hundreds of variations, and it is impossible to be sure of a match or harmony without seeing the colors together.

5. Take your measurements for length and width *before you go shopping*. Plan the style of heading and other details at home. Do not try to do in the store what you should have done at home.

6. Remember to inquire about shrinkage and allow accordingly.

7. Test all curtain materials by holding them up to the light and studying the effect as light shines through. In the case of draperies you may find that it is necessary to line them. If so, be sure that you choose a lining which will add to the pleasing effect. Some cretonnes and other materials have a way of looking sleazy and faded when the light shines through them. This type of fabric is not a good choice unless you intend to line them. Unbleached muslin is a satisfactory and inexpensive lining for most cretonnes.

8. Try to get the best value for your money. Remember that good taste is more important than a fat pocketbook. Sometimes a cotton print from the dress counter will be just the thing.

When you are buying homespun for draperies, it is well to look at homespun bedspreads. One bedspread, cut down the center makes the two curtains for one window. Occasionally, you will find bedspreads cheaper to buy than homespun by the yard, and often you can find colors and patterns which are not available in yard goods. Homespun draperies have the advantage of having enough weight not to require lining.

SUGGESTIONS FOR FURTHER STUDY. 1. Decide upon the ideal type of curtaining for your own room. Make a scale drawing of the window, and draw the arrangement of curtains that you would like to have. Get a sample of the material you would like to use. Make a brief written statement telling why you chose the color and style.

2. Collect samples of wallpaper, cretonnes, and slip-cover materials. These samples should be big enough really to show the colors and patterns. One-half to one-quarter yard is adequate. Perhaps your school will have such a collection. Try to make pleasing combinations with these samples.

3. Make a collection of pictures from newspapers and magazines showing curtain arrangements. Write one sentence under each picture stating your opinion of its art quality.

4. Make a sketch of a window in your home, and draw the arrangement that you think should be used.

5. List all the names of curtain materials that you know or that you can find in newspaper and magazine advertisements. Get a sample of each type and learn to recognize each kind of fabric. Arrange for an identification test of curtain materials. Your teacher will put samples of ten curtain materials on exhibition, each one numbered. Make a list of the numbers and write down the correct name of each fabric.

A TEST ON YOUR STUDY OF CURTAINS

I. Be prepared to give a clear, definite answer to each of the following questions:

1. Vera Norton is trying to select the color of the new curtains for her own room, which is small and rather dark. It is furnished with maple furniture, green rugs, yellow walls and ceiling, and has notes of orange in the smaller articles. She is undecided between dotted Swiss curtains of yellow or of green. Which will make a better effect? Why?

2. Mrs. Mason is planning new curtains for her living room, which is small and rather crowded with furniture and decorative accessories. Would you recommend curtains of plain color or curtains with a figure? Why?

3. Some rooms require only glass curtains; other rooms require only draperies; other rooms require both glass curtains and draperies. Describe a room which requires each of these treatments. How does the curtain fulfill a practical need in each case?

4. In your own room do you think it would be better to use curtains which are part of the background or curtains which stand out as a center of interest? Why?

5. What are the general rules which will help you to decide how long your curtains should be?

6. What principle of design will help you to drape your curtains attractively?

170

II. Plan a color scheme for the room shown on page 26 in which the curtains become part of the background. Next, plan a color scheme in which these curtains become a pleasing center of interest.

III. List 12 points which should be considered in the selection of curtains for a living-room window which opens on a small garden.

IV. Some of the following statements are true and some are false. List the numbers of the statements on a separate sheet of paper, and write *true* or *false* after each number.

1. Figured curtains are generally more pleasing when used with plain or textured wallpaper.

2. Flame-colored draperies form an effective background.

3. Glass curtains should always hang in straight folds, because when looped back they always form ugly lines.

4. A floral pattern in curtains may harmonize nicely with a plaid slip cover and a striped rug.

5. Horizontal lines in the drapery pattern increase the apparent size of the room.

6. Glass curtains should always be just 12 inches from the floor, and draperies should be 6 inches from the floor.

7. Pale blue is a good color for a glass curtain in a small, dark room with northern exposure.

8. Either a plain color or a pattern may make a room seem smaller than it really is.

9. Texture is an important factor in the beauty of a curtain material.

10. Stylized design is considered more interesting and beautiful than realistic design for decorative fabrics.

Chapter 8

BACKGROUNDS TO LIVE WITH

~~~~~~

The walls, floor, and ceiling of a room constitute the background of a room. These are the surfaces against which the furniture and other furnishings are seen. It is important to have good backgrounds so that the beauty of furniture, draperies, pictures, and decorative accessories may not be lost. A beautiful mahogany chair, lovely in line and color, placed against a wall covered with a bold red-and-green wallpaper, loses much of its charm in the overpowering effect of the background. A fine blond-wood table standing on an emerald-green rug loses some of its delicate beauty. A ceiling that is painted a shiny, glaring blue hangs over the room, distracting our attention from the attractiveness of the room below.

The importance of good backgrounds cannot be stressed too much. Poor backgrounds are not only disagreeable to look at, but they also detract from the effectiveness of the other furnishings.

WHAT IS A GOOD BACKGROUND? What are the qualities which make a wall a good background? The wall is a vertical support that helps to hold up the roof. Its characteristics are solidity and flatness. Good decorative design in wallpaper will not destroy the effect of a flat, solid wall. A paper that displays realistic flowers and vines rambling hit or miss all over the walls is not likely to emphasize flatness or solidity. This disorganized effect is illustrated in the upper sample of cretonne shown on page 160.

Floral forms are also used in the design of the wallpaper shown at the left of the opposite page, but this pattern is organized instead of confused. The forms are flat and stylized producing an effect of much greater character and interest than in a naturalistic design.

Thomas Strahan Company

Left: Handsome and formal in effect, this wallpaper is nonrealistic and highly stylized. It uses the French medallion motif. Right: This damask pattern, popular in Colonial days, is still well liked. It is an excellent selection for a background effect.

This paper adorns the wall without detracting from its solidity or flatness.

The pattern uses a motif known as the French medallion. It is formal and handsome in character, and is best suited for use in large rooms furnished in eighteenth-century styles. The original of this paper was found in a home in Stonington, Connecticut, under several other papers in the back parlor. You will be interested to know that the house was once occupied by the famous artist, James MacNeil Whistler, who painted the great picture called "Mother." (See page 252.)

The wallpaper shown at the right above is known as a damask paper, a type very popular in Colonial days. Its name refers to the type of pattern, which has a very slight contrast in values. The design is well

173

Thomas Strahan Company

Left: This pattern is suitable for use in small rooms and hallways. Notice the harmonious shapes and relationships among the different elements of the design. Right: This paper is an English toile reproduced for modern use. The motifs are based on life in England about 1800.

organized, though not bisymmetric as in the case of the medallion paper at the top left of page 173. The effect is much less forceful than in the other paper. The delicate value contrast creates a textured quality, and makes a good background for pictures and other furnishings.

The wallpaper shown at the left above is copied from a pattern found in an old Colonial house in Kingston, Massachusetts. No one knows whether the paper was placed on the wall during the eighteenth century or at a later time. This type of pattern has been popular for a long time. It is called a diamond or diaper pattern and appeals to many people. Since it is a small pattern it can be used in small rooms. When printed in colors which do not have such a decided contrast in values, the effect is almost like a textured paper at a little distance. The paper which is pictured was printed in tones of light gray, dark red, and white. Used with white woodwork in a small breakfast room with a white dado (wainscoting), the effect is delightful.

The wallpaper shown at the right above is a different type. The original was the bottom layer of papers in the stairwell of a beautiful

174

home in New Durham, New Hampshire, built about 1800. One hundred and fifty years later the pattern is still popular. It is known as an English toile and is related to the cretonne toile shown on page 161. This paper is suitable for large rooms and blends with the Colonial style. It is less formal than the first wallpaper that we studied.

NEW STYLES IN PAPERED WALLS. In recent years it is no longer considered necessary to paper all four walls of a room with the same wallpaper. Three walls may be papered with a plain or textured paper and the fourth wall with a patterned paper in matching color tones. The large figured paper on page 173 and the toile paper on page 174 are suitable for papering a fourth wall. This style of wallpapering often adds interest to a room which might otherwise seem monotonous.

TEXTURES IN WALLPAPER. Plain wallpapers depend for their beauty on color and texture. Some papers are given a pleasing texture by a fine intermingling of colors. A paper which appears to be a warm gray at a little distance may prove upon close examination to consist of a finely gradated mingling of dull blues and tans. A paper printed with flat gray cannot give the same pleasing textural effect. Sometimes texture is achieved through small indistinct patterns which appear at little distance to be finely modulated color tones. Even when a pattern is fairly distinct, as in the paper shown at the left on page 173, the total effect may be that of texture rather than a definitely marked design.

SUGGESTIONS FOR FURTHER STUDY. 1. Collect as many samples of wallpaper as possible. Dealers are generally willing to give away old sample books. Odd pieces of leftover wallpaper can be brought from home. Classify the wallpapers according to the following types: realistic, stylized, textured. The decision should be made by class vote after each paper is discussed.

2. Try to find pleasing combinations of plain and pattern papers for a combination effect in the same room.

3. Try hanging pictures on each piece of wallpaper. Select the ones which you think make good backgrounds for small pictures about eight by ten feet.

PAINTED WALLS AS BACKGROUNDS. Many walls are finished with paint instead of wallpaper. Plain, colored walls can make perfect backgrounds, provided the color tones are correct. Vivid hues, such as emerald green, crimson, Chinese red, and royal purple, do not make good backgrounds. Intense color is more forceful than neutralized hues and is unpleasant when it presses in on you from the walls of the room. Instead of emerald, use moss green, aqua, or pastel tones. Instead of crimson, try dusty rose, coral or salmon pink.

The lighter colors make a room seem larger, and the darker tones bring the walls closer together. The latest trends in interior design include darker color than has been customary for walls. Even though fashionable, dark walls are not advisable for small or dark rooms. The dark greens, browns, and blues are very effective, however, in large, light rooms where furniture is of blond wood and the upholstery fabrics are light in color. The dark background shows off the light colors of the furnishings with pleasing contrasts. This type of color scheme is shown on pages 179 and 347.

Do you like your paints shiny or dull? Texture in paint finishes is just as important as in wallpapers. Some paints are very glossy, others are dull, and some have a partial gloss. They are known as high-gloss, flat, and semigloss paints. Besides choosing the color which you want, you must choose the type of finish.

Most people feel that the high-gloss paints and varnishes are suitable for kitchens and bathrooms because we like shiny surfaces in these rooms. Smooth, shiny surfaces suggest cleanliness, and are easy to wash. In other rooms the semigloss or flat finishes are more pleasing. High-gloss paints and varnishes reflect the light in a very obvious way. This texture does not combine pleasantly with the textures of rugs, draperies, and polished furniture.

> An experiment with paints. To become familiar with the different kinds of paints suitable for the finish of walls and woodwork, it is necessary to experiment with the actual paints. Secure different kinds of paints, including enamel, flat paint, and calcimine. These can be bought in small quantities for the purpose of experimentation. Paint an area of about two feet square on a wooden board or on a piece of composition board with each kind of paint which you are able to secure. After these are dry, set them up and inspect them for their relative merits as to pleasing quality.

The ceiling is a background. Although we do not see furniture or pictures with the ceiling immediately behind them, the ceiling is really part of the background. Think of the room as a big box in which the furnishings are placed. The bottom, top, and sides of the box are continuous surfaces lining the inside of the box.

Ceilings are above our heads, and we do not feel comfortable if they seem about to fall. If they are too dark in value, too intense in color, or are covered with a bold and striking pattern, the feeling of too great weight is produced. Rooms with heavy beamed ceilings often give this impression. A good rule is to make the ceiling lighter in value than the walls and to give it a color that tones in with the dominant color of the room.

There is an exception to the rule under certain conditions, however. A room with a very high ceiling in a darker tone than the walls will give the effect of lowering the ceiling. Of course, you would not choose a tone so dark that it is heavy in effect. Suppose that you are using pale maize-yellow for three walls of a room with a high ceiling and a deep aqua on the fourth wall. The aqua tone used on the ceiling will help to "lower" the ceiling.

The choice of a wallpaper for the ceiling is a special problem. Many people prefer to have the walls and ceiling covered with the same paper. Of course, this requires a wallpaper pattern that looks well upon the ceiling. A different paper on the ceiling requires a molding or border around the edge in order to make a good finish for the top of the walls. Often the wallpaper borders which match the paper are very ugly. Some people solve this problem by using a narrow wooden molding around the top of the room. If you are using a striped paper, you can use a stripe cut from the paper for a finishing border.

A special problem in wallpapering has to be solved in rooms with sloping ceilings. The most successful treatment is to use the same paper on walls and ceiling. This makes it necessary to choose a paper which is simple in design, such as that shown in the cottage bedroom on page 178.

How should woodwork be treated? The woodwork, or trim, as it is sometimes called, is part of the wall and for that reason should be considered as part of the background. The most successful treatment is to keep the color of the woodwork the same or very close to the same as that of the walls. When paint is used for the walls, it is a good idea to use the same color for painting the woodwork. When the walls are papered with a plain color, the woodwork can be painted to blend in with the color of the paper.

Ivory or white woodwork has been popular since Colonial days. These tones are very satisfactory for combining with various colors. The white woodwork in the room shown on page 179 combines pleasantly with the blue wall to create a delightful effect. The white frames on the pictures, the white curtains, and the white flowerpots echo the larger white area of the built-in cabinet. The blue of the wall is echoed in the blue linoleum. Thus the furnishings of the

Ponderosa Pine Woodwork

Wallpaper with a simple allover design is best for rooms with sloping ceilings. Notice the storage spaces and the dressing table built into the end of this cottage bedroom.

room are seen against a very charming blue-and-white background.

The fireplace wall in the room shown on page 180 is wood paneling painted light ivory. It combines pleasantly with the wallpaper used on the other three walls. The ivory tone blends beautifully with the greens, yellows, and browns of the other furnishings. The polished brass of the fireplace accessories accents the color scheme.

Painted woodwork is generally more satisfactory than natural wood stained and varnished. Stained woodwork has a way of standing out boldly and seeming cheap and ugly. Dark rectangles of doorways and window frames cut up the walls and often create a disagreeable background.

Suggestions for further study. 1. Do you prefer papered or painted walls? What are the practical considerations in caring for each type?

White woodwork with blue walls and floor forms the background for this charming room.

2. Would you like to change the background of your own room? If so, how would you do it? Why?

3. What is your opinion of the color of the walls in your classroom?

A beautiful paneled wall. Notice the fine proportions in the mantel and in the panels.

WOOD PANELING FOR WALL FINISHES. Instead of having papered or painted plaster walls, many modern homes are paneled in wood. This is a revival of historic styles. During the eighteenth century, homes in both America and England had rooms which were completely or partially paneled. Those who have visited Mount Vernon; Carter's Grove in James City County, Virginia; the Jeremiah Lee Mansion, Marblehead, Massachusetts; or other old Colonial houses have seen some of this beautiful paneling.

In the homes that are built today, wood paneling has been adapted to smaller rooms and a more informal way of life than was characteristic of the great house of the Colonial era. Knotty pine is especially popular for wall paneling. The dining room shown on page 182 and the bedroom shown on page 183 are finished in knotty pine. Notice how well it remains in the background. Good pine paneling has a pleasing effect with its mellow brown tones and its dark knots which provide an agreeable variation in texture. Notice how well the built-in corner cupboard fits into the background. It is desirable that all built-in features should stay in the background and yet add in-

180

terest to the room. The small dining table with its bowl of flowers and Windsor chairs blends perfectly with the pine paneling to make a charming effect. Certainly, knotty pine is a background to live with.

The bedroom shown on page 183 appeals to those who like their rooms quiet and restful. The background plays an important part in securing this effect. The plain textured rug, the paneled wall, and the simple pattern of exposed rafters combine to create an atmosphere of dignity and serenity.

The pine-paneled living room in the illustration on page 184 has a quiet elegance. Would you not like to sit by the fire in this room watching the flickering shadows and dancing flames? Raised moldings underneath the mantel and around the cornice add a touch of ornamentation. Pine-faced beams on the ceiling also add to the charm of the room. This effect is more suggestive of the historic interiors of the past than the effect of the dining room or bedroom which we just discussed. It is not nearly so elaborate, however, as some of the old rooms with fluted pilasters, arched doorways, and mantels with superstructures.

PLYWOOD PANELING FOR WALL FINISHES. Plywood paneling is a new type of wall finish developed in modern times. It provides a beautiful finish and is cheaper to install than solid wood paneling. Plywood is made by veneering a hardwood onto a cheaper wood. It is produced in mahogany, maple, walnut, birch, and other fine woods. The plywood comes in large panels of various sizes and thicknesses. Thus, wood paneling is available for many homes where solid wood is prohibited because of the greater expense.

The hallway and stairwell shown on page 185 have walls and ceilings finished in plywood. Notice the small, rounded moldings which finish the corners where edges of plywood panels meet. The effect is different from the traditional-style paneling, but it is also beautiful. Its smooth, unbroken surfaces are characteristic of effects in modern design.

The design of the stairway is worth studying. Notice the slight curve at the top and at the bottom, and the interesting curve of the handrail. The tall stair-well window has been left uncurtained. Glass shelves with pots of trailing ivy and other plants add a decorative touch.

Another effect in plywood paneling is shown on page 187. The wood, which is birch, has a beautiful, satin finish and soft, mellow color which make a splendid background for the furniture, draperies, and pictures.

181

This small dining room with knotty-pine paneling has quaint charm.

The picture on page 186 shows some plywood paneling being installed over an old papered wall. One of the advantages of plywood paneling is the ease with which it can be put up either on new walls or over old walls.

BACKGROUNDS OF MAN-MADE BOARDS. Modern science has found a way to make building boards from wood fibers, sawdust, and other materials. These are sometimes called composition boards and are sold under various trade names. Their cost is less than for wooden boards, and so we have an economical type of material for finishing walls and ceilings. The room illustrated on page 188 has walls made from one of these synthetic materials. In this case the paneling is put

The pleasing quality of this bedroom depends chiefly on the simplicity and charm of floor, walls, and ceiling.

on in horizontal strips which create a horizontal line movement. It is a good background for modern-style furnishings.

In the room shown on page 189, synthetic-board panels have been used to create an opposite effect. Here the line movement is vertical rather than horizontal. It increases the height of the room. On page 188, the horizontal lines increase the width of the room. The horizontal feeling is characteristic of the modern style, and the vertical movement is in keeping with traditional styles.

In the modern living room on page 190 composition-board panels were used to finish the sloping ceiling. Narrow, flat strips, called batten strips, are used to cover the ends of the boards where they

Knotty pine is used for the walls in this beautiful living room.

The stairwell and hall in this illustration are finished in plywood paneling.

Plywood paneling is easily installed over old plaster walls.

meet. This results in a kind of plaid pattern which breaks up the large ceiling area.

COLOR IS IMPORTANT. Color is very important in securing a pleasing background effect. If the color of the walls is too intense, for example, "electric" blue, the walls are no longer a good background. If the color is too grayish, the effect may be dull and monotonous. The blue tone used for the walls in the room shown on the opposite page is well chosen. It is an interesting color yet neither so bright as to be distracting nor so dull as to be uninteresting. Since this room received plenty of sunlight, the coolness of the blue was a happy selection.

The hall which can be seen through the doorway at the left is papered in yellow because it is small and dark.

The basic color scheme is a triad—red, yellow, and blue,—but if you think of it as pale blue, dusty pink, and primrose yellow it may

 (*Text continued on page 190*)

The delightful colors used in this New York City apartment make it seem lighter and larger than it really is.

Birch plywood paneling makes a delightful background.

Good backgrounds are created by the use of synthetic wall materials. The horizontal paneling gives the illusion of extra space.

This attractive traditional room has a composition board background. Notice how the vertical paneling adds height to the room.

The ceiling of this modern living room is finished with panels of composition board.

(Continued from page 186)
seem more charming. The furnishings were planned by a young couple who could not afford to spend much money. Through clever planning and a good choice of color they managed to achieve a pleasant and livable home. They say that color provides 90 per cent of the effect and that it cost nothing extra!

NEW KINDS OF WALLS. Twentieth-century styles in house design include several new kinds of walls. New types of materials have been made and old materials are used in new ways.

The Dow Chemical Company

Plastic tile in lovely colors provides new, gleaming beauty for kitchen and bath-room walls.

Plastic tiles for bathroom and kitchen walls provide exciting new beauty. These tiles, as shown in the bathroom above, have a mar-bleized or mottled texture and come in a wide range of pretty colors. They are smooth as glass and easy to keep clean. Splashing water

Patterned glass provides a beautiful, sparkling background and lets light through into dark corners.

does not mar them. Once more we find that beauty and utility go hand in hand.

Another new type of material used for modern backgrounds is patterned glass. It is particularly useful in dark rooms. The glass partition shown above takes light from the kitchen to the dining room and at the same time provides a sparkling, gleaming background. It is sometimes used as walls for the shower bath or as a partial screen between entry and living room. Panels, partitions, or entire walls are made from patterned glass. It has the advantage of enduring beauty, is easily kept clean, and never needs painting or polishing. Again we find that beauty and utility are partners.

We have already discussed the use of curtains for wall coverings, but a discussion of backgrounds should include floor-to-ceiling curtains. The picture on the opposite page shows some very beautiful window curtains which become a wonderful background when they

Floor-to-ceiling draperies in beautiful fabrics make an attractive background when drawn.

are pulled at night. It is interesting to know that these curtains are made from Celanese, a kind of rayon which is one of the new twentieth-century materials.

Another invention of the twentieth century is the modern folding door which is a space saver and provides an attractive background when closed. This type of door is shown in the picture on page 194. As you can see, the door folds upon itself in an accordion-like way. It slides on a track installed across the top of the doorway. The doors are covered with a plastic material which is easily cleaned.

In this interior the folding doors can be pulled across the wide opening between the kitchen and breakfast nook, hiding the kitchen and providing a pleasant background. These folding doors require no space for swinging out into the room, and are particularly useful in small rooms and hallways. Closet doors often open out in such a way that they interfere with the placing of furniture, but fold-

Modern folding doors are space savers and provide a pleasing background when they are drawn shut.

ing doors require no room at all. These doors are obtainable in a wide range of colors and can be selected to blend with any color scheme.

Brick walls outside the house are an old story, but brick walls for interior finishes are new. This is the case of a new use for an old material. The rooms illustrated on pages 12, 75, and 78 show how beautifully a brick wall can serve as an interior finish.

SUGGESTIONS FOR FURTHER STUDY. 1. What wall finish would you like for your own bedroom? For your living room of the future? Discuss points of beauty and utility in these finishes.

2. Collect pictures of historic rooms. Study the backgrounds. Do you know any modern rooms which seem to be related to historic styles?

3. Collect pictures of modern rooms and arrange an exhibition of them. Be prepared to discuss the beauty and practical considerations for each type of background.

Bigelow-Sanford Carpet Company, Inc.

The "tweedy" texture of this carpet blends delightfully with the stone fireplace, paneled walls, and upholstery.

THE FLOOR IS PART OF THE BACKGROUND. Along with the walls and ceiling, the floor must be treated as a background. Its special function in the decorating scheme is to co-ordinate all the elements in the decorating scheme. The floor covering may serve as a foundation for all the decorative elements. Much of the furniture is seen against the floor. If the floor covering blends in color, texture, and pattern with all these elements, it has a harmonizing effect. For example, the carpeting in the room shown above blends beautifully with the stone fireplace, the wood paneling on the walls, and the modern furniture. It has a "tweedy" texture of blended tones of orange, brown, and gray-blue. These tones are echoed in the gray stone of the fireplace, the brown sheen of the wood paneling, and the blond wood and orange upholstery of the furniture. The texture seems just right for holding together harmoniously the roughness of the stone, the ribbed texture of the upholstering materials, and the smoothness of the woods.

195

Charming simplicity of materials and design make this room beautiful.

THE FLOOR COVERING CAN CREATE AN EFFECT OF SPACE. Plain, one-color, room-size rugs or over-all carpeting creates an effect of greater space and restfulness.

In rooms where the rug shows a foot or so of floor around its edges the effect of space is lessened. This happens because the eye is interrupted in its movement before it reaches the wall. When the rug also has a definite pattern, there seems to be still less space. When you are choosing a floor covering, decide whether you wish to create a feeling of greater space, or to have the effect of smaller and cozier areas. This is a matter of personal preference.

MODERN RUGS HAVE VARIED TEXTURES. A plain rug depends on color and texture for its interest. The choice of color should always be guided by suitability for a background. A brilliant blue which seems to "jump up" at you as you enter the room does not make a good background because it is too intense. On the other hand, the color should not be so dull and neutralized that it has no life.

Many new types of texture have been developed in recent years. Tweedy textures, such as is shown on page 195; soft, fluffy textures, shown on page 117; deep, shaggy textures, as on the opposite page; and shorter, shaggy types. Another type known as sculptured or carved shows the design in a raised pattern against a lower background of the same color.

HARMONY IN BACKGROUNDS. The small room, a den, shown on page 196, is beautifully harmonious in its background areas. The lustrous, painted paneling of the walls makes a perfect background for the ship painting and the fireplace. The doors on either side of the fireplace are cut into the paneling with no disfigurement of the lovely surface. The books on their shelves also serve as background and quietly add a bit of interest. The plain plaster ceiling is completely unobtrusive. The floor with its shaggy rug contrasts pleasantly with the other surfaces. What more could one wish in the room where one intends to read, study, or think?

BARE FLOORS AND SMALL RUGS. Hardwood floors are beautiful, and some people feel that a fine floor needs no rug at all but should be enjoyed at its best. Other people feel that a few small rugs provide more comfortable walking but also show off the beauty of the flooring. The large room in the illustration on the next page has a fine floor and is only partially covered by the lovely hooked rugs. Notice the placing of the rugs, which is in harmony with the lines of the room. Since this is a large room we need not feel that the broken floor area interferes too greatly with the feeling of space.

LINOLEUM GOES ANYWHERE IN THE HOUSE. Once upon a time linoleum belonged strictly to kitchens and bathrooms, but now, because

197

Arkansas Soft Pine Bureau

The rugs in this room have been wisely chosen and carefully placed.

of its beauty and suitability, it is welcome in any room in the house. A great variety of pleasing effects can be secured with linoleum floor covering. By this means it is possible to have almost any color that you like for your floor. The stairway, hall floor, and living-room floor in the picture on the opposite page are soft green. The marbleized texture contrasts pleasantly with the plain border, and the white strip around the edge of the border repeats the white of the stair spindles, doors, and other woodwork in an interesting way.

The ease of cleaning and taking care of linoleum floors is an important feature and adds to their desirability. The lustrous sheen of well-polished linoleum adds to the appeal of this type of floor covering.

Linoleum makes a beautiful floor for any room in the house.

OTHER TYPES OF MODERN FLOORS. Asphalt tile, rubber tile, and flagstone are used for the floors in many contemporary houses. The bathroom shown on page 55 has an attractive asphalt tile floor. Other tile floors are seen in the rooms on pages 73, 78, and 165. Pleasing designs and colors are obtainable in both asphalt and rubber tile. Some people prefer the rubber tile for greater comfort in walking and standing on the floor.

Flagstone is a natural rock and therefore a hard and durable substance. Many entrance halls, recreation rooms, and dining rooms are finished with flagstone floors.

PATTERNS IN FLOOR COVERINGS. Rugs, carpets, linoleum, and tile floors are made in a variety of patterns. The problem in selection is similar to that in the choice of wallpaper.

Remembering that a floor should seem flat and smooth and stay in its place, which of the linoleums shown on the next page seem the best selections for an average-sized kitchen? Which pattern, A or B, do you feel would keep the floor as a good background? Patterns C and D are similar in color and effect except for the black lines in D. Do

A   B

C   D

The Armstrong Cork Co.

Some linoleum patterns make better backgrounds than others. A and C are better backgrounds than B and D, because they are not so forceful.

you consider these lines an improvement? All of these linoleum patterns have good design quality. There are no naturalistic pictures of flowers and foliage. But the discriminating person will find A and C more pleasing for use as floor coverings.

An Oriental rug with harmonious, well-related design.

FURTHER STUDY OF THE FLOOR AS A GOOD BACKGROUND. 1. Find two pictures of linoleum, one showing a good and one a poor background. Give the reasons for your selection.

2. Cut two pictures from magazines, one illustrating a good and one a poor background. Write the reasons for your selection.

3. Collect five samples of colored cloth or paper that would make good colors for plain rugs.

4. Find in catalogues and magazines pictures of rugs showing patterns. Exhibit these during your class time and decide by class vote which ones would make the best backgrounds.

5. Arrange a time and place when the class can discuss some real rugs. There may be rugs in the school building, small rugs can be carried to school, or a visit can be made to a store.

We need the principles of design for help in selecting good rug patterns. We know that harmony and a unified effect are important. The Oriental rug shown on page 201 is a good example of harmonious and unified design. The eye travels smoothly over the surface of the rug. There are many beautiful patterns in Oriental rugs, but some patterns are not pleasing. True Orientals are very expensive, but this does not guarantee beauty of design.

Since early Colonial times hooked rugs have been used in American homes. Many homemakers enjoy making them from yarn or from strips of cloth cut from discarded clothing. Whether these rugs will measure up to the standard for art quality depends chiefly upon the choice of a pattern and the combination of colors. Some designs for hooked rugs are shown on the opposite page. Each has the delightful charm which belongs to good hooked rugs.

The first one is a nice example of an old hooked rug. The pattern is thoroughly conventionalized and fits the shape of the rug. There is an interesting combination of light and dark in the rug. This type of rug is well chosen when we need a spot of interest, but it does not make a good background. The second rug is also a good example of pleasing design. It is less forceful than the first rug but is no less satisfactory. The floral pattern fits into the rectangular shape in a very pleasing manner. We have no feeling that the flowers are realistic. The whole effect is quaint and charming.

CHOOSING THE RIGHT RUG. Following is a summary of the points expressed in the discussion of rugs. If you remember these points when you select a rug, they should help you to make a wise choice.

1. The color of the rug should blend with the other colors in the room. The color should also be dark enough and dull enough so that the rug does not "jump up" off the floor.

2. Design in a figured rug should be harmonious and interesting.

3. A large figured rug which covers most of the floor should have a quiet and inconspicuous pattern in order to make a good background.

4. A small figured rug may be used as an accent in front of a fireplace, desk, or other piece of furniture.

Two beautiful hooked rugs from early American homes.

5. A figured rug should not be chosen for a room in which many of the other furnishings are also figured.

6. The texture of the rug should be pleasing and should harmonize in character with the other furnishings in the room.

7. One large rug will make the room appear larger. It should extend to within six to twelve inches of the wall. This also helps the room to appear unified. It "holds the room together."

8. Several small rugs will make a room appear smaller.

A TEST ON THIS CHAPTER

I. You should be able to make a list of ten standards by which to judge the background of a room. They should be of the same type as those listed on pages 47 and 117.

II. Plan the background which you think would be ideal for your own room at home. Collect samples of real materials if possible or pictures showing what you would use for floors, rugs, walls, and ceiling. This will be a test of what you have learned in this and previous units of study. You should be able to plan the background of your room so that the colors are right and the values in the proper relation to one another; to choose the right kind of wallpaper; and to change any bad proportions. Make a drawing of one wall in your room and color it according to the samples which you collect.

III. If you have thoroughly mastered the contents of this chapter you should be able to do the following exercise without difficulty. This should be a class exercise for which only twenty minutes should be allowed.

IV. What is wrong (if anything) in each of the following cases?

1. Sand-colored walls, ivory woodwork, green and rust predominating in cretonne draperies, red mahogany furniture, green upholstering material, and a blue-and-gold Chinese rug.

2. A child's nursery with pale yellow walls, red-and-blue draperies, blue furniture, toy shelves and bookshelves painted yellow with red edges, and a green-and-white rag rug.

3. A child's bedroom in a monochromatic harmony in tones of green—delicate green walls, white woodwork, furniture a darker moss green, curtains and bedspread in chintz with tones of bright green, black, and white, the floor covered with broadloom carpeting in a brilliant emerald green.

4. An early Colonial dining room, sand-colored walls, blue-and-rose cretonne draperies, red mahogany furniture, hooked rugs in blue, rose, and gray with accents of black.

5. A Colonial bedroom with a figured Colonial wallpaper, maple furniture, chintz draperies, chintz-covered chair and chintz bedspread, hooked rugs with bold patterns.

6. A small living room with damask draperies, plain walls, tapestry-covered chairs and davenport, several small Oriental rugs.

7. A living room with maple furniture, cretonne draperies, chintz-covered chairs and davenport, floor carpeted with broadloom, a hooked rug in front of the fireplace and an Oriental rug in front of the davenport.

V. Your teacher will hang fifteen pictures of rugs with patterns where the class can see them and give each picture a number. You will judge the rugs for the quality of their design, rating them good, medium, or poor. Make a list of the numbers of the rugs which you will put into each group. Each student should work individually and without consulting her classmates. After the judging is completed, compare your lists to see how well the members of the class agreed.

Chapter 9

FURNITURE FOR EVERYDAY LIVING

W hen you buy furniture, think well about the service and pleasure that it will give in the everyday life of your home. Every piece should be selected to fill a specific need. In addition to its useful qualities, every piece of furniture should be beautiful in design, color, and finish—something that is a joy to look at any day in the year. Other points for consideration are durability, ease with which it can be cared for, and its suitability for the room where it will be placed.

As always, utilitarian values and beauty of appearance are partners. Let us first consider some points in pleasing effect.

LOOK FOR GOOD LINES. Lines and shapes are just as important in furniture as in lamps or china. Rhythmic repetition of similar lines and easy transition from one line to another create a harmonious design in furniture. This point is illustrated in the two chairs shown on page 206. Both these chairs are patterned after historic styles. The chair at the right is called *Windsor* and the other, *ladderback*. In both designs there is a pleasant rhythmic repetition of lines and shapes.

In the Windsor chair the curved lines in the top of the back and the seat repeat each other. The slant of the legs, the arms, and the back also repeat each other, creating a unified feeling. In the ladderback chair there is a rhythmic repetition of line, in the slats in the back, also in the four posts, and again in the supports in the lower part of the chair, which echo the shape of the seat. All lines are practically at right angles to each other, and this repetition of square corners helps to give a unified effect. The curved lines in the slats of the back add a pleasing variety without seeming inharmonious or

Henry C. Steul and Sons, Inc.   Winthrop Furniture Co.

Two chair designs with rhythmic lines. Left: A ladderback chair. Right: A Windsor chair.

inconsistent with the straight lines used in the other parts of the chair. Imagine the slanted legs of the Windsor chair placed on the ladderback chair!

STRENGTH AND REFINEMENT EXPRESSED IN LINE. A pleasant rhythm of line cannot be produced unless the lines themselves are refined and graceful. Compare the curved lines in the two chairs pictured on the opposite page. In the first chair the lines are restrained and graceful in curve, and in the second they are clumsy and awkward. Possibly the two chairs are equally comfortable to sit in, but a purchaser with good taste will not hesitate a moment to select the first chair. It suggests elegance and refinement, while the second is ponderous and heavy.

Lines can express strength or weakness, quiet or unrest. Surely the lines used in furniture should express strength and quiet. Also on page 207 the same desk is shown with two different sets of curved legs. As we look at the two pictures we immediately become aware that the legs on the first desk seem much stronger and more har-

Good and bad designs in upholstered chairs. Left: Graceful lines and pleasing proportions. Right: Ugly lines and clumsy proportions.

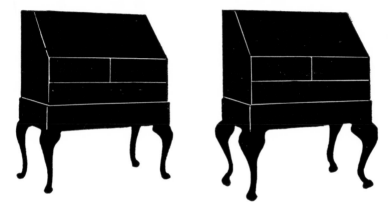

A contrast of strong and weak curves in desk legs. Left: Strong, graceful curves. Right: Weak, restless curves.

monious with the body of the desk. The curves of the legs on the second desk are more pronounced, with the result that they seem weak and hardly able to support the weight of the desk. Nor do they harmonize with the straight lines in the upper part of the desk. Such curves give a restless effect, and indeed it needs but a slight exercise of one's imagination to make one see this desk walking across the room!

LINES IN MODERN FURNITURE. The modern dining group on page 208 shows the use of straight lines and square corners which is characteristic of most contemporary furniture. There is a very satisfactory rhythm in the repetition of straight lines and rectangles. The squares of the chair seats and backs, the rectangles of the table top and buffet

207

The Merchandise Mart; by Thomlinson of High Point

This modern dining-room group has an interesting design of rhythmic lines and shapes. It has a pleasing effect of stability and strength.

front harmonize agreeably. They express strength, solidity, and comfort. The chair seats are large enough and the backs are slightly curved to make a very comfortable chair at mealtime.

Interest and variety in the design is secured by the V-carved legs on the table and chairs. The tapering shapes suggest an elongated V, so they are called V-carved. Notice also that the support for the chair arm is an inverted V-carved piece that adds considerable interest to the chair design.

FURTHER STUDY OF GOOD LINES IN FURNITURE. 1. Comment on the lines of the furniture shown on pages 385, 388, and 391. Remember that criticism should include favorable as well as adverse comments.

2. Find pictures of two pieces of furniture, one good in line and one bad. Write explanations of why one is good and why one is bad.

3. Make a sketch of some piece of furniture at home which you think could have better lines. Make straight front or side views in

Interesting and monotonous spacing in chair backs. Left: Monotonous because of even spacing. Right: Interesting variation of spacing.

order to avoid the difficulty of drawing in perspective. It may not be necessary to draw the whole piece of furniture. For example, you can draw a table leg or the top of a bed. Make a second sketch showing how you think it can be improved.

4. What is your opinion of the curved legs illustrated on page 211?

LOOK FOR GOOD PROPORTIONS IN FURNITURE DESIGN. The difference between monotonous spacing and more interesting spacing is illustrated in the backs of the two chairs shown above. In the first chair the slats and the spaces between the slats are exactly alike. The effect is monotonous. In the second chair, a silhouette of a Sheraton, the spaces between the slats are wider and the slats themselves are narrower. The result is much more pleasing.

The tall chest of drawers in the illustration on page 210 has pleasing proportions. The width is in pleasing relation to the height, and the graduated spacing in the drawer fronts is interesting. How ordinary the effect would have been if the chest had been square and the drawers had been evenly spaced! The low chest with the mirror above is also interesting in its proportions.

Now study the proportions of the various pieces of furniture used together in the room. They seem harmonious in size and effect. No single piece is so large or so small that it is out of scale. This is something to consider when you are purchasing a new piece of furniture. Is it too large for harmonious effect with the other pieces already in the room? Is it too small? One should also consider the amount of floor space required for a piece of furniture. A large piece of furniture may seem twice as large if crowded into a small room. The furniture shown is large and heavy, but in this case the floor space is adequate.

SUGGESTIONS FOR FURTHER STUDY. 1. Give your opinion of the proportions in the two chairs shown on page 207.

209

Hooker-Bassett Furniture Company, Inc.

Proportions in the design of this furniture are harmonious. The furniture is also in pleasing proportion to the size of the room.

2. Comment on the proportions of some piece of furniture in your classroom.

3. Collect pictures of sideboards, chests, and other pieces of furniture which you think have interesting proportions. Be prepared to explain why they are good.

ORNAMENTATION ON FURNITURE. Many styles in traditional furniture are ornamented. The modern style is almost entirely free of ornamentation, depending on fine structural design, wood, and finish for its beauty. Occasionally we find a piece of contemporary furniture which has a little ornamentation, such as the shaped metal drawer pulls on the chests shown on page 22. Basically the modern style does not include decoration. If you are considering the purchase of a piece of traditional furniture, you should study the way in which any decoration adds to or detracts from the general effect. Poor ornamentation has ruined the beauty of many a piece of furniture.

Now compare the two highboys shown on the opposite page for beauty of decoration. Carving is used for ornamentation on both highboys. On the highboy at the left the carving is used to emphasize the structure. Grooved posts are used at each side, on the finials, and

Two early American highboys. Left: Good design in every detail; pleasing proportions, graceful lines, restraint and beauty of decoration. Right: Pleasing spacing, but its beauty is ruined by heavy and fussy ornamentation.

in the fanlike central decorations. The carving is simple and pleasing. Quite different is the carving on the highboy at the right. It is fussy, restless, and ostentatious. It is full of weak, sprawly curves that certainly do not emphasize the shape of the highboy. Next compare the metal drawer pulls on the two highboys. Those on the first are small and pleasing in effect. Those on the other highboy are so large that they add to the confused and overdecorated effect.

Another type of decoration frequently used in the legs of chairs, tables, and cabinets is called turning. Both chairs in the illustration on page 206 have turned legs and stretchers between. The turning here is in good proportion to the rest of the design. In some cases the turning is heavy and bulky, so that the general effect is bad. You will find it interesting to study the turning on the pieces of furniture

211

which come under your observation. The turning on a piece of furniture may mean the difference between good and bad design. You will observe that in some pieces of furniture, such as gateleg tables and some chairs, the only form of ornamentation is turning.

Another type of decoration sometimes used on fine pieces of furniture is marquetry. Different-colored pieces of wood or other materials are inlaid on the surface of the wood to form a pattern. Marquetry requires great skill, and furniture decorated with it is expensive. Sometimes it is imitated by painting on the surface that mimics an inlay. At a little distance the effect may be that of marquetry, but close inspection and feeling of the surface of the wood always reveals the imitation. Painted decoration may be very good, but when we have it on our furniture we should not pay the price of genuine marquetry.

Painted decoration can be judged by the same rules that apply to other forms of decoration. It should not be overelaborate, it should emphasize structural design, and it should be conventional in character. The front of a kitchen cabinet is not the place for a spray of naturalistic looking roses. A conventionalized pattern is more suitable and pleasing.

SUGGESTION FOR FURTHER STUDY. Collect and mount pictures of furniture with some ornamentation. It is interesting to have an exhibition of these pictures on the classroom bulletin board. Each member of the class should supply at least two pictures and write a criticism below each. After all members of the class have had an opportunity to examine the pictures, there should be a class discussion of the furniture and the criticisms.

GOOD DESIGN IN UPHOLSTERING AND SLIP-COVER MATERIALS. Since so much of the furniture which we use today is upholstered, we should consider the art problems related to design in upholstering materials. We like the same qualities of design in upholstering materials which we like in curtain materials.

If a conspicuous pattern is used for upholstering, no other equally conspicuous pattern should be used in draperies or rugs. Patterns used in the same room should not compete with one another or the result will be disturbing. Decide whether the curtains or the furniture is to be a center of interest and select your patterns accordingly. If one pattern is large and conspicuous the other patterns should be smaller and less vivid in color.

The upholstering material used on large chairs and davenports forms rather large spots of color in the room. In our study of color we learned that the larger the spot the more neutralized the color should be. This is a situation in which this rule should be applied. The davenport will be more suitably upholstered in a dull, rich red than in a scarlet, or in a moss green rather than an apple green. Very intense color will call too much attention to the furniture instead of making it fit invitingly into the whole scheme of the room.

The problem of selecting suitable upholstering materials depends to some extent upon texture. The smooth, lustrous surface of satin and silk damask harmonizes best with the more formal and richly furnished type of room. The sheen of silk or rayon blends with the elegance of design in Sheraton or Louis XVI furniture, but we would not think of combining it with the more simple design and rough texture of wicker porch furniture. The room furnished with Colonial type furniture calls for homespuns, wool or cotton tapestries, chintz, or cretonne. In selecting an upholstering material one of the most important considerations is to choose a material that is harmonious in texture and character with the piece of furniture itself and with the rest of the room.

In recent years slip covers for furniture have become very popular. They serve to protect fine upholstering or to conceal an ugly piece of furniture. They can be laundered, whereas it is impossible to launder the upholstering on the chair itself. For both practical and artistic reasons the slip cover is useful in achieving a comfortable and attractive room. The slip cover will conceal a color or pattern that is wrong and the expense is much less than for reupholstering.

SUGGESTIONS FOR FURTHER STUDY. 1. It will be necessary for you to have actual samples of upholstering materials in working out this problem. Bring samples from home, and get others from the stores. Learn to recognize at least five upholstering materials in common use.

2. Make combinations of figured upholstering materials and curtain materials. Work in groups of two or three, and when you have found a combination that you think is good ask the class to discuss it.

3. What kind of material would you choose for a wicker chair? For a fine walnut davenport? For a small bedroom chair?

4. Arrange a lesson in the study of slip-cover materials. Criticize and compare patterns and colors.

CONSIDER PRACTICAL USE. When you buy furniture, consider the particular use for each piece. Chairs are needed for many purposes—lounging, sewing, reading, sitting at a desk or at a dining table. You

213

Heywood-Wakefield Company

This lounge chair is easily turned around and moved about because of a concealed mechanism.

must be sure to select the kind of chair that will serve your purpose best. Each of these uses demands a chair that has certain characteristics. The chair at the writing desk should be of the right height to afford working comfort, and should not have arms that extend far enough to interfere with drawing close to the desk. The first requisite of a lounging chair is comfort. One assumes a very different position when resting than when working at a desk. When resting we are generally inclined to lean back a little and stretch the legs slightly forward. A good lounging chair provides for this. The back tilts at just the right angle. The seat is low enough so that the feet reach the floor easily, and must neither be too deep nor too shallow. The whole chair is soft and comfortable. The horsehair parlor set of the nineteenth century, with the hard, slippery seats, provided none of the essentials for lounging. It might seem by contrast that any of the oversize furniture of the present time must be comfortable, but such is not the case. Some of the chairs are so large and massive that the average person is lost in them. Few people can sit in a very large chair and reach the floor comfortably with their feet. If one sits far enough back to lean comfortably against the back of the chair, the feet are off the floor and it is difficult to rise. Before purchasing a lounging chair one should try sitting in it several times, testing its comfort thoroughly.

214

Consider H. Willett, Inc.

Pleasing design in a dressing table and mirror.

The chair shown on the opposite page may at first seem large and unwieldy for moving about until you learn that it is fitted with concealed "dolly" wheels that swivel and are fitted with ball bearings that permit the chair to turn all the way around and at the same

Three types of desks which meet different needs. A: A secretary desk. B: A table-top desk. C: A chest desk.

time permit the chair to be moved easily from one part of the room to another. One of the difficulties with heavy lounge chairs is moving them for cleaning or other purposes.

Every piece of furniture should be considered from the standpoint of suitability to use before it is purchased. Suppose you are buying bedroom furniture. Do you want a dressing table or a chest? If you cannot afford both, you should decide which will serve your needs best. Compare the dressing table and mirror on page 215 and the chest and mirror on page 210. The dressing table is made with knee room so that one may sit down to use the mirror, while to use the mirror of the chest one must stand. However, the chest has drawer

216

D E

F

Sligh Furniture

Table top desks in contemporary style. D: Typewriter desk (closed). E: Typewriter desk (open). F: Desk with drawer space.

space; this may be an important point to consider. If you have no other place to keep your belongings, you may prefer to have the chest.

When you select a desk, consider your most important requirement. Which of the styles shown on these two pages would suit you best? The secretary desk has space for books above and generous drawer space below. But this desk cannot be put in front of a window, and it is a large, heavy piece of furniture not well suited to a small room. The table-top desk has less drawer space, but it can be placed in front of a window. The table top is an excellent working surface where you can spread out your books and papers. The chest desk is not so large and heavy, but has no space for books.

The typewriter desk shown in two views, open and closed, at the top of this page provides both a table and storage for the typewriter. The typewriter shelf is supported by a mechanism which drops down and slides back into the upper part of the compartment. There is

Modernage Furniture Corp.; Man-Low

Modern furniture showing simplicity of design, horizontal lines, blond finish, and absence of decoration. The center piece is a secretary desk.

space for **paper** and other supplies at the bottom of the compartment and in the drawer above the kneehole space.

Still another type of desk is shown in the bottom picture. This is a kneehole desk with plenty of room for the knees and four wide drawers on the left-hand side. Notice that no drawer pulls are visible. There are slots underneath the edge of each drawer with enough room for the fingers.

A modern type of secretary desk is shown above. The front pulls down for a writing surface as in other secretary desks, but provides a rather small space. The bookshelves are arranged at each side instead of at the top. There are more shelves inside the doors. This desk is a very attractive piece of design in the modern style. Notice the emphasis on horizontal lines and the absence of any decoration. It depends for its beauty on the lovely blond finish and the fine lines and proportions.

Still another consideration is the style of the furniture. The woman who bought a fine Duncan Phyfe table for her dining room was disappointed because it did not harmonize with the rest of the furniture in her house. She had hesitated between a Duncan Phyfe table and a tavern draw-top table. Both are good design but quite different in character. The Duncan Phyfe is delicate and graceful, expressing a quiet elegance. The tavern table is square and sturdy in character.

In the effort to secure harmony do not make the mistake of matching pieces of furniture so well that the result is monotonous. It is for this reason the "sets" of living-room furniture seldom make a pleasing effect. Bedroom and dining-room sets of furniture do not offer this same problem in monotony because of the variations in form of the different pieces of furniture, but in the living room the chairs and davenport are so nearly alike in size, shape, and color that the combination lacks variety.

ADDITIONAL PROBLEMS FOR STUDY. 1. Criticize the following selections from the viewpoint of suitability:

A spinet desk for a woman who has a great deal of correspondence and writing to do.

A dressing table in a bedroom where the only other articles of furniture are a bed, a small table, and a chair.

2. Select pictures of living-room pieces that you think will combine well.

3. Write a paragraph telling what new piece of furniture is most needed in your home. What requirements should it fulfill from the standpoint of suitability?

BEAUTY OF WOOD AND FINISH. In order to appreciate beauty of wood and finish in furniture, it is essential to study real woods and finishes. Arrange to study pieces of furniture or samples of wood with good finishes. Mahogany, birch, walnut, gumwood, maple, and oak are commonly used, and therefore you should have a sample of each of these woods. What differences can you discover in the grains of these different woods? You will observe a certain likeness between birch and mahogany, but upon closer inspection you will note the short, straight, dark lines in mahogany. Birch has a pleasing grain and is used in good furniture. Most people, however, find the variations in the grain of mahogany even more pleasing. Gumwood and walnut have certain similarities of grain, but after some study you should be able to see the differences.

Our study of woods should bring us to a realization of the fact that the gum and birch have a claim to beauty as much as mahogany and walnut. Even though mahogany and walnut are most beautiful, gum, birch, and other woods have certain claims to merit. A table made from gumwood or birch may be a good table from the standpoint of both durability and beauty. It is only when a table of gumwood or birch is misrepresented as walnut or mahogany that we object. We do not want to pay a price for which we do not receive full value. Many furniture manufacturers have felt this so keenly that they have encouraged a movement to have every dealer "name the woods" and sell every piece of furniture for exactly what it is.

A PROBLEM FOR INVESTIGATION. Investigate the local stores. Do the dealers "name the woods," and are the pieces tagged so as to name the kinds of wood used in each piece of furniture?

A CONTEST IN RECOGNITION OF WOOD. Collect samples of as many different kinds of wood as possible. These should be stained and finished so that they have the same appearance as in furniture. Write to furniture manufacturers, and get help from the woodshop teacher. Study these pieces until you feel sure that you can recognize them. Arrange a contest in one of two ways. Use fresh samples of the same woods which you have not used in your study, or arrange to go to a furniture store where you can identify the woods in the different pieces of furniture. Your teacher will decide what pieces you should try to identify. Make a list and try to name each correctly.

Look for a good finish on your furniture. Avoid a cheap, shiny finish and enjoy the soft, polished surfaces in fine furniture. No matter how good the design in the table nor how beautiful the grain of the wood, it can be ruined by a high-gloss varnish. It was an old saying among cabinet-makers, "Fill the wood with oil and polish it with wax." We need only compare a piece of furniture having a waxed and rubbed finish with a cheap varnish finish to appreciate the difference.

The beauty of finish in a piece of furniture includes a good finish on all parts of the piece. This means a smooth, lustrous finish on the chair legs that are turned, in the carved ornament that decorates the curved leg of a Queen Anne chair, in the grooves around the edge of a table top, or on the corner posts in a Colonial chest. In cheaper finishes we find the top and larger surfaces well finished but the details are left rough. Examine some pieces of furniture for the quality and beauty of their finish and you will see how finish can contribute to real beauty in furniture.

Your study of finishes should include color. Traditional mahogany furniture is finished with red and with brown stain. Ask a furniture dealer to show you both finishes. Then you can select the color which blends well with your other furnishings. Contemporary mahogany furniture is often blond. Walnut is finished in dark or light tones of brown. One tone may suit you better than the other. Maple furniture is finished in several different tones. Some is very bright red-orange in tone. This is the least beautiful of the maple finishes. Most attractive is the soft brownish-yellow tone. Before you buy a piece of maple furniture look well at its color.

Mahogany, maple, oak, and other woods are bleached and finished in a very light blond color for much modern-style furniture. The secretary desk shown on page 218 is blond mahogany.

SUGGESTIONS FOR FURTHER STUDY. 1. If possible, visit a furniture factory or repair shop so that you can see how furniture is put together.

2. Examine the furniture in your home and at school to see how much you can tell about the quality of its construction.

AN EXTRA PROJECT. The study of period furniture is interesting to those who enjoy learning about life in past centuries. Select one or more of the following periods as your interest and time permits:

Jacobean (Tudor)	Sheraton	French Provincial
William and Mary	Adams	The Three French
Queen Anne	Colonial	Louis's
Hepplewhite	Empire	
Chippendale	Victorian	

Make an evaluation of the style you study in terms of the following criteria:

1. Expression of rhythmic line and proportion.
2. Characteristic ornamentation.
3. Functional quality for period in which style was first introduced.
4. Is the style still popular and reproduced by furniture-makers?

LOOK FOR GOOD CONSTRUCTION. Durability is an extremely important quality in furniture. Good design, fine wood, and beautiful finish in your dining-room chairs will not make up for poor construction. A chair which soon becomes wobbly and breaks down is not a good buy.

If you are considering the purchase of a chair, examine the joints to see if they are strong. The diagrams on page 222 will show you one good method of joining the back legs and chair rail (edge of the seat). This is called a dowel joint. Notice how the corner block is

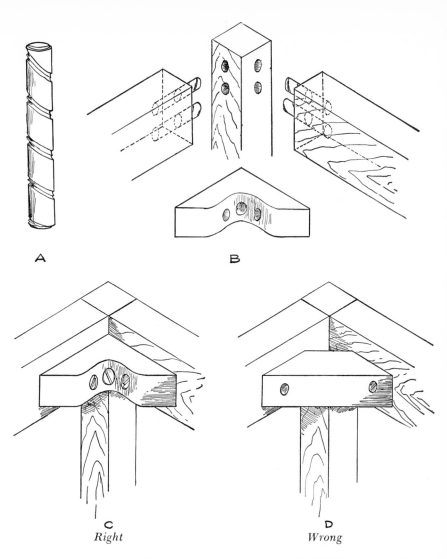

A   B

C   D
Right   Wrong

Diagrams showing the correct use of the dowel joint in wood furniture construction. A: Wooden rod called a dowel. It is grooved to permit the escape of air bubbles in the glue which is used to strengthen all types of joinings. B: Diagram showing how the seat rails are fitted into the chair post (leg) and strengthened with a corner block. The dowels fit into the holes in the chair post and into holes drilled into the rails as shown by the dotted lines. C: Parts fitted together. Notice the center screw in the corner block which draws the leg tight against the rails and corner block. Screws into each rail help to make the joint tight and firm. D: A poor type of corner block because it does not fit into the corner and is nailed instead of screwed.

222

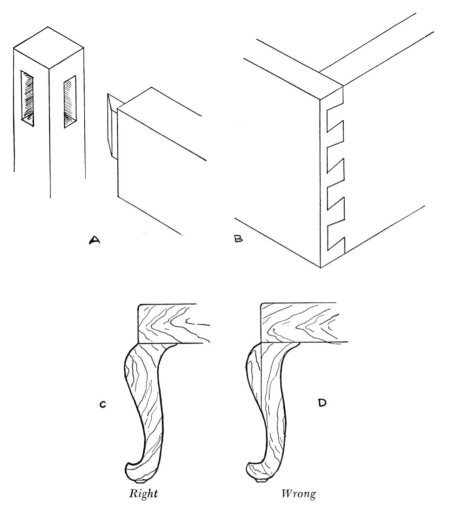

A   B

c   D

Right   Wrong

Diagrams showing points to look for in judging furniture construction. A: A mortise-and-tenon joint is a strong joint and is used in good furniture. A projecting piece called the tenon is cut on the piece to the right which fits into the mortise or hole in the piece at the left. C: A curved leg should be cut from one solid piece. D: A curved leg should not be cut from a piece made by gluing two pieces of wood together.

screwed in for re-enforcement. The center screw helps to pull the leg tight against the block and rails.

Another good joint is called the mortise and tenon. You can see how this is made in the diagram above.

223

A dual-purpose table for games or dining.

In some pieces of furniture you can see what type of joint is used, but in upholstered chairs and davenports the joints are likely to be completely hidden. Since you cannot take one of these pieces apart in the shop, you will have to rely on the seller to give you information about the construction.

JUDGING UPHOLSTERED FURNITURE. Almost all the construction and much of the material is hidden in the case of upholstered furniture. You must rely on the seller for truth regarding the quality of the springs and the material used for webbing, padding, and workmanship. If possible, get a guarantee or label concerning these things. Many states now require a label on upholstered furniture stating the contents used inside the cushions and built-in spring sections.

Sponge rubber is a new, modern material which is becoming very popular for loose cushions. It has no springs to get out of order and always holds its shape.

> SUGGESTIONS FOR FURTHER STUDY. 1. Arrange for a class period when you will examine the construction of furniture. Borrow chairs and other pieces from other rooms in the school, or visit a room where there are several pieces.
>
> 2. Ask the woodworking teacher to demonstrate different kinds of joints used in construction of furniture.

DUAL-PURPOSE FURNITURE. The great aim in modern home design is to create a more livable home. Furniture designers are seeking new

224

ideas and new ways of doing things which will help to achieve this objective. Dual-purpose furniture, which many people find very useful is being produced. If you have a limited budget and one purchase can be made to serve for two, so much the better. Often one piece of furniture which serves for two is particularly advantageous in small apartments.

The combination game and dining table shown on the opposite page would be a wise choice for a home with limited space. When open, the table is 36" x 72" and when closed it is 36" x 36". It is simple and functional with a parquet top which adds interest to the severity of the design.

In the pictures on page 226 you can see how some cocktail tables serve a dual purpose. In the upper picture, the four square cocktail tables are grouped together to form one large, handsome table, effective as a background for a large flower arrangement or useful for serving after-dinner coffee or a living-room buffet supper. When seats are more essential than tables, Presto! Change! Someone snaps thick rubber foam cushions onto the tables and they become comfortable seats. Or if someone desires an hour of de luxe lounging, one of these seats will make an admirable ottoman for the chair shown at the left in the picture.

MODERN FURNITURE IS SECTIONAL. Contemporary furniture designers have taken great pains to design furniture which fits together along the wall. You would not suspect that the piece which stands against the right-hand wall in the picture on page 227 is really made up of three separate pieces. The center part is a chest with four drawers which are opened by using the finger-tip space underneath the edges of the horizontal paneling. The pieces at either side of the chest are called junior wardrobes. The doors open in the center and four sliding trays can be pulled forward. These trays and the drawers in the chest are divided into compartments. Wouldn't this be a help in keeping your belongings in order!

The daybed is also a dual-purpose piece of furniture. By night it is a bed and by day, a davenport.

Some sectional furniture is made in a style which fits a corner, such as the sectional sofas shown on page 116. It is said of the modern style that it makes use of neglected corners. For example, the table shown on page 226 uses space which otherwise might be wasted. Does it not seem to you that these pieces which fit into corners add unity to the whole effect?

NEW IDEAS IN FURNITURE DESIGN. Contemporary furniture designers are striving constantly to create new types of furniture which will

Sligh Furniture

Tables that lead a double life! Top: They are combined to make one large decorative table. Bottom: Two of the tables now wear cushions which transform them into comfortable seats.

Sligh Furniture

This group of furniture is designed to provide comfortable living in a small bachelor apartment, but it can be used advantageously in many other ways.

be truly functional in our modern way of life. Every year, furniture companies are introducing innovations which depart radically from the furniture forms of the past. Many of these will add considerably to the ease of living and beauty of the American home. Naturally the wise homemaker will not buy these new types of furniture without first considering carefully whether they will suit her needs and her taste. But among these new ideas she is sure to find some that will solve her particular problems in home furnishing.

The picture on page 229 shows a new idea for a dressing table. The bed footboard is formed by a lift-top dressing table in the center with a chest on either side. The top when lifted reveals a fluorescent light, and the drawers on either side provide convenient storage. In a room where wall space is limited, this type of arrangement is especially desirable.

The headboard is as functional as the footboard in this compact arrangement. The cabinets at either side have swinging drawers, as shown on page 228. The top and bottom drawers take care of the various odd articles, beads, cold cream, and facial tissues which you might wish to have handy. The center space provides a convenient place for books or other reading material.

You will be interested to know that the bedspread and draperies are made from a fine-quality burlap and the walls are covered with burlap.

Popular Home Magazine; United States Gypsum Company

This picture shows the detail of the bedside cabinet in the headboard shown on the opposite page.

Forms and materials unknown in traditional furniture styles are used in the new styles which you may choose for your home. The room on page 230 has a new-type desk which appeals to many people. The base is made of gleaming metal tubing. There is no wood to polish or refinish, and there is plenty of room for feet and knees. It is also easy to clean underneath the desk. The upper part of the desk is fitted with sliding doors and compartments for storing papers. A perforated metal wastebasket is suspended underneath the right-hand side of the desk top. It can be opened easily by pulling it out. On the other side of the desk is a trap door which can be lifted for access to storage space underneath.

Notice the very nice grouping of the lamp and the decorative map above the desk. The background in this room is finished with a wallboard cleverly stained to resemble pine paneling. The wallboard has the advantage of being fire resistant.

Popular Home Magazine; United States Gypsum Company

Functional design of headboard and footboard provides convenience and saves space. (Designed by Henry Glass.)

BE TOLERANT IN YOUR TASTES. Are you one of the people who feels that only the "old" styles are beautiful? That only traditional styles will last? Or are you one who thinks that only modern design is the answer to beauty and comfort in the home? That everything predating the twentieth century should be thrown out the window? These opposite points of view are the cause of endless arguments and much disagreement.

Differing ideas and tastes are quite understandable, but a bit of tolerance for other points of view can lead to broader understanding and appreciation of the beauty in the world. Those who admire only the traditional furniture forms can find beauty to enjoy in modern styles if they are willing to admit that traditional is *not the only kind of beauty* in home decoration. On the other hand, those who are devoted to the modern style can also find enjoyment in the traditional if they can practice a little broad-mindedness. Of course, you

Popular Home Magazine; United States Gypsum Company

A new concept in desk design.

are entitled to your preference in styles, but need this mean that your chosen style is the only one in the world with a claim to beauty?

STANDARDS FOR GOOD FURNITURE

When you select furniture, check each piece for the following points:

1. Is its structural design pleasing and harmonious? Are the proportions of its different parts interesting or monotonous? Is there a good rhythm of line throughout the whole? Is it well balanced or is it top-heavy?

2. Is the ornamentation in good taste? Does it enrich the surface and emphasize the structural form, or is it fussy and elaborate?

3. Is it thoroughly suited to its use?

4. Does it provide the proper amount of drawer space? If it is a chair, is it comfortable?

5. Is the material used for upholstering well designed?

6. Is its color and scale of pattern suitable?

7. Are the wood and finish pleasing?

8. Is it well constructed?

TO TEST YOUR APPRECIATION OF FURNITURE DESIGN

I. Study the illustrations in other chapters in this book which show furniture. Select a piece of furniture which you think shows excellent design. Be prepared to tell the class why it is good.

II. Study the furniture shown on pages 264, 303, 349, and 382. Answer the following questions:

1. Which pieces of furniture show strong graceful lines? Weak lines?

2. Which pieces show good proportion? Bad proportion?

3. In which pieces is the ornamentation good? Why?

4. Which pieces would you combine in the same room?

5. Which pieces would be inharmonious in the same room?

III. Collect pictures of furniture that you would like to have for some room in your home.

Chapter 10

PICTURES FOR YOUR WALLS

You may buy pictures for your home in a dime store or in an art gallery. Of course, in the art gallery you will pay a great deal more than in a dime store, but, even so, you might buy a picture that would not be good decoration for *your* home. You might also buy in a dime store a picture that would be very poor decoration for your home. It is a matter of taste and personal preference.

WHAT SUBJECTS IN PICTURES DO YOU LIKE? The pictures on your walls should mean something to *you personally*. Naturally you will like pictures of things which are interesting to you in life. If you are especially fond of animals, you will like animal pictures. If you are fond of sports, you will like sporting pictures. If you love outdoor life and travel, you will like landscapes and outdoor scenes. If you are greatly interested in people and human nature, you will choose portraits and pictures of people. There are dozens of subjects which may appeal to you personally.

When you buy a picture for your home do not select just any pretty little picture that has no special meaning to you. If you give someone a picture as a gift, try to choose one that will appeal to that person's special interests. It will not be possible to discuss in this chapter all the different subjects which might appeal to you. We shall discuss only a few modern pictures by American painters that may serve to suggest to you the kind of pictures you would like to have for your own home. If you are historical-minded, you may prefer pictures from past periods of art. Some people like the religious pictures of the Renaissance, the eighteenth-century English portrait

232

paintings, or the seventeenth-century Dutch and Flemish paintings. Many people prefer twentieth-century painting because it deals with a subject that is part of our own lives. Of course, you may like several different types of pictures; in this case, you will include them in your selection of pictures for your walls.

ORIGINAL PAINTINGS OR REPRODUCTIONS. Not many people can afford to buy oil paintings in the exclusive shops of the art dealers. A great many people can afford to buy reproductions of the greatest and most valuable paintings in the world. Many of these reproductions are made in color, and they can be used most effectively in room decoration. Some of the most successful rooms created by interior decorators have been planned around colored prints reproduced from fine paintings. On pages 403 and 404 you will find a list of places where you can secure good colored reproductions of great paintings.

Any of us would rather own an original oil painting than a reproduction from the same painting. But you should remember that not all oil paintings are good art. Some of them are very bad art. Just because a picture is "hand painted" does not mean that it is a good picture. It is better to own a *good reproduction* of a good picture than a *poor original* painting. Learn to be critical about pictures. This is not a thing that you can learn from a few pages in a book. You will learn by continued experience in looking at pictures and comparing them. Always look at a picture to see if it shows you the kind of thing you really like to see in a picture.

SUGGESTIONS FOR FURTHER STUDY. 1. Discuss in class the subjects for pictures which each member would choose for her home.

2. Collect catalogues from the companies listed on pages 403 and 404. If possible, examine the colored prints from these sources. Perhaps your public library will have some of these prints.

LANDSCAPES FOR OUTDOOR LOVERS. Probably landscapes are popular because so many people are fond of the outdoors. There was a time in history when landscapes were not considered worthy subjects for the painter's brush. They were used only as backgrounds for portraits or religious paintings. Landscapes are now considered quite worthwhile subjects for any painter's brush.

The two landscapes shown on page 234 were painted in two distant parts of the country, the east and the west. "Mrs. Scott's House" by Edward Hopper was painted in the rolling hills of New England.

Randolph-Macon Woman's College

In the collection of Mr. and Mrs. Roy R. Neuberger; photograph Macbeth Gallery

Two modern American landscapes. Top: "Mrs. Scott's House" by Edward Hopper. Bottom: "The Rainy Season" by Peter Hurd.

"The Rainy Season" by Peter Hurd was painted in New Mexico. Each picture tells us a great deal about the hills and the country where it was painted. Mrs. Scott's little house clings firmly to the top of its sunlit hill. The house is alone, but not lonely. Sunlight bathes it in a lovely light. The hills are warm and friendly because it is summer. Notice the rhythmic repetition of the long, beautiful curves over the tops of the hills. Notice, too, the fine pattern of dark and light created by the sunlit house against the shadow on the next hill. Certainly the artist must have been thinking in terms of rhythmic lines and patterns of light and dark. Such pictures are not created by accident.

Have you missed any small details in the house or hills? The artist did not show separate boards in the house and barn or any separate blades of grass on the hills. Such details would have spoiled the strong, bold effect of his picture. If we bothered with such details, we could not see the great beauty of the picture itself.

There is vast expanse of land around the house in the Hopper painting, but there is still greater expanse in the painting by Peter Hurd. Here, the artist has tried to make us feel the great reaches of the hills of New Mexico. A silvery light floods the landscape. An overcast sky is to drop its rain on the hills below. In the foreground a rancher has stopped his team and looks out over the hills. A cowboy on his pony has stopped nearby. A strange light plays over the hills.

Peter Hurd paints the country that he knows. He lives on a ranch in New Mexico and divides his time between ranching and painting. This picture has a lovely rhythmic pattern in the forms of the hills. Our eyes slide down one hill and up another with the greatest of pleasure. The beautiful light that plays over the hills gives great beauty to the landscape.

The painting on page 236 by John Rogers Cox gives his version of the rolling prairies of the Middle West. A golden wheat field stretching far off to meet the great sky piled with mountainous gray clouds, creates the impression of illimitable space. The composition is planned with almost geometric precision. Right-angle crossroads, a straight row of telephone poles, neat, square-cornered fences, and the regular grass borders along the wheat fields, combined with the heaped-up curves of the clouds, create a severely formal and striking effect. Obviously this is not a photographic portrayal of a particular crossroads. It is much more than that; it is a highly individualized expression of the spirit of the Middle West. The artist creates a mood

235

"Grey and Gold" by John Rogers Cox, a painting of the wheat fields of the Middle West.

in a far more effective way than any photographer could possibly do it. In Cox's painting we not only get an impression of how the rolling prairies look, but also what they are *like*.

CITY PICTURES FOR CITY PEOPLE. Some people like the city better than the country, and so they are interested in pictures of the city. Modern artists have found many subjects for painting our cities. Some of them choose to paint the boulevards, parks, and splendid business streets. Others choose shabby, dingy sections.

Roy Hilton, a Pittsburgh artist, has been interested in recording his impression of the Pittsburgh region, especially the industrial and more crowded areas. In his painting, called "Above the River" (opposite page), a house is perched on the side of the hill, a very high house, towering above the street. Steps in front of it and beside it lead to still higher buildings farther up the hill. There are many dwellings in Pittsburgh like this one, high, narrow, and reached only by many steps. Instead of being built to harmonize with the contour of the ground, they stick straight up like giant fence posts. In "Above

236

"Above the River" by Roy Hilton, an interpretation of the Pittsburgh scene.

the River" Hilton has captured the characteristic quality and effect of Pittsburgh in one of its aspects.

People who like "pretty" pictures do not understand why some artists choose to paint such scenes. Why should an artist wish to paint something that is ugly, drab, and depressing? Perhaps because he is wearied with the superficial prettiness of traditional subjects

"At the Soda Fountain" by William J. Glackens portrays a typical American scene in any corner drugstore.

and turns to everyday reality. At the same time, he discovers a kind of beauty which is inherent in the scene and puts it into his canvas for our pleasure.

In the Pittsburgh painting, Hilton has emphasized the structural forms of the ground, the houses, the steps, and the street. The eye travels back and forth around these forms, always by a route which emphasizes the third-dimensional quality and depth of the picture. The forms have bulk and solidity. In a way, this kind of painting provides us with a greater sense of reality than when we are looking at the actual scene. "Above the River" has achieved this quality of essential realism, and at the same time it creates a mood, an effect of harsh, bleak beauty.

PAINTINGS OF LIFE IN AMERICA. Modern artists have discovered that scenes taken from life in America make good pictures. Some artists in the past have thought that only pretty things were suitable subjects for pictures. Other artists insisted they could make pictures from scenes in everyday life. Instead of choosing beautiful country scenes or pretty ladies for their paintings, these artists chose street scenes, life in the city, on a farm, and similar scenes.

Can you imagine making a splendid picture from a scene in the drugstore soda fountain? Or at a family reunion? That is exactly what American painters have done in the paintings reproduced on pages 238, 240, and 241. "At the Soda Fountain" is a delightful picture by William J. Glackens. To enjoy it most you should see it in color. One girl wears a pink dress and the other a yellow one. The green ginger-ale bottle and the pineapple in the background make nice bits of color. Even in the black-and-white reproduction you can see the glow of light which the artist painted into this picture. Even the shadows are vibrant with color.

Notice how the figures of the two girls and the boy behind the fountain are arranged to make an interesting composition. The eye travels easily up the arm of the girl at the right, over the top of the boy's head, and down over the head and arm of the girl at the left. It makes a sort of triangular composition which is very pleasing. Out of the confusion and multiplicity of articles at the drugstore soda fountain, the artist organized a simple and harmonious picture.

"Schellhammer Family Reunion" (page 240) by Virginia Cuthbert shows quite another aspect of American life. The occasion is a picnic when members of the family have gathered from far and near. Most of the women are engaged in setting the tables, and most of the men stand about waiting the call to eat. Back of the house some of the boys are throwing horseshoes. Other interesting details are carried out in the various parts of the picture.

In creating this painting, the artist did not try to paint just one family reunion exactly as she saw it. She tried to paint a picture that was typical of the family reunions held every summer in western Pennsylvania. She chose a family name that was common in the county where she, herself, had spent many summers. After the picture

Courtesy of the artist

"Schellhammer Family Reunion" by Virginia Cuthbert shows another bit of life in America.

had been exhibited in several galleries, she received letters from all parts of the United States asking about the family and the house. Many people thought it might be their family or their house. This proves that the picture does typify the old American custom of family reunions at summer picnics.

The painting on the opposite page, called "Weighing Cotton," was done by Thomas Hart Benton, and it, too, is a depiction of the American scene. Benton was born in Missouri and has painted many pictures which tell about life in his part of the country. "Weighing Cotton" records one phase of life as the artist has seen it. We see the pickers filling their long, oddly shaped bags with cotton, and others waiting to have theirs weighed.

SUGGESTIONS FOR FURTHER STUDY. 1. Select five places in or near your community (either country or city) which you think would make good subjects for paintings. Compare these with the selections of others in your class.

240

"Weighing Cotton" by Thomas Hart Benton, an interpretation of life in the cotton-growing states.

2. List five subjects which are typical of life in America that might be used as subjects for paintings.

PAINTINGS OF PEOPLE. The most popular picture subjects with many people are pictures of other people. This is especially likely to be true of people who are greatly interested in human nature and society in general. The picture on page 242, called "A Young Woman," was painted by Isabel Bishop, a New York artist. It represents a type of girl that the artist saw on the streets near her studio. This girl in the picture is not a pretty society girl type; she is a good-looking, sturdy American girl. She gives the impression of strength and ability. Whatever her job she will learn to do it well. She probably knows her way around the streets of the city. Isabel Bishop likes to paint the girls that she sees in the little park near her studio. Mostly they are office girls. The artist herself must be interested in people and human nature to paint these types so well. She has an individual

241

"A Young Woman" by Isabel Bishop shows a type of girl which the artist saw on the streets of New York.

way of using her paint. You can see it in this painting, and when you see another you will know it is by the same artist.

The painting shown on page 243 is also the picture of a girl. It is

Department of Fine Arts, Carnegie Institute

"Anne in White" by George Bellows is a charming portrait of the artist's daugh-ter.

called "Anne in White" and was painted by the girl's father, George Bellows. A good portrait not only shows a good likeness but reveals something of personality and temperament. What does this portrait tell you about Anne as a person? Most people say that she is shy, quiet, and "a nice girl." We feel sure that she would have charming manners and never be noisy or bold. Portraits can tell a great deal about people. A good portrait painter must be able to paint character as well as noses and eyelashes!

243

When artists paint pictures of people, their aims may be quite different. When Isabel Bishop painted "A Young Woman" she was interested in showing a type of girl that she sees on the streets near her studio. When George Bellows painted "Anne in White" he wanted to show her personality and temperament. Other artists who paint pictures of people may be interested in showing still other effects. For example, an artist may wish to create a beautiful decorative effect with his drawings of the human figure. We enjoy such pictures for rhythmic movement, interesting proportions, good balance, and pleasing emphasis in the composition of the figure.

Other artists who paint pictures of people intend to tell a story in each picture. Such pictures are illustrations. They may be dramatic, amusing, sad, or imaginative, depending upon the story. You will find it interesting to study the illustrations in current weekly and monthly magazines. Learn the names of the illustrators whose names you like best, and note their ways of drawing figures, expressing character, and telling a story. With a little study you will be able to recognize their work before you see the names.

A CLASS DISCUSSION. Can a photograph or a painting tell a story more effectively? Why?

NONREALISTIC PICTURES. All the paintings that we have discussed express some form of realism; that is, they represent some aspect of nature as it really is. Another type of picture, quite opposite from the realistic, has become popular with many modern painters. There are many kinds of nonrealistic pictures, and we do not have space in this chapter to discuss all of them.

"Israel," shown on the opposite page, is a painting by Samuel Rosenberg. It is painted in a style which is generally called semiabstract. Here the artist has taken the figure of a Jewish rabbi sitting in the synagogue and has given it a kind of design treatment. The head has been elongated and squared into a blocklike shape, the diagonal lines of the face are emphasized, and most realistic details are omitted. Shapes and forms in other parts of the canvas echo the straight and diagonal lines of the head and face. The colors are rich and deep suggesting the quality of stained glass. It seems as though the painter might have seen this old rabbi sitting in the darkened interior where the light from stained-glass windows played tricks with reality.

Why did the artist choose to treat the figure in this semiabstract fashion instead of a more realistic manner? Had he shown the old rabbi as he really looked, interest would have been centered on that

244

"Israel" by Samuel Rosenberg is a semiabstract painting in which the artist directs our thoughts to the history of a people rather than to a description of one man.

one man, his appearance and his character. The abstract figure compels us to think, not of one man, but of many men, of the whole Jewish people, their history, and their sufferings. In other words, we are forced to think in terms of larger thought consciousness. Although we think in terms of abstract ideas, yet our emotional re-

245

An amusing bit of fantasy called "Siesta" painted by Doris Lee.

sponses are involved. When the artist shows us what he thinks and feels, as he does in this case, the result is known as expressionism.

FANTASY, NONREALISM, AND SURREALISM. The modern movement in painting includes a definite tendency away from reality. One type, known as surrealism, is based on the psychology of the subconscious mind. Surrealistic paintings express the unreal quality of things felt and seen in dreams. In some, the effect is created by incongruity, the putting together of objects and scenes which would not normally be found together. The results may be strange, weird, and fantastic with no purpose other than to plunge the observer into a queer, dreamlike state. Some surrealistic paintings are playful and some are serious. Some have meaning and some do not, but all are nonrealistic.

The picture reproduced above is an amusing bit of fantasy by Doris Lee called "Siesta." Perhaps it is based on the unconscious desire for certain types of physical comforts. The girl is peacefully reposing on a nice soft bed surrounded by open country. She has everything that she could want for a bit of luxurious relaxation—a book, a bowl of luscious cherries, chocolates, and birds to sing sweetly. What more could she desire for solid comfort? There is only one jarring note in this dreamlike state of perfect bliss, the rooster which will crow loud and long!

WHY NONREALISTIC PICTURES? Why is it that so many present-day artists prefer to paint nonrealistic pictures? To many people, their paintings are strange and childish. Some believe that modern artists cannot draw, and therefore make up a "crazy" kind of picture which does not require skill in drawing. It is not true that they cannot draw. Many of them are excellent draftsmen, but they have definite reasons for preferring to do nonrealistic painting. They believe that people who like naturalistic pictures should be satisfied with photographs. They ask, why should the artist waste his time copying nature? Let the camera do that. They believe that the artist should create something from his own thoughts and feelings, something that the camera cannot reproduce. Some of them like to paint in abstract terms to make you think and feel in terms that is not possible with a realistic painting. Others like to paint in terms of fantasy, as Doris Lee did in "Siesta." Be tolerant of modern painting and you will find much to enjoy. Try to understand what the artist was aiming at in his picture, and then judge how well he accomplished his objective.

ETCHINGS AND LITHOGRAPHS. The pictures which we have just been discussing are oil paintings. Although not many of us can afford to hang original oil paintings on our walls, most of us can manage to secure some reproductions of fine paintings. However, there is another possibility in securing pictures for our walls. Original etchings and lithographs can be secured at reasonable prices, and they make very good wall decoration. The etching shown on page 248, called "Peace in the Valley," was done by Luigi Lucioni. The scene is Vermont, as you might guess from the rolling hills and magnificent elm tree. Etchings are made on copperplates. The artist etches lines into the plate which produce the picture. From this plate several prints are made, but only a limited number of perfect impressions can be made from one plate. After that the plate is destroyed. Each print is an orginal etching. Most etchings are black and white.

Lithographs are also made by printing from a plate which the artist prepares, but the process is different from that for etchings. The artist draws with a special lithographic crayon on a specially prepared stone or possibly on an aluminum or zinc plate. Prints are made from the plate, and each is considered an original lithograph.

An etching by Luigi Lucioni called "Peace in the Valley."

To understand fully how lithographs and etchings are produced, it is necessary actually to see the process. However, you can learn to detect the difference between these two types of prints by examining them closely. Study the etching by Lucioni above and you will see that it was done by the use of many fine lines. This is much easier to see in an original etching than in the reproduction in this book. The fine lines in an etching are made with a needle which cuts through a coating of wax on the plate.

THE PICTURES IN YOUR HOME. As a summary to this brief study of modern painting, let us consider the important points which should enter into the selection of pictures for the decoration of your own home.

1. Choose a subject which means something to you personally. If you like surrealism, do not hesitate to select a surrealistic picture even though your friends are scornful of your choice.

2. Decide what you desire from your pictures. Do you want the type that provokes serious thinking about the problems of the world,

or do you prefer quiet subjects with no meaning other than a decorative spot on the wall? Either choice is good if it serves your needs.

3. Bear in mind that your house is not an art gallery. You cannot plaster your walls with pictures and expect to have a restful and beautiful home.

4. Consider each picture thoughtfully before you decide whether to hang it on your wall. First impressions are not always lasting ones. A picture selected in haste may soon become a bore, and one which is at first rejected may become interesting after further acquaintance.

5. Select simple and functional frames for your pictures. Heavy, elaborate frames are not necessary for the protection of a picture or to set it off from its surroundings. A frame should harmonize with the picture in color, weight, and general appearance.

SUGGESTIONS FOR FURTHER STUDY. 1. If you are interested in securing etchings for home decoration, write to the Associated American Artists, 711 Fifth Avenue, New York City for their catalogue and prices.

2. Appoint a committee to secure information about lithographs.

3. If possible, arrange a demonstration of printing an etching or a lithograph.

JAPANESE PRINTS FOR WALL DECORATION. Still another kind of picture for your walls is the Japanese print. The one shown on page 250 is an old one and is very valuable. Other prints and copies from them are not so expensive. Many people like these prints for wall decoration, but others do not like them because they do not understand their meaning and beauty. They say the people do not look "natural." The Japanese artist does not try to make his people look realistic. He is interested in beautiful lines and forms. Look at the lady shown in the print. Let your eye follow the graceful curves of the kimono. The smaller curves in the hand and face blend delightfully with the curves of the costume. Next notice the swinging rhythms of the cherry tree branches. All the lines flow together in a most beautiful pattern. Think of the Japanese print as a design and you will understand its meaning and beauty more easily.

Japanese prints are made by printing from wood blocks. Since several prints can be made from the same blocks, you may find several prints that are alike.

SUGGESTIONS FOR FURTHER STUDY. 1. Practice reading character from portraits. Secure copies of famous portraits and try to read character

A Japanese print called "Lady Standing Under a Cherry Tree."

from each one. Remember that character is what a person is like, not how he is dressed nor what he does for a living. How well does your character analysis of portraits agree with that of others in your class?

2. Collect prints of the type of picture which you enjoy most.

Start a scrapbook of your favorite pictures. Be selective. It is better to have a few good prints than many poor ones.

3. Flower prints and bird prints are good wall decoration. Collect flower and bird prints for a class exhibition. You will find many attractive ones in magazines and in the dime stores.

FRAME YOUR PICTURES CORRECTLY. Many a good picture has been ruined by its frame. The purpose of a frame is to serve as a boundary line and to set the picture off from its surroundings. Pictures are framed in order to protect them and to set off their beauty. The picture is the center of interest, not the frame, and never should the frame call attention to itself or detract from the picture in any way. Strangely enough, the fashionable thing in picture frames a few years ago was an overornamented, bright gilt type of frame that shrieked for attention. Such a frame attracts so much attention that it is almost impossible to look at the picture. Imagine a bright, glistening gilt frame on a picture full of dull, rich tones, and you can readily see that such a frame fails to fulfill its artistic mission.

In the upper picture on page 252 the frame acts as a boundary to the picture and sets the picture off from its surroundings. The picture is a reproduction of the famous painting, "Mother," by Whistler. This is a masterpiece of painting. Every art principle is admirably expressed. Can you point out how perfect balance, fine rhythmic movement, interesting proportion, and emphasis are attained? It seems impossible that anyone should take liberties with such a beautiful picture, but look at the lower picture on the same page. The beauty of the picture is ruined—all one can see is the ugly mat. A frame should never change the size or shape of a picture even slightly. The artist has planned the picture as it should be and the *frame should fit the picture.*

The weight of the molding used for the frame should be determined by the color and other characteristics of the particular picture. Pictures with strong color and strong contrasts of dark and light, those expressing considerable action or movement, and oil paintings require heavier frames. See the frame on "Line Storm" by John Steuart Curry on page 253. Care should be taken, of course, not to go to the other extreme and use moldings that are so heavy that they overwhelm the picture. Pictures that are lighter and more delicate in character are better framed in lighter-weight moldings. The etching shown on page 254 is well framed in its narrow, black molding because it is delicate and fine in character.

The desirability of the mat, sometimes used, depends on the size

Two styles in picture framing. Top: A simple molding which is harmonious with the picture and sets it off to advantage. Bottom: Horrible effect produced when the frame mutilates the picture.

252

This painting, "Line Storm" by John Steuart Curry, is dramatic and has strong contrasts of light and dark. Therefore, it is best framed with a wide molding. The light value of the frame sets off the dark tones of the picture.

and character of the picture. It should be thought of as part of the frame because it serves also to set off the picture from its surroundings. Most pictures look better framed close, but in the case of a very small picture, delicate in character, a mat is desirable. It is customary to use mats on etchings and frequently on water colors.

Color is a very important point in choosing the picture frame. A rule that is generally safe to follow is to make the color of the frame a little lighter in value than the darkest value in the picture. The color of the frame should echo the color in the picture. Dull-gold frames can be toned with the dominant color in the picture, thus making the frame blend with the picture; and yet if the frame is nearly as dark in value as the darkest tones in the picture, it makes a good boundary and holds the picture together. The old-fashioned bright-yellow gilt frames were never good in color because they were too conspicuous and never echoed the color in the picture. Nor is the black or dark-brown wooden frame good on a colored picture because it, also, fails to repeat the color of the picture.

This etching is well framed with a white mat and a narrow black molding.

MARGINS FOR PICTURE MATS. Etchings, lithographs, and some other prints are generally framed with mats. This offers a problem in proportions. How wide should the margin be on the top, sides, and bottom? There is no rule to tell you exactly how many inches should be allowed, but there are general rules which will guide you in deciding upon the proportion of widths for these margins.

1. The bottom margin should always be widest. Our feeling that the base of a design should be large enough to support the top has resulted in a rule for page margins. The bottom margin should al-

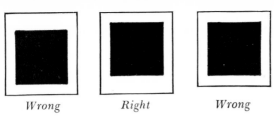

| Wrong | Right | Wrong |

Diagrams showing three possible ways of mounting a square picture. The middle one is correct, because the bottom margin is wider than the top and side margins. This is necessary for a feeling of stability.

ways be wider than the other margins. Compare the three different ways in which the margins are arranged in the above illustration. Do you not feel that the first arrangement is upside down and that the third arrangement looks cut off? The wider margin at the bottom in the second arrangement gives the most satisfactory effect. A wider margin should be left at the bottom in mounting pictures, writing a letter, arranging a page in a notebook, or wherever margins are required. The wider margin at the bottom gives the proper feeling of support.

2. *For a square picture, the top and side margins should be the same width.* The etching shown on the opposite page is approximately square, so equal margins at top and sides with a wider margin at the bottom are most satisfactory for a mat on a square picture.

3. *For a vertically shaped picture the top margin should be wider than the sides.* Since the picture has an up-and-down movement it is essential that the margins repeat this feeling. The better effect in the first picture on page 256 is the result of a top margin wider than the sides and, as always, the widest margin at the bottom.

4. *For horizontally shaped picture, the top margin should be narrower than the sides.* In this case the movement of the eyes is from side to side, and the margins should echo this effect. The first picture on page 257 is mounted more pleasingly than the second one. The second one shows how disturbing it is when the proportions of the margins are reversed.

EXPERIMENTS WITH MARGINS. Select a picture which you wish to mount and experiment until you have found the margins that are most satisfactory. Lay the picture on a large piece of mounting paper and use rulers or strips of paper to block off the edges of the mount. Experiment by moving these strips near to and farther away from

← *Correct*　　　　↑ *Incorrect*

The Art Institute of Chicago

This illustration shows the same picture mounted correctly and incorrectly. Since it is a vertical picture, the top margin should be wider than the side margins. The bottom margin should be widest.

the picture. Watch the effects as the proportions of the margins change, and decide which are best suited to the picture. Do not be satisfied until you are sure the margins are the best that you can possibly make. It is this sort of experiment that helps us to develop a feeling for fine proportions.

SPACING WHICH PRODUCES A UNIFIED EFFECT. Often we wish to group a number of objects to make a unified effect. For example, we may wish to hang several small pictures on one wall, or to mount several pictures and clippings on the page of a scrapbook, or to arrange several articles on a shelf in a china cupboard. In each of these arrangements, the space between the articles should be less than the margins around the outside. Otherwise the effect is scattered. Notice the arrangement of the camera pictures on page 8.

The two printed pages of an open book should be thought of as two parts of one design, or as a horizontal panel. If the spacing is correctly planned, the space between the two pages will be less than the outside margins. Since the two pages make a horizontal panel, the top margin should be narrowest, the side margins wider, and the bottom widest of all.

256

Correct   *Incorrect*

These illustrations show correct and incorrect mounting for a horizontal picture. The side margins should be wider than the top margin, and the bottom margin should be widest of all.

PROBLEMS IN GROUPING TO SECURE UNITY. 1. On one page arrange two or more pictures or some pictures and paragraphs of written material. Remember that the page is to have a unified and not a scattered effect.

2. Arrange several pictures on a bulletin board so that the effect is unified.

3. Arrange three or more small pictures on a wall so as to make a unified and pleasing group.

HANG YOUR PICTURES FOR BEST EFFECT. If a picture is worth hanging on the wall, it is worth hanging so as to show it off to advantage. Here are rules for hanging pictures:

1. It is best to hang pictures so that wires do not show. It is now possible to buy special hooks for this purpose which are very small and do not mar the wall but which support considerable weight. When it is necessary to use wires, two wires should be used which hang from two hooks on the molding, rather than the one wire which hangs the picture from one hook. The one wire makes a triangular shape which is not in harmony with the shape of the picture and which leads the eye upward away from the picture.

2. Pictures and tapestries should be hung near the eye level instead of near the ceiling. It is ridiculous to hang pictures so near the ceiling that they cannot be viewed easily. Rather than do this, it is better not to hang them at all. Such an arrangement gives a wall a scattered appearance lacking in unity.

3. Two or more pictures on the same wall should be carefully placed with relation to each other. Avoid "odd" arrangements. A

Associated American Artists, Inc.

The pictures here are hung so that they become part of the whole design with emphasis on horizontal lines.

stairstep arrangement is bad because it leads the eye up to the ceiling. Irregular, scattered arrangements should always be avoided. As the eye passes from one picture to another it must pursue a jumpy up-and-down path that makes a poor rhythmic movement.

4. Pictures should be hung flat against the wall. If the picture tilts away from the wall at the top it does not seem securely fastened, and sometimes makes an ugly shadow at the edge of the frame. If the screw-eyes to which the wires are fastened are placed near the top of the frame they will prevent the frame from tipping forward.

5. A picture or tapestry should not be crowded into a space that is too small for it. There should be sufficient wall space around it so

This group of pictures is hung so as to make a very interesting center of interest above the davenport.

that the general effect is not cluttered. For a picture to be seen to the best advantage, there must be plenty of space around it.

6. Select the best-shaped wall space for each picture or tapestry. A vertical picture fits best into a vertical-shaped wall space, and a horizontal picture fits best into a broader space.

7. Pictures and tapestries should be hung with respect to the pieces of furniture that are placed against the wall. The picture or tapestry should form a part of the group with the furniture rather than be isolated. The groupings of pictures shown on these two pages are well related to pieces of furniture. Unless a picture is hung near a table, davenport, or other piece of furniture, it is likely to look "lost."

Suggestions for further study. 1. Criticize the way the pictures are hung in your school building. Remember that criticism includes good as well as bad points.

2. Have you rehung any pictures at home? Tell how you made an improvement.

3. Find a picture in a magazine which shows a picture hanging on

a wall. Be prepared to show this picture to your class and tell them why it is well hung according to the rules you have just learned.

4. Set a small group of furniture on one wall of your classroom. Use a table, bookcase, or desk on which you arrange some decorative accessories. Try hanging a picture above this group. Move the picture around until the class agrees that the best place has been found. Remember that the picture should be a part of the group.

Chapter 11

CHOOSING AND USING DECORATIVE
ACCESSORIES

Decorative accessories may contribute much to the livable and comfortable atmosphere of a home. Clocks, mirrors, vases, pictures, candlesticks, and ash trays all help to make a house more livable. Without them rooms are bare and fail to give the feeling that they are lived in. With *too many* articles of this kind, rooms have a cluttered and confused appearance. Mantelpieces, tops of pianos, and bookcases loaded with pictures, vases, and statues make a room seem crowded and untidy. Numerous pictures plastered on the walls, sofa pillows heaped on the couch, and tables overweighted with lamps, books, bowls, and ornaments are in decidedly bad taste. To those of discriminating taste the bareness that results from an absence of decorative accessories is preferable to the confusion of too many.

But neither extreme is necessary. If one owns many interesting and beautiful pictures, tapestries, pieces of pottery, copper, or brass, they need not all be displayed at the same time. Indeed, to make a display of them is exactly what should be avoided. It suggests too much the department store or the museum. We should use only those things which fit into our rooms without cluttering or over-decorating them. If we have more things than can be used at one time, some of them should be kept stored away. They can be exchanged at intervals for those in use, thus obtaining variety in decorative accents.

The selection of our decorative accessories should receive as careful consideration as that given to other furnishings. The same prin-

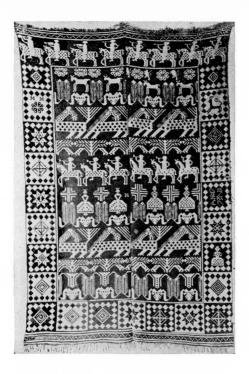

Carnegie Magazine

Swedish weaving made in 1773. It was probably used as a bed-cover, but it is suitable for a wall hanging because of the interesting stylized pattern.

ciples of art studied in relation to tables, rugs, and curtains apply to the design and decoration of clocks, sofa pillows, and picture frames. The art quality of home furnishings is by no means a question of cost. To be sure, some of the most beautiful things are the most expensive, but so are some of the ugliest. We must learn to judge for ourselves.

DECORATIVE ACCESSORIES FOR THE WALLS. Our first thought in planning to make a wall space more interesting is a picture. Pictures suitable for home decoration were discussed in Chapter 10. In this chapter we are concerned with other kinds of decorative accessories for the walls.

Mirrors, tapestries, plaster plaques, and clocks all make good wall decoration. They are frequently more desirable than pictures because they may be less expensive and they may give variety. Too many pictures in one room may seem monotonous, and a mirror or tapestry may offer harmonious variety. To some people, a "piece of cloth" hung on the wall is queer. To other people, a beautiful design in a textile is just as beautiful as a picture. In this class is the delightful Swedish tapestry shown above. The jolly little animal forms,

262

A modern cretonne pattern suitable for a wall hanging. The motif is "The Ride of Paul Revere."

trees, girls, and flowers make a charming effect. This is a kind of fabric known as double weaving. It was woven by a Swedish housewife more than one hundred and fifty years ago.

Of course, it is a valuable museum piece, and most of us cannot afford such expensive tapestries for our walls. Very good design and color in tapestry can be obtained at inexpensive prices, however. The cretonne shown on this page was sold at fifty cents a yard. The theme used here is "The Ride of Paul Revere." The pattern is flat, conventionalized, and well organized. It is entirely decorative in character, and the pattern has interest. The colors are dull tones of olive green, soft yellow, and orange in small spots—a perfect adjacent harmony. A yard of this cretonne made a very nice wall decoration above a big green davenport.

In selecting a wall tapestry we should avoid the pictorial and choose conventionalized and decorative patterns. A picture may be truly pictorial and give a realistic impression of things as they actually are, but it should be the purpose of the tapestry to present a design which is conventionalized, flat, and entirely decorative in character.

263

The old Colonial mirror makes a very good wall decoration.

In the above illustration we see how attractively a mirror may be substituted for a picture. This old Colonial mirror has beautiful proportions and is well suited in style to the desk above which it is hung. Here, also, the decorative treatment of the frame makes it an interesting wall decoration. When selecting a mirror, we must remember that overornamentation is objectionable and that the use of too many restless curves in the frame cannot produce a harmonious, dignified effect.

WALL PLAQUES FOR DECORATION. Ceramic tiles make good wall decoration when they are chosen for their art quality and used correctly on the wall. Many of the rules which apply to hanging pictures also apply to hanging wall plaques. For example, they should be placed so that they are related to a group of furniture and other accessories. The clever and amusing pair of wall plaques shown on pages 266 and 267 would make a good decoration above a bookcase or desk. The plaques are called "Downbeat" and "Trumpeter." The artist has stylized the figures with strong, rhythmic lines that are very expressive. One can almost hear the wild swing of the music!

Other ceramics, such as the shallow tray shown at the top of page 270, can also be hung on the wall for effective decoration. Plate hangers, available in many stores, will hold them safely.

SUGGESTIONS FOR FURTHER STUDY. 1. Borrow several kinds of wall tapestries and hang them in your classroom. These should include cretonnes, India prints, Chinese embroideries, block-printed linen, and real tapestry panels. Study each piece for qualities of design and color.

2. Visit a store or art gallery where you can see fine textiles suitable for use as wall hangings.

DECORATIVE ACCESSORIES FOR MANTELS, TABLES, AND BOOKCASES. There are dozens of articles which serve as decorative accents on mantels, tables, bookcases, desks, and chests. Vases, boxes, ash trays, candlesticks, clocks, and similar objects may add to the beauty of our rooms. They may also, of course, subtract from the beauty of our homes. Ugly, fussy, gaudy decorative accessories can make the best of rooms look cheap and ordinary. A *few good accessories* can make an ordinary room more interesting.

The choice of good accessories does not depend upon your pocketbook. It depends upon your taste. Good design and color are no longer confined to exclusive art stores and gift shops. Very nice examples of pleasing design and harmonious color can be found in the dime stores. They are even to be found in the chain grocery stores. Green glass bottles of interesting shape may be containers for prune juice, but they make excellent containers for ivy or other cut plant materials. Cider bottles of dark amber-colored glass are excellent

This delightful ceramic wall plaque is by the American artist Dale Nichols and is called "Downbeat."

decorative accessories for some rooms. The bottles in the middle of each window in the illustration at the top of page 350 are cider bottles. Each one cost twenty-nine cents filled with cider, which is a reasonable price for cider. On a printed label accompanying each bottle, the manufacturing company stated that the bottles were copied after early American bottles. Naturally this adds to their interest. One of them has been used successfully as a base for a lamp.

Several illustrations in this book show good decorative accessories used in room decoration. The candlesticks shown on page 16 are splendid design. The blue pottery container for the lilac branches

266

"Trumpeter" is the companion wall plaque to "Downbeat" on the opposite page, and is also by Dale Nichols.

on page 19 has fine design and color. It's cost was twenty-five cents.

ORNAMENTATION ON DECORATIVE ACCESSORIES. We have learned that decoration should enhance structural design, and this is just as true for the small articles of furnishing, which we call decorative accessories, as for furniture. The Italian vase shown on page 268 is beautifully decorated with a free pattern of bird and floral forms. As you can see from studying the decoration, the pattern is applied with freehand brush strokes. The contour of the vase is excellent, and the decoration fits it splendidly. A border fits around the collar of the vase, and another around the bottom. The center of interest, con-

An Italian vase decorated with free design. The decoration is applied with free-hand brush strokes. It fits the contour of the vase very nicely. The center of interest, consisting of large bird forms, is placed at the bulge of the curved contour.

sisting of the bird forms, is placed at the greatest bulge of the curving sides. Altogether, the effect is delightful. This vase is an old one of considerable value which most of us could not afford to buy.

In the opposite illustration is a box decorated with a similar type

A Mexican "thumbnail lacquer" box. The green lacquer was scratched out with a thumbnail while still soft. This is another example of free design. No two panels are alike. Each panel fills the space very successfully.

of design which is more likely to come within reach of our pocketbooks. It is a Mexican box decorated with "thumbnail lacquer." Green lacquer is applied over ivory lacquer, and while the green lacquer is still soft, the pattern is scratched out with the thumbnail. This is also free design. No two panels are alike. Charming animal and floral motifs fit their spaces perfectly. The box itself is of the simplest thin wood construction, but its decoration makes it beautiful.

MODERN DESIGN IN DECORATIVE ACCESSORIES. The modern decorative dishes on pages 270 and 271 were designed by famous American artists. The shallow tray at the top of page 270 is suitable for an ash tray or a nut or candy dish. It is a "free shape" which is most intriguing. Why should dishes be round? Isn't this free shape much more interesting? The design is called "Little Harbor" and was done by Joe Jones, who often paints the sea in his easel pictures. How many motifs can you find that tell the story of the safe little harbor?

The decorative bowl at the top of page 271 is also an interesting free shape. The artist is Julio de Diego. The bowl, which may be used for fruit or flowers, is a rich autumn-brown outside and sea green inside. Notice how delightfully the abstract decorative pattern enhances the contours of the bowl.

Associated American Artists, Inc.

This shallow dish in free shape was created by Joe Jones, a very well-known American painter.

Associated American Artists, Inc.

"Stately Duck" by Carl Walters, which is very stately indeed.

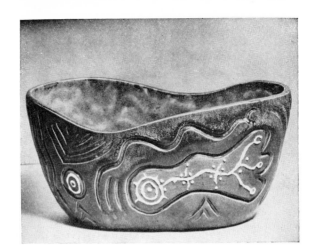

Associated American Artists, Inc.

This free-shape bowl is pleasingly ornamented with an abstract pattern. The designer is Julio de Diego.

Associated American Artists, Inc.

"Cock o' the Walk" by Gwen Lux, and very cocky he is!

271

STYLIZED DESIGNS IN STATUETTES. Miniature statues are very popular. They can be bought at any price, ranging from a few cents to many dollars. Some are ugly, some are amusing, and some are beautiful. Once more it is your own good taste that will help you to choose those which are interesting and beautiful. As in other art products, price is no indication of art quality. A fancy gold statue set with diamonds can be gaudy and ugly.

The two ceramic birds shown on pages 270 and 271 are far from realistic representations. "Stately Duck" by Carl Walters at the bottom of page 270 is a dignified little bird with a solemn eye. The head is crackled white with black markings and the body is greenish black. Notice the fascinating rhythm of the markings as they swirl around the neck and breast.

The bird shown at the bottom of page 271 is a creation by Gwen Lux and is called "Cock O' the Walk." Certainly he is well named. Did you ever see a more boastful and cocky creature? He flaps his wings and crows to assert his importance! His ruffled feathers are amusingly expressed with sketchy, irregular markings. Can you imagine a more complete contrast in "personality" than the "Stately Duck" and the "Cock O' the Walk"?

ARE YOU A COLLECTOR? Do you collect little horses, dogs, or other ceramic figures? It is an interesting hobby, but you will have the most fun with it if you collect according to a plan. Some people have as their only aim the biggest collection possible. Others find it much more interesting to collect pieces which will represent different types. Suppose you are collecting horses. Instead of trying to acquire more than anyone else has, try to collect horses which express different ideas. For example, you might wish to collect only stylized or "design horses." Some of the types would be a streamlined race horse expressing speed, another might be a heavy, draft-horse type, another a gaited saddle horse, and so on. In each case you would be selecting horses which express ideas rather than just adding ten more horses to the first hundred.

CLOCKS CAN BE BEAUTIFUL. Among the useful accessories in home furnishing is the clock. In times past, the clock has been dressed up in everything from a Greek temple to a cuckoo-bird cage. Clocks are most attractive however, when they look like *clocks*. The design shown on the opposite page was produced by a very old clock-manufacturing company, but it is a very up-to-date design. One cannot help but enjoy the smooth flowing lines of the mahogany base which holds the circular clock gracefully. There is no ornamentation to dis-

This clock design is functional and beautiful.

tract one or to disguise the clock. *It is a clock and looks like a clock.* Again we have a design that is thoroughly functional and at the same time attractive.

SPECIAL ACCESSORIES FOR THE HOLIDAYS. The fanciful little figures illustrated on page 274 are candle folk, though they need not necessarily be burned as candles. The nativity scene has great charm. Mary, Joseph, and the baby animals pay their respects to the Christ Child in the manger. The scene is set by the edge of a mirror lake among pine branches and holly leaves.

USING YOUR DECORATIVE ACCESSORIES. What to do with your treasured collections and other decorative possessions is sometimes a problem. Remember always that they are intended to add beauty to a room, not to give it a cluttered appearance or to add hours of work dusting and caring for them. Do not allow your walls, tables, mantel, and desk to become crowded with your tapestries, pictures, vases, and statuettes. If you have more than you can display advantageously at one time, let them take turns.

273

A charming table setting for Christmas Day.

The problem is always to make a pleasing arrangement on the mantel, over the table, or wherever it may be. Do not think, "Where can I put this?" Instead ask yourself, "What can I use here to make a good arrangement?" The arrangement with the small chest shown on the opposite page was carefully planned. The miniatures on the wall are hung so that the lamp and candle do not cross them. The bowl of ivy and the vase on the chest add interesting variety of spacing. The whole effect is unified and harmonious.

Study your room and plan how you can use your accessories to the best advantage.

A CHAMBER OF HORRORS! We cannot pretend that all the decorative accessories in the ten-cent stores, or in the exclusive art shops, are good design. Some of them are very bad indeed. Of course, no one wishes to spend money for ugliness and absurdities. Here is a description of some atrocities seen on one trip to the stores. A flying duck carrying artificial flowers on its back! The very idea is absurd. No respectable duck would fly around with flowers sprouting from its back! The flowerpot set in a horse is just as bad. It is made like a horse, and a clumsy horse at that. What horse would allow plants to

274

A pleasing arrangement of decorative accessories and chest.

grow from his backbone? Another horror is a plaster head of a pretty girl. She looks as though her head had been neatly cut off from its body and pasted against the wall. This little novelty exhibits a truly terrible kind of realism. It has a real feather and a real ruffle pasted on the plaster head! Then there is an ash tray made like a toy sailboat. Why a sailboat should make a good ash tray no one knows! You are supposed to scrape your ashes on the edge of the sail and drop them into the boat. As a matter of fact, you would be more likely to tip the whole thing over!

The most dreadful idea of all was a string holder made in the shape of a girl's face. The string comes from her mouth!

These accessories did not cost much money. They varied in price from five cents to twenty-five cents. But whatever the price, they were expensive, because such choices are a waste of money. Equally ugly and ridiculous decorative accessories are to be found in exclusive art stores and gift shops—for example, a ten-dollar fish bowl consisting of a large bowl balanced on the nose of a big black pottery seal; a five-dollar kitchen clock with a frame that looks like a teakettle; and a three-dollar ash tray made to represent a pair of hands which hold the ashes.

Suggestions for further study. 1. Collect vases and bowls for use during one class period. Criticize each piece for contour and for decorative design.

2. Study the decorative accessories shown on pages 43 and 44. Do you consider their choice and use good or poor? Why?

3. Have a class discussion regarding the choice and arrangement of accessories on tops of dressers and dressing tables.

4. Cut two pictures of decorative accessories from newspapers or magazines, one good and one bad design. Mount them and explain why each was chosen.

A test on decorative accessories

I. Collect pictures of decorative accessories from newspaper and magazine advertisements. Select the three which are best in design and the three which are poorest. Mount them and write a criticism of each design. Exchange papers with another member of the class. Check the criticisms which have been made, and add any others that may occur to you.

II. This is a test of your ability to judge art quality in decorative accessories. The instructor of your class will exhibit five articles which vary from good to bad in quality of design. Write a criticism of each article.

III. Answer the following questions:

1. Is an expensive, hand-painted, imported French toilet set with portraits of Marie Antoinette painted on the backs of the mirror and brushes in good taste? Give your reasons.

2. Is a large, realistic china dog, curled up as though asleep, a good decorative accessory to place beside the fireplace? Why or why not?

3. Would you choose a plain bronze ink bottle or a bronze lion's head with a hole in the top for your pen?

4. Would you choose a pair of book ends which consist of large rectangular blocks of glass, or a pair with pretty little china figures as decoration?

Chapter 12

GARDEN BEAUTY INSIDE THE HOUSE

Flowers and potted plants in the house add a touch of beauty that speaks of gracious living. A bowl of zinnias on the table and a pot of ivy on the mantel are accessories which add charm to the routine of everyday life. There is a fascination about live, growing things which appeals to almost everyone. Those who wish to live pleasantly do not mind taking the time and trouble to cut some garden flowers and arrange them for the house or to water and care for their potted plants.

There are numerous pictures in this book showing lovely rooms enhanced by plants and flowers. Turn through the pages and notice the bowl of bittersweet on the chest shown on page 43, the huckleberry leaves in the white urns on the mantel shown on page 78, the spring flowers on the table shown on page 146, the blooming plants on the stone ledge next to the fireplace illustrated on page 195, and the ivy plants on the chest shown on page 391.

BEAUTY IN MANY PLANT MATERIALS. Perhaps you do not have a garden and cannot afford flowers from the florist. This means that you cannot have cut flowers in your house all summer, but there are other ways in which you can manage to have the beauty of plant life. You might occasionally buy a few flowers from a farmer's market for special occasions, or you might find wild flowers growing where you are allowed to pick them. If you look, you can find beauty in flowers that are generally considered weeds. Very attractive bouquets can be made from Queen Anne's lace and black-eyed Susans. Goldenrod, joe-pye weed, and other common plants provide very good material for effective decoration. In the fall, there are autumn leaves and many dried materials such as milkweed pods, plume grass, and bittersweet which make excellent arrangements.

Besides these cut materials you can use potted plants and bulbs for home decoration. Narcissus bulbs in a low bowl are pleasing from the moment they begin to sprout until they bloom. An African violet, a pot of ivy, sansevieria, cactus, and philodendron are available in small sizes for a minimum expenditure, and you have the pleasure of watching them grow.

If you care enough for garden beauty in your home, you can find a way to have it.

FLOWER ARRANGEMENT IS IMPORTANT. Garden flowers are beautiful. Why cut them and bring them into the house unless you treat them with respect? It requires no great genius to make a nice arrangement for your table or mantel. It *does* require care and thought. Flowers cannot be jammed carelessly into a vase if they are to show off to the best advantage. Here again the principles of art and color harmony are important. Your study of design and color will give you a good start in flower arrangement.

Flower arrangement has become a great hobby with many people. Flower shows are held by garden clubs all over the country, with prizes offered for the best arrangements. Flower arrangement is a form of art that is popular with everyone. Those who do not have the courage to enter a competition may have fun arranging flowers in their own home. In this unit of work we are concerned especially with flower arrangements for our own homes.

CHOOSE THE RIGHT PLACE FOR YOUR FLOWER ARRANGEMENT. Your first thought in making a flower arrangement should be concerned with where you will use it. Do you need one for the dining-room table, for the mantel, or for a bookshelf? Or are you going to enter it in a flower show? A flower arrangement for each of these places has particular requirements. The dining-room table requires one that is not too tall and that may be viewed from any angle. The mantel requires one that fits into the arrangement of decorative accessories and is seen only from the front, with the wall for a background. The same things are true of an arrangement for a bookcase except that the arrangement of decorative accessories will be different. A flower arrangement for a flower show must conform to the specified requirements.

When you select your flowers in the garden, think where you will use them. It will help you to pick the right colors, the right kinds, and the right amount. If you want them for the living room and the color scheme is green and rust, then bright pink roses will not look so well. Yellow or white ones will harmonize better. If you want a low mass arrangement for the dining-room table, then zinnias and larkspur will be better than gladioli.

If you know where you are going to use a flower arrangement, you will not pick a great many more flowers than you need. It is best not to use more than one or possibly two arrangements in the same room. A bouquet is generally a center of interest, and we know that only one chief center of interest is pleasing. Too many bouquets will make your rooms look like the horticultural hall at the county fair!

Of course, we cannot always choose the special kind of flowers we should like to have. The garden does not always supply them, and our friends sometimes present us with their own choice of flowers. In such cases we must decide where the flowers will appear to the best advantage. Instead of sticking them into a vase and then looking around for an empty spot to put them, consider first where the flowers will look best, and make an arrangement for that particular place. This will make a great difference in the success of your bouquets.

Flower arrangements in our homes should harmonize with the color scheme and fit into the arrangement of decorative accessories. A bouquet should never look as though it were added to the room after all other arrangements were made. It should be a part of the arrangement. The bowl of marigolds shown on page 105 is a part of the arrangement on the small table. The arrangement of lilac branches on the chest in the picture on page 19 is part of the decorative scheme.

The flower arrangement shown on page 280 was definitely planned as part of the whole arrangement on the desk top. Deep pink weigela and pinkish-lavender wisteria in a rose-pink pottery vase blends beautifully with the dull red mahogany desk and the summer landscape. The little old-fashioned lady figures are blue and pink, and the book covers are green, gray, and rose. The lines of the weigela branches and the wisteria blossoms lead the eye swiftly into the composition. Since the flower arrangement is large it is placed nearer the center than are the books. Altogether, the effect is stable and restful. Imagine the unfortunate result if the books and the flower arrangement were transposed!

Always think about your flower arrangements with relation to the other decorative accessories near at hand. It is just as easy to place the arrangement advantageously as to put it in the wrong spot.

This flower arrangement is well placed in relation to the decorative accessories on top of the desk.

CHOOSE THE RIGHT CONTAINER. There should be harmony between the flowers and their container. Short-stemmed flowers should not be stuck in the top of tall vases, as on page 281. The proportions between the vase and the flowers are uninteresting. A general rule followed by many experts in flower arrangement is to make the flower arrangement one and one-half times as high as the container. Or if it is a low container, as on page 283, one and one-half times the width of the container may be used. This is only a general rule, however, and many successful arrangements vary from it. Long-stemmed flowers stuck into a small container are just as bad as short-stemmed flowers in a tall container. Choose your container with an eye for proportions, both for practical reasons and beauty of effect.

CONTAINERS SHOULD STAY IN THE BACKGROUND. A container should not be so elaborately decorated that it draws attention to itself rather than to the flowers. The flowers should always be the center of interest. Neither of the vases on page 281 is a good container because

280

of the undesirable ornamentation. The spray of flowers on the vase at the left attracts as much attention as the flowers at the top.

The color of the container is also important. It should not be more forceful than the colors in the flowers. For instance, a brilliant pink vase would overwhelm the delicate pink of apple blossoms, and an intense orange bowl would ruin the beauty of pale yellow daffodils. The color of the container should blend with the color of the flowers and leaves. The tall vase shown on page 285 is a dull green which harmonizes well with most stems and leaves.

COSTLY CONTAINERS ARE NOT NECESSARY. It is not necessary to buy special vases and bowls for flower containers. With a little ingenuity, you can find all sorts of interesting containers. Shiny tin cans from which the labels have been removed make very good containers. One of the small tin cans which comes with frozen orange juice is excellent for a small arrangement. A row of these shiny little cans set close together makes a very interesting container for a long-shaped arrangement suitable for the dining table. A tin can set inside a basket makes a good container.

Exploration of the kitchen will produce many interesting con-

Two very poor flower arrangements. Left: Short-stemmed flowers should not be stuck in the top of a tall vase. Right: The effect is monotonous, because the flowers and vase are equal in proportion. Containers should not be elaborately decorated, for they attract too much attention.

281

A mass arrangement combining several kinds of flowers. Grouping of each kind of flower is more pleasing than a hit-or-miss arrangement. The two gaillardia blossoms make a good center of interest.

tainers—an oblong aluminum baking tin, a dark-green glass bottle which contained prune juice, a small yellow mixing bowl, a white china bowl from the best set of dishes, and other everyday articles.

PLAN YOUR ARRANGEMENT. After the right container has been found, the next problem is to decide on the general plan of the arrangement. Here you must call on all your knowledge of the principles of design and color. A good arrangement must have emphasis,

282

Arrangement by Mrs. G. L. Lincoln, Madison, Wis.

An arrangement of gladiolas and Phitzer's juniper which has a horizontal rhythmic movement.

pleasing proportions, rhythmic feeling, and balance from side to side and from top to bottom. All these things you must think about at once! Let us see how the design principles are expressed in the flower arrangements pictured in this section.

EMPHASIS IN FLOWER ARRANGEMENTS. Look at the arrangement on the opposite page and you will see at once that the two large gaillardia make a good center of interest. Without them, the arrangement would lack a focal point. Several different kinds of flowers were combined in this arrangement, and the two largest and brightest were selected for the center of interest. Notice their position in the arrangement. A good rule to remember is that the center of interest should be low and near the center.

In the arrangement of gladiolias and Phitzer's juniper on page 283 a center of interest was created with a horizontal group of the largest, fullest blossoms. For this type of arrangement it is a good idea to let the flowers cover the edge of the container. This helps to make a unified effect or to "tie" the bouquet and container together. Notice also the delightful rhythmic lines in this arrangement created by the stalks of flowers and branches of juniper.

PROPORTION IN FLOWER ARRANGEMENTS. We have already learned one rule for flower arrangements that depends on this principle of art. The plant material should be one and one-half times as high as the container. Of course, there are exceptions to this rule. It is often better to let a tall, slender leaf or spike of flowers extend two or three times as high as the container. This is shown in the arrangement of gladioli on page 285. The tips of the leaves and buds extend twice as high as the container, but the principal mass of the flowers conforms to the rule. In this arrangement, the container was placed on a square block base. This adds a third element to the arrangement. It is pleasing in its effect, because it adds weight to the bottom of the design.

The principle of proportion is a reminder that equal spaces are monotonous. If you cut all the stems the same length your flower arrangement is sure to be monotonous. See how this was avoided on page 285. Gladioli generally come with long stems all about the same length. Some people feel that to cut them is wrong, but you cannot make a good arrangement unless you cut some of them. Some expert flower arrangers lay their flowers in groups on a table, and decide which groups should be short stemmed before even beginning to make the arrangement. Thus they get variety in the spacing of their bouquets.

RHYTHM IN FLOWER ARRANGEMENTS. The crab-apple blossoms shown on page 286 have been arranged to make a rhythmic line harmony. It is especially easy to see rhythmic movement in this type of arrangement. Here the eye travels easily back and forth along the delightful swinging curves. There is a lovely rhythmic repetition of the same curve in the branches and in the container; this creates a close harmony of lines.

Often the shape of the container gives the keynote for the treat-

An arrangement of gladioli with a strong vertical rhythm. One tall spike of flowers is balanced by two leaves and a smaller flower.

ment of rhythmic line in the arrangement. In the picture on page 287 the rounded contour of the vase is echoed in the curve of the artemisia and in the shape of the blossoms. The drooping stems at the

Crab-apple blossoms in a pottery vase. There is a nice rhythmic movement in the branches which echoes the shape of the vase.

left blend into the same circular movement. The flowers and vase are unified partly by the flower forms which droop over the edge of the vase, half concealing its top. In the above picture you will see that some of the apple blossoms fall below the edge of the vase. This is

Single white chrysanthemums and artemisia in a pottery vase. This arrangement shows especially nice relationship between flowers and container.

also true in the pictures on pages 282 and 285. It helps to "tie" the two parts of the design together.

Good rhythmic movement in a flower arrangement never allows crossed stems. A crisscross arrangement of stems and leaves is bad.

Suggestions for further study. 1. Point out how rhythm is expressed in the arrangements on pages 287 and 289.
2. Make a diagrammatic study of the rhythmic line in the arrangement on page 283. Draw an oval representing the container. Then draw seven circles representing the flowers. Last draw seven lines representing the lines of stems and branches.

Balance your arrangements. Formal balance is seldom used in flower arrangements. Plant materials do not lend themselves to bisymmetric balance. Informal distribution of "weights" in flower arrangements seems more natural and appealing. (Remember the seesaw on page 15?) Study the balanced effect in the arrangement on page 287. Imagine a dividing line down the center, then notice how the white chrysanthemums lean far to the left and are balanced by two larger blossoms near to the center and a spray of artemisia which swings to the right and back again. The feeling of balance is especially pleasing.

Suggestions for further study. How is a balanced effect obtained in the arrangement of gladioli on page 285? In the arrangement of milkweed pods on page 291?

Color harmony in flower arrangements. Nature presents us with many beautiful colors in flowers. It is our problem to use these beautiful colors in a beautiful way. We have already mentioned the first color problem in making a good flower arrangement—the selection of the right color for a container. When more than one kind of plant material is used in the arrangement, we have another problem in combining colors. Even the addition of extra foliage is a color problem. Not all greens in leaves are harmonious. Some are yellowish and some are bluish. Some greens are silvery and others are frosty white. Some are fine textured and others are coarse. Naturally, some combinations are harmonious and others are not.

The best way to tell whether colors harmonize or not is to "try them on the eye." Continued practice will tell you when they blend. As someone has said, "One look-see is worth a million tells." Your previous color study should help you to see color harmony in flower arrangements.

Every type of color combination imaginable is possible with flowers. Here are a few suggestions. A fine monochromatic harmony can be made with deep blue bachelor's-button, blue larkspur, and pale blue forget-me-nots. Another good monochromatic harmony can be

Flower Grower Magazine; photograph by Jack Roche

This lovely winter bouquet would bring beauty to any room.

made from bright yellow-orange zinnias and pale yellow-orange snapdragons. A delightful adjacent harmony can be created using blue, pink, and purple asters. Another lovely adjacent harmony can be made from yellow, orange, and deep red-orange marigolds. Many complementary combinations are possible. Pale pink roses with their own pale green leaves and stems, lilac with yellow tulips, purple and yellow iris, orange nasturtiums with deep blue verbenas are all good complementary combinations. Triad combinations are also easy to make. For example, pink sweet peas, blue ageratum, and pale yellow snapdragons make a pleasing triad harmony.

Remember that color combinations from the color circle are not always harmonious. Scarlet phlox certainly does not blend with delicate salmon pink sweet peas. Pastel blue ageratum does not harmonize with bright yellow marigolds. In general, the brilliantly colored flowers do not blend with the delicate tints in other flowers. Remember also that the brilliant colors do not harmonize easily. The brilliant scarlet phlox will not blend with equally brilliant orange marigolds.

In combining different colors always lay the flowers together before making an arrangement. Do they blend, or can the harmony be improved by removing one color? In other words, try it on the eye.

BEAUTY IN DRIED ARRANGEMENTS. When winter months come, it is no longer possible to have garden flowers in the house, but it is possible to have another kind of garden beauty. It is just as easy to have as many lovely bouquets in the house in the winter as in the summer and at very little expense. Dried arrangements like those shown on pages 289 and 291 are available to anyone who plans ahead and gathers the material in the fall. There are many garden flowers which you can grow for your winter pleasure, and many that grow in the fields which can be had for the trouble of picking them. Among the garden flowers that are desirable for winter bouquets are ageratum, cockscomb, strawflowers, honesty, statice, and many types of zinnias. In the fields you can find teasels, goldenrod, thistles, cattails, joe-pye weed, Queen Anne's lace, and others.

These should be gathered when they are in their prime, that is in full bloom. Every leaf should be stripped off and the bunches of flowers tied and hung upside down to dry. Later they can be put in large suitboxes to protect them from dust until you wish to use them.

The milkweed pods and dry branches in the arrangement on the opposite page are lovely in rhythmic movement. One cannot help but enjoy it even though it is made from a common weed. The bouquet shown on page 289 is lovely and long lasting. It is full of

Mrs. David R. Kellogg

Milkweed pods and bare branches in a pottery pitcher. This is a fine use of a common weed. It makes a lovely rhythmic arrangement.

beautiful, soft colors ranging from the dull reds of the cockscomb through browns, tans, yellows, and greens.

CHRISTMAS GREENS. At the holiday season we decorate with Christmas greens—pine branches, holly, and other greens. This is an op-

Several types of holders which are useful in holding flower stems in place.

portunity to use other very effective plant materials for decorative arrangements. Very often, the greens are made into wreaths or sprays which are hung on the door or in the windows. They remain fresh for a long time, but eventually become dry and brittle. Keep some of the greens in water and they will remain fresh for weeks.

A low, flat container filled with cedar sprays makes an attractive table decoration for winter. Pine cones pressed into the little branches help to make the arrangement even more attractive. Keep the pine cones stored away in a box between seasons and you will get many years of use from them. During the holidays you may wish to use Christmas tree ornaments in combination with the greens for a lovely decoration. Remember your art principles when you make your arrangements of Christmas greens.

You must have good holders. None of these flower arrangements can be made without suitable holders to keep the flowers in place. You must have something in the containers to keep the flower stems from wobbling and slipping about. Several different types of holders are shown above.

The flexible-wire holder shown at the upper left corner is a satisfactory type of holder because it keeps the flowers firmly in place. The wires can be bent to hold the stems at any angle desired. Below

A good decorative arrangement making use of chestnut branches and mullen.

the flexible-wire holder is a glass-block holder. This is the least satisfactory of all the holders. The holes never seem to be in the right
places or the right sizes for the stems. The lead-strip holder shown
hooked over the top of the glass vase is especially good for tall glass
vases. It is flexible and can be bent to suit the arrangement. It can be

hidden with leaves or foliage. The stems will show, of course, in a glass vase. In no case should the holder show when an arrangement is finished.

Below the glass vase is a needle-point holder. These needle-point holders can be obtained in several different sizes. They are very satisfactory bcause they hold the flowers firmly in place when the stems are pushed down upon the needle points. Crumpled chicken wire shown at the upper right is satisfactory for tall pottery vases. When pushed down firmly into the vase, it will hold flower stems very well. Below the chicken wire is a bird-cage holder. This is satisfactory for many types of containers, especially for low ones where a spreading arrangement is desired.

There are several homemade holders which are very useful. A potato cut to fit the bottom of the vase and pierced with an ice pick makes a good holder. Sand in the bottom of the container can be used for small flowers such as pansies and nasturtiums. A forked stick wedged into the top of the container serves to keep the flowers in place. Bits of hemlock or spruce stuffed into the container will also keep the flowers from slipping about.

SUGGESTIONS FOR THE STUDY OF FLOWER ARRANGEMENTS. 1. Collect pictures of flower arrangements. Many appear in magazines and newspapers. Criticize each arrangement for good and bad points.

2. Your teacher will hang ten pictures of flower arrangements in your classroom. Each one should have a number. List the three which you consider most interesting and the three which you consider least pleasing. Compare your selections with those made by other members of the class. Be prepared to tell *why* you made each selection.

3. Bring flowers and containers to school. Divide the class into groups of two or three to each group. Let each group make the most interesting arrangement possible. The rest of the class will criticize the arrangement according to the rules on pages 295 and 297.

4. Hold a flower arrangement contest. Perhaps the local garden club will sponsor it and help with your show. Your flower show might include such classes as these: an arrangement for a luncheon table; an arrangement for a bookshelf; an arrangement in adjacents; an arrangement for a kitchen window sill; an arrangement using dried plant materials.

5. Read and report on one of the flower arrangement books listed in the bibliography at the end of this book.

POTTED PLANTS FOR DECORATIVE EFFECT. Day-by-day enjoyment of your potted plants will increase 100 per cent if you make them part of the general decorative scheme. If you have only one plant, it should have its own place on a table or elsewhere. It should provide a point of interest in the room and not appear to be an extra which has to be crowded into the space. The pots of ivy shown on page 150 form a center of interest on the mantel and add interest to the general effect. The sansevieria on the table shown on page 193 has been assigned to a spot which it fills very pleasantly. Its height helps to tie the lower shelf of the step table to the tall lamp and shade, thus creating a unified effect.

When you have several plants, try hard to find an interesting way of showing them off. In the picture on page 45 several potted plants are used to create a delightful window garden. Notice that each plant has plenty of room, so that it can be enjoyed for its special kind of beauty. The long lines of the window boxes which hold the pots help to unify the design of the window garden.

The picture on page 195 shows two very interesting arrangements for potted plants. Some of them are set directly on the stone ledge at the left of the fireplace. The coffee table also provides an interesting arrangement for plants. One end of the table is made in the form of a tray which holds some philodendron plants. Their glossy green leaves create a pleasing feature.

The picture on the next page shows still another way of using potted plants as part of a decorative scheme. A glassed-in living porch is made more interesting by the plants set on the window sills. This window wall might have been very bare-looking without the plants.

SUGGESTIONS FOR FURTHER STUDY. 1. Use one class period for making pleasing arrangements using a potted plant, books, lamp, pictures, or decorative accessories.

2. Report on interesting ways of making plants a part of a decorative scheme. Describe arrangements that you have seen in rooms or found in pictures.

SUMMARY OF RULES AND SUGGESTIONS

The principles of art give us several rules and suggestions for making good flower arrangements.

1. Decide first where the flower arrangement is to be used.

2. Select a container harmonious in color and shape with the flowers to be used in it.

3. In line arrangements work for interesting repetitions of pleasing lines.

(*Text continued on page 297*)

The potted plants in these window niches add interest and variety to the living-room–porch.

(Continued from page 295)

4. The lines of the plant materials and the shape of the container should be harmonious.

5. In mass arrangements group the flowers to avoid monotonous effects.

6. The center of interest should be low and near the center of the arrangement.

7. The flowers should be larger than the container, but not so large as to appear top-heavy. That the flowers should be one and one-half times as high as the container is a general rule.

8. Balance arrangements from side to side. Informal balance is useful.

9. Combine colors that blend harmoniously.

10. Beautiful arrangements may be made with common materials and containers.

To test what you have learned about flower arrangement

On a separate piece of paper, write *true* or *false* for each of the following statements:

1. A good flower arrangement looks well anywhere.
2. A perfect flower arrangement is attractive from any angle.
3. Containers should harmonize in *color* and *form* with the flowers.
4. Vases decorated with floral patterns are always suitable for flower containers.
5. Properly crossed stems add interest to an arrangement.
6. Great care should be taken to cut stems in varying lengths for the same arrangement.
7. Large, heavy flowers should always be placed at the top of an arrangement.
8. When different kinds of flowers are combined, each kind should be grouped.
9. A good arrangement never has any leaf or blossom hanging down below the rim of the container.
10. Weeds can be used to make beautiful arrangements.

Chapter 13

LIGHTING FOR BRIGHTER LIVING

One of the great differences between the homes of yesterday and those of today is lighting. Our furniture, wallpaper, and draperies may be patterned after historic styles and our houses may be Cape Cod cottages or Southern Colonial, but the lighting is different. It is a long step ahead from candlelight to modern electric lighting. Reading, sewing, studying, or writing after dark must have been a dim business, indeed, for our ancestors.

The beginning of better lighting for everyday living was brought to pass when Thomas A. Edison invented the incandescent light bulb. In the early days of this new type of lighting, a single bulb was hung in the middle of the room where it beamed brightly. True, it gave more light than the outmoded candle, but it was far from adequate. Though it burned more brightly, it also glared in the eyes of those who faced the center of the room and at the same time left the outer edges of the room in comparative darkness.

ADEQUATE LIGHTING FOR THE MODERN HOME. What does adequate lighting for comfortable living include?

1. It makes tasks anywhere in the house easier to do.
2. It reduces eyestrain and provides more comfortable working conditions for working after dark.
3. It has flexibility—the right light in the right place.
4. It adds glamour and charm to the everyday scene.

This problem requires a careful room-by-room study of lighting needs. What activities are carried on in each room and how can adequate light be provided?

There is plenty of light by day and by night in this kitchen.

The kitchen. Adequate lighting for this room includes both a central light on the ceiling and several other lights located in the work areas. Many activities are carried on at the sink, preparing vegetables, filling water glasses, washing dishes, and so on. Adequate light can be supplied from a lighting fixture directly above the sink, as shown on page 54, or it may be recessed in the ceiling, as shown above. This kind of built-in trough is called soffit lighting. Another kind of arrangement for area lighting is shown on page 302. Here the light is hidden behind a valance board, preventing glare in the eyes but shedding plentiful light below. It can be used over the sink area or in any other room in the house. If the sink should stand below some cabinets, as on page 300, lights should be placed underneath the cabinet. Isn't this a glamorous effect? The lustrous sheen of the stainless steel lighted from above is truly luxurious.

Concealed lighting underneath the cabinets serves both utility and beauty.

Lighting for the kitchen range can be managed in any of the same ways as for the sink area. If the range stands against a blank wall it can be lighted by a fluorescent frosted-glass reflector mounted above it. This sheds light below on the cooking activities and serves as a shelf above.

The food-preparation area in the kitchen also needs special lighting. If pie-making and similar processes are carried on at a counter below storage cabinets, the lighting problem is easily solved, as in the case of the sink shown on page 54.

Lighting in the kitchen should eliminate shadows from all work areas. Central lighting plus additional lights directly over the work areas provide adequate lighting. If you have ever had the experience

Here is an interesting lighting effect—decorative as well as useful.

of working in a kitchen with only central lighting, you know that your own shadow is continually frustrating your attempts to see.

The dining room. Lighting requirements in the dining room are opposite to those in the kitchen. Here, it is the center of the room which needs the most light. Instead of work areas located around the edge of the room, it is the dining table in the center which should be especially well lighted. The most satisfactory arrangement is a center fixture which directs the light downward or upward or a combination of both. The downward light gives the greatest amount of light over the table, accenting the gleam of silver and glass, but at the same time it tends to create shadows in the farther parts of the room. When the light is thrown upward, it is redirected downward and provides a more even distribution of light with fewer shadows. A combination of both upward and downward lights creates a higher degree of illumination with a brighter effect on the dining table.

In some dining rooms, recessed spotlights are built into the ceiling, thus providing for highlighting the table. In this case some supple-

Valance lighting creates good general illumination and pleasing effect.

mentary lighting, such as side lights or valance lighting, is desirable.

An unusual lighting arrangement for a dining room is shown on page 301. Plywood panels are alternated with lighted niches. This provides sufficient light for the table in this dining alcove and at the same time creates a soft, lovely illumination. Useful as well as decorative, the lighted niches dramatize the accessories very agreeably.

The living room. Lighting requirements for the living room include general lighting for conversation, listening to the radio, or similar activities, and also lighting at specific locations for reading, sewing, playing the piano, writing, or other activities. For general illumination and creating a pleasant effect, valance lighting, as shown above, is very attractive. In this room the valance extended all the way across the side of the room. Three single windows gave a choppy appearance to the wall until the room was renovated, and the wall was made a focal point through the use of a wall curtain,

Fluorescent cove lighting provides pleasant illumination, and a portable incandescent floor lamp offers light at a specific location.

the wall-to-wall valance, and a continuous line of illumination. When valance lighting is used, drapery materials should be chosen which reflect light satisfactorily. Dark colors and rough textures tend to absorb the light and, therefore, are not wise selections.

Another type of overhead lighting, shown in the picture above, is called cove lighting. The cove extends the entire length of the wall and tends to give the effect of a low ceiling. The intensity of the lighting is low enough for watching the television screen in comfort and makes pleasant illumination for conversation or entertaining. Fluorescent lighting is installed in the cove.

The incandescent-type portable floor lamp at the left is turned on to give concentrated light for reading, sewing, or playing games. Portable lights should be conveniently located at all chairs where one might wish to read, sew, or do other close work. Another method of providing adequate light for close work is the fluorescent wall

*Bracket lighting above
the desk is both useful
and beautiful.*

bracket, as shown on this page. These fixtures add pleasing variety to
the decorating scheme.

The bedroom. In the bedroom, as in every other room, adequate
lighting must be planned around the special needs. Sleeping, dressing, facial make-up, and often sewing, reading, and writing, require
special types of lighting. For general illumination any of the types
which we mentioned for other rooms can be used. A ceiling light,
which need not be placed in the center, valance, or cove lighting
may be used. For facial make-up, twin lights on the dressing table
or fluorescent tubes on either side of the mirror are desirable.

Various types of lighting are available for use at the head of the
bed. Your choice will depend on the general style of furnishing and
your personal preference. Table lamps at either side of the bed are
convenient and blend well with traditional styles. If you do much
reading in bed you may wish to have a wall bracket with fluorescent-
tube lighting installed above the head of the bed. Or perhaps you
will prefer the twin lights shown on page 100.

The bathroom. Three lighting fixtures are considered adequate
for the bathroom, one on either side of the mirror and one on the

ceiling above the washstand. The side lights may be either fluorescent tubes with plastic or glass shades or incandescent lights. In the bathroom shown on page 73 recessed lights are used.

SUGGESTIONS FOR FURTHER STUDY. 1. Draw a floor plan of a room in your house showing where the lights are located. If you think the arrangement can be improved upon, draw another plan showing the ideal arrangement.
2. Make a list of the points that should be remembered in lighting the different rooms in the house.

GOOD DESIGN IN LIGHTING FIXTURES. There is probably no other small article of furnishing which adds to or detracts so much from the beauty of a room as the wall bracket or central lighting fixture. In the daytime these fixtures are conspicuous because of their placing, and at night they become centers of interest when they are lighted. The central fixture and the wall bracket sketched below are particularly ugly because of their weak, fussy curves, uninteresting proportions, and overornamentation. Each of them shows a bad mistake from the standpoint of suitable design.

A fixture which hangs from a ceiling should never give the impression of such weight that one questions its security. The center fixture is much too heavy to give a restful, stable effect. The wall bracket is not pleasing because of its pretentious, foolish ornamentation. In an *electric* light fixture it is indeed silly to imitate old-fashioned candles dripping with wax. The ruffled cup at the bottom of each candle, supposedly to catch the candle drippings, is an added absurdity.

Now turn your attention to the center fixtures and wall brackets shown on page 306. The center fixtures are plain, without ornamen-

NO! 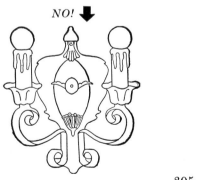   NEVER!

305

Better Homes and Gardens Magazine

Chase Brass and Copper Co.

Pleasing designs in ceiling and wall fixtures which will harmonize with either traditional or modern styles of furnishing.

tation, depending upon good structural design for their beauty. Instead of being suspended by a chain so as to threaten our heads, they are fastened close to the ceiling. Their lines blend into the flat surface of the ceiling, and we feel there is no danger of their dropping upon us unawares. Both of them may be termed thoroughly modern in design and well suited to use as *electric* light fixtures. Here there is no attempt to imitate styles of the past.

The two wall brackets are equally well suited for use as electric light fixtures. The first design may suggest an old-fashioned lamp or candlestick with its chimney, but it is equally pleasing as an electric fixture. The second design is thoroughly modern in its appearance. These brackets, as do the central fixtures, depend chiefly upon good structural design for their beauty. Graceful curves and interesting proportions are the very basis of their attractiveness. The turnings

Choose any of these lamps above . . .

but none of these below.

in the first wall bracket and the grooves in the second merely serve to emphasize the basic structure.

GOOD DESIGN IN LAMPS. Overornamentation seems to be a common fault in the design of lighting fixtures and lamps. In our search for beauty we overload our lamp shades with ruffles, bows, lace, and artificial flowers. Lamp bases are overdecorated with meaningless scrolls and are made in strange forms.

The table lamps in the lower row on this page all show mistakes in design. The first is bad, almost ludicrous, because of its perfectly round shape with a decorated washtub turned upside-down above it.

The second lamp is poor design because the base is clumsy in proportion and shape. The column-like lower part and the urn-shaped upper part of the base practically divide the base into two parts. There is no unity between the upper and lower parts of the lamp base, and though the result may not be actively disagreeable we feel that it is ordinary and uninteresting. The lamp shade itself is good

307

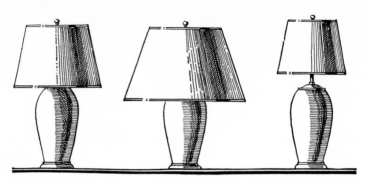

The proportion of the shade in relation to the base is important. Left: Pleasing proportion of approximately two to three. Center: Shade is too large. Right: Shade is too small.

in shape and proportion, but it cannot save the base from seeming mediocre.

The third lamp is obviously bad because of the realistic figure used to hold up the lamp shade. We do not like to think of a figure so real in its effect standing endlessly with the burden of the lamp shade on her back. The lamp is further made ridiculous by the silly bow pinned to the edge of the shade.

The lamps in the upper row on page 307 show good points in design. In each of them you will be able to pick out simplicity of design, good lines, a lack of ostentatious ornamentation, pleasing proportions between base and shade, and suitability to use.

Very often people have pottery bowls or vases made into lamp bases. Then they are confronted with the problem of selecting a shade that is in the right proportion to the base. In the drawings on this page three different sizes of shades have been tried on the same base. The first seems most harmonious in its proportion, the second is so large that it is apparently about to drop over the base, and the third is so small that it has a skimpy appearance. The height of the shade above the base is also an important factor. If the shade is too low, as in the second lamp, or too high, as in the third lamp, the whole effect cannot be pleasing.

SUGGESTIONS FOR FURTHER STUDY. 1. Collect pictures of lighting fixtures and table lamps showing good design. Be prepared to show your pictures and explain why you think the design is good.

2. Find at least ten pictures in other chapters of this book showing good design in table lamps.

3. Arrange for a demonstration of correct lighting by an expert who can show you the correct measurements for the height of a

The Heifetz Manufacturing Company

Top: Floor lamps receiving awards in the Good Design Exhibit sponsored by the Museum of Modern Art. Left: First prize for floor lamps by Gilbert A. Watrous. Right: Honorable mention for floor lamps by A. W. Geller and Marion Geller.

Bottom: Table lamps receiving awards in the Good Design Exhibit sponsored by the Museum of Modern Art. Left: First prize designed by Joseph Burnet. Right: Honorable mention designed by Robert Gage.

lamp and its distance from you when reading, studying at a desk, and before a mirror for facial make-up. If possible secure a copy of the following: The Magazine of Light, Vol. 19, No. 4, 1950. Lamp Department, General Electric Company, Nela Park, Cleveland, Ohio.

NEW DESIGNS FOR TWENTIETH-CENTURY LAMPS. Historically speaking, electric lamps can trace their ancestry back through kerosene lamps and candlesticks of other centuries, so it is natural that the first designs for electric lamps were adapted from forms used for earlier types. Quite often an old oil lamp has been wired for electricity, thus retaining the "quaint" effect. The lamp at the right on page 179 may have been converted to electricity from an old kerosene lamp or perhaps it was a gas-burning lamp. Possibly it was made to imitate an old lamp so as to express nineteenth-century character. However, the wire running from its base betrays the fact that it is lighted by electricity. The kerosene container is not needed for any utilitarian purpose, only for camouflage. Is this functional design?

Designers of the twentieth century feel that electric lamps should express their true character. An electric lamp should look like an electric lamp and not an imitation of an old oil lamp.

The illustrations on page 309 show lamp designs which won awards at the Good Design Exhibit in the Merchandise Mart in Chicago, sponsored by the Museum of Modern Art of New York and the Merchandise Mart. If these styles seem strange and queer to you, remember that we are looking for new and different designs which are suitable to *electricity*. New ideas, new concepts, and new materials have been introduced into these designs. Perhaps they are no more strange than the streamlined automobile in comparison with the stagecoach of two hundred years ago!

The long-necked floor lamp won first prize in the nation-wide competition. The long stem which contains the wire passes through the steel ball on top of the base on angle so that the light can be raised or lowered and swing in any direction. The ball rests on a very powerful magnet which is set at the peak of the tripod base. The lamp shade is fiber glass and can be turned up for indirect lighting or down for direct lighting.

The floor lamp in the upper right of page 309 works on an entirely different principle and won an honorable mention in the Good Design competition. The tripod legs are used to hold a polished brass urn which holds the light bulb. The shallow metal reflector on the top pivots to reflect the light in any number of desired angles.

The table lamps illustrated are completely different in type and each is excellently adapted to its purpose. The lamp at the left won first prize for table lamps. The light source, contained in a satin-polished brass urn is completely separated from the rest of the lamp. A perforated metallic reflector above is supported by three metal legs. When the urn is centered below the reflector, the result is fine general illumination. When the urn is moved slightly away from the center, the light is thrown in that direction.

The lamp shown at the lower right also won an honorable mention and features four masonite panels which surround a central light source. Each panel is movable, swinging on a center axis. Many different lighting effects can be secured by manipulating the panels at various angles to each other.

To test your taste in lamps

I. What is your opinion of the lamps shown on pages 18, 153, and 167? Which ones do you like best? Why? Which one would you select for your own living room? Why?

II. You should now be able to judge the art quality of lighting fixtures and lamps according to the principles of design. Your teacher will display six designs for lighting fixtures and lamps. Write a criticism of each design, telling why it is good or bad. If you think one of the designs is partly good and partly bad, tell what is good and what is bad in that design.

III. Make a list of five questions which you will ask yourself before you choose a lamp or lighting fixture. These questions should be of the same type as those on pages 230 and 231.

Chapter 14

HOMES FOR TODAY AND TOMORROW

B eauty of architectural design is just as important in a three-room
cottage as in a ten-room mansion. Sound construction and good
materials are also important both in large and small houses. Functional design is another quality which is of utmost importance in
any house. When one buys a house, its size is controlled to considerable extent by the cost, but no one should feel that beauty and utility
are not possible in the small, low-cost home. Have you not seen a
little house, lovely as a dream, that you would far rather live in than
a great monstrosity of a house, hideous as a nightmare? Beauty is not
measured in terms of size or price tags.

Good design in house exteriors

Good architectural design means that the architect has used the
principles of design in a pleasing way. In the following pages we
shall discuss the use of these principles in several house designs.

GOOD BALANCE IN EXTERIOR ELEVATIONS. The problem of balance
in a house elevation is the same as an arrangement on a mantel or
bookcase. Instead of balancing vases, pictures, and other decorative
accessories, the architect balances doors, windows, chimneys, and
gables.

The house shown on page 314 is an excellent example of formal
balance. The doorway is placed in the exact center with one window
and gable directly above. This central part of the design is flanked

on either side by windows, pilasters, and chimney arranged in a bi-symmetric pattern.

This house was built nearly two hundred years ago and has an interesting history. At one time it was the headquarters of General George Washington, and later it was the home of the poet Henry Wadsworth Longfellow. It is an imposing house, suggesting the importance of the eminent citizens who were the original occupants. Its formal, solid style expresses the formality of the way of life in the eighteenth and early nineteenth centuries. Thus it is functional for the kind of living for which it was designed. As a home for present-day living, it is not well adapted.

The design of the small house on page 315 is a good example of informal balance. The doorway and gable above it are located in the approximate center of the wall. The big chimney and the windows at the left balance the large gable on the right. Notice that the chimney which is "heavy" in appearance is placed near the center so that it will balance the big gable to the right.

The first diagram below the picture shows this arrangement of architectural features. The diagram at the right shows what would happen (in visual effect) if the chimney should be moved to the other side of the design.

Do you notice the different kind of effect in the general character of the house which results from the use of informal balance? This house has none of the formality or pretentiousness of the house on page 314. In spirit it seems much better adapted to our kind of life in the twentieth century.

RHYTHM IN HOUSE EXTERIORS. The house shown at the top of page 316 is an excellent example of rhythmic line and form. The slanted roof lines, the chimney contour, and the pediment above the doorway form a harmonious and pleasing effect. For a very disagreeable line movement look at the lower house on the same page. The lines in the decoration of the gable and in the windows lead the eye in at least five different directions at once!

Rhythm in the exterior of a house is also expressed in the orderly and symmetrical arrangement of doors and windows. In the house shown at the top of page 317 the doors and windows are arranged in an orderly rhythmic repeat which is pleasant. Compare this with the bottom house on page 319, where the windows on the side of the house have apparently been placed with no regard for orderly arrangement in a hit-or-miss pattern. Windows often are well placed on the front of a house but are left to chance on the sides and rear. There is no need to restrict beauty to the front of a house!

The Craigie-Longfellow house, built about 1760, is a good example of formal balance.

GOOD PROPORTION IN EXTERIORS. The architect's first problem in proportion is to choose a general shape which has good relationship of height to width. If you were asked to choose the house which has the better proportions in the illustrations on page 317, you would choose the upper because the horizontal rectangle is more pleasing than the square. We generally like houses of horizontal proportions because they seem to be more harmoniously related to the ground.

A second problem in proportion is the spacing of doors and windows so as to avoid monotony and to achieve interest. The first house on page 317 has interestingly spaced windows. Notice that the upper windows are not so tall as the lower windows and that the lower story of the house appears higher than the upper.

Another problem in proportion arises when two materials are used in the exterior of the house. The two pictures on page 318 show a good and a bad answer to this problem. In house A we find an interesting proportion between stone and wood. The stone predominates. In house B we find a most uninteresting combination of brick and wood. It is a half-and-half arrangement which gives the impression that the upper part of the house does not really belong to the lower part.

EMPHASIS IN HOUSE EXTERIORS. Every house exterior should have a center of interest just as in any other design. The doorway is a

314

A

B

The design of the small house (top) expresses informal balance and good rhythmic movement. The two diagrams (bottom) show the difference between good (A) and poor (B) arrangement of the same architectural features.

natural center of interest, and architects frequently emphasize it, as shown on pages 318 and 326. Chimneys are sometimes featured as the dominant part of the design, as in the houses shown on pages 316 and 370. A porch or a group of windows may also serve as a center of interest as seen on pages 324 and 365.

Each view of a house should have just one important center of interest. When two or more elements vie for attention the result is unfortunate. In the lower house on page 316, the porch, the round

(*Text continued on page 318*)

315

The Creo-Dipt Co., Inc.

*Two house designs which show the differ-
ence between good and poor line movement. Top: Pleasing effect produced by
lines of roof, chimney, and pediment. Left:
Ugly effect created by lines of windows,
porch, and roof.*

316

The Creo-Dipt Co., Inc.

Two houses which show the difference between good and poor proportions in house designs. Top: Pleasing rectangular shape with interesting window spacing. Right: Uninteresting square shape with ugly window and porch spacing.

317

Olsen Homes

Two materials have been used in the construction of each of these houses. Top: Interesting proportions between stone and wood. Left: Uninteresting proportions of wood and brick.

(Continued from page 315)

window, and the decorated gable all compete for attention and the effect is confusing.

A HOUSE SHOULD FIT ITS SITE. A good house design always harmonizes with the place where the house is built. A house that looks well on flat land may look very much out of place on the top of a

*Two houses on the side of a hill.
Top: This house fits the hill.
Right: This house was not de-
signed for a hillside.*

hill. A tall, narrow house does not fit the top of a hill. It gives the impression that a high wind might blow it away.

One of the special problems in planning a house is encountered by those of us who live in a hilly country. Most houses are planned to fit a flat piece of ground. Unfortunately, many people build the kind of a house on the side of a hill which is meant to be built on a flat piece of ground. For example, look at the second house shown above with its great expanse of ugly basement wall. Most of the space within this ugly basement is wasted.

If only the builder of the house had planned his house to fit the hill he might have had one or two lovely rooms on the lower level with wide windows looking out across a magnificent view. But instead he followed the traditional house plan. Probably he could not conceive a living room at the "back" of a house or bedrooms on a level with the ground at the "front" of the house.

Now notice the other house on the side of the hill shown on page 319. It fits the ground so nicely that at first you may not realize that the house is two stories deep on one side and one story deep on the other. The bedrooms on the upper floor are practically on a level with the garage. The whole effect is unified and harmonious.

SUGGESTIONS FOR FURTHER STUDY. 1. Collect pictures of houses which express the principles of design.

2. Arrange an excursion to view the houses in the neighborhood. Make it an aim of your expedition to discover the houses which are the best examples of balance, rhythm, proportion, and emphasis. You will find many violations of these principles. Suggest ways in which these mistakes might have been avoided.

3. Make a simple line drawing showing the front of your home or any other house that you may choose. Show it as it is and as you would like to remodel it.

4. Be prepared to discuss the following topics at your next class meeting. Give your opinions and have arguments and illustrations to support your ideas.

Do you consider it right for a city to make building regulations in the residence portion of a city restricting the types of house which may be built? Can it be legally done by zoning laws?

Could a community develop public opinion which would check the building of rows of many houses exactly alike?

What civic responsibility does one have in planning the exterior of a house?

5. If any members of the class own cameras, an interesting exhibition can be arranged. Try to get pictures of houses that illustrate as many of the points as possible that have been discussed in this problem. Mount the pictures and put them on a bulletin board. Then see if the rest of the class can tell what each picture was meant to illustrate.

Color problems in the exterior of the house

Have you ever noticed as you walk down the street that some houses seem to shriek for attention because of their vivid hues and that other houses we do not see because of their drab, uninteresting color? Both the gaudy, yellow house with its red roof and the dull, slate-colored house fail to blend with their surroundings. Perhaps their owners like these colors and therefore desire to use them in large quantities. But no matter how well we like a thing, it is sometimes disastrous to use it in large doses.

Bright color is used on a signboard to attract attention, and to use the same color on a house accomplishes the same result. Most of us do not intend to paint our houses for the purpose of advertising them. On the other hand, it is not necessary to paint them a mud color in order to keep them in the background. What can we do then to make our houses fit into their surroundings?

First of all, we must remember that the walls of a house form a large area and that we cannot use intense color successfully in large areas. Consequently, instead of using a screaming yellow, it will be better to use a soft cream-ivory. Next we must consider the surroundings of the house, the houses near at hand, and the greens of the grass, shrubs, and trees. The color of the house must be such that it blends successfully with these if we are to have a pleasing effect.

The white house with green shutters has been popular for many centuries and continues to be satisfying. The green shutters echo the green of the foliage and tie the house harmoniously to the landscape. Sometimes a white house seems bare and bleak. This generally happens when bluish white is used instead of cream white. Blue is a cold color and cream is warm. Other colors frequently used with success are buff, gray-brown, and gray-green. These colors fit themselves into the natural surroundings of trees and grass better than reds, blues, and purples.

When houses are so near together that they are viewed at one glance, their colors should not quarrel. This may make it impossible for us to use the color that we should really like. But in the long run the color which blends with the neighboring houses is a happier choice. If our house stands between two white houses, it is taking an unfair advantage of our neighbors to paint it a chocolate brown or a slate gray. Often we are tempted to carry out our individual ideas as to the color of a house regardless of the surrounding houses, but we cannot successfully treat a house as an individual unit when it is seen as part of a group.

In our attempt to "dress up" our house in distinctive coloring we sometimes use many colors. In a house recently observed the lower part was painted green, the upper part painted buff, the shingles stained red, and the porch and trimmings painted brown. Needless to say, the house appeared to be a hodgepodge; it could hardly appear anything else. This is a glaring example of bad color combination in house exteriors. A house should be a unified whole, and its color can do much to help in this respect. It is a good general rule to say that the whole house should be painted one color.

Manufacturers have come to realize the possibilities of fine color effects in house exteriors and are producing shingles, tiles, and bricks in a wide range of colors. Have you ever really studied the color in brick walls? Go where you can see a brick wall of a house and examine it. Is the color a smooth, flat red or yellow? Or is the color mingled? Stand close to the wall so that you can see the separate colors. Then look at it from across the street to get the blended effect. If you continue your study of color in bricks, you will find that it may range from an orange-yellow, through orange, red-orange, red to violet.

It was the old-fashioned idea to produce bricks that were perfectly smooth and flat in color. But now we have discovered how much more charming is the effect if the color is mingled and if the surface of the bricks is left rough in order to produce a pleasing quality of texture. Compare for texture the different brick walls which you see. The color of the mortar does much to add to the general color effect. Sometimes it is white, sometimes black, and sometimes colored to blend with the color of the bricks. Examine the walls which you see and notice how different effects are obtained.

Manufacturers of shingles have also realized the possibilities of color effects, and people have been quick to appreciate the artistic results. Shingles are frequently used to cover the whole house as well as the roof, as shown on page 334. Since the shingles are stained rather than painted, the texture of their wood is apparent. This contributes much to the general pleasing quality of shingle roofs and shingle-covered houses. As you study color in shingles you will find as much variety in the blending of colors as in bricks.

As you are engaged in your study of brick and shingle-covered houses you will doubtless find many stucco houses. How many different texture effects are you able to find? Can you find any in which the trowel marks are left as a part of the texture? How many different colors have you found used in stucco? You will notice that the warmer colors—yellowish tan and even pink—are more pleasing than the cold, colorless grays. If you have visited southern California or seen colored pictures of the houses there, you will know that brighter color is used in the stucco houses than is used generally in colder climates.

SUGGESTIONS FOR FURTHER STUDY. 1. Select a brick house in the neighborhood and discuss the color you think would be most suitable for painting the wood frames of the doors and windows.

2. Copy the colors which you find in the most interesting brick wall that you have seen. You can use either crayons or paints to reproduce the blended effects in the bricks.

3. Be prepared to discuss the following topics in class:

Is it more suitable to use vividly colored house exteriors in a tropical climate than in a more temperate climate? Why?

Do you think it improves the texture and general color quality of a brick wall to paint it? Why or why not?

What is your opinion of the color in the exterior of your school building? Could it be improved?

Do you think there is a good chance for a harmonious, unified effect in a house that is made with the lower portion of stucco and the upper portion of wood, with a conspicuous stone chimney and with a brick porch? Why?

Styles in houses

Houses of today, like furniture and room interiors, are designed in both historic and modern styles. Many of them are patterned after Colonial styles, the Pennsylvania farmhouse, the Spanish mission, the tall, steep-gabled English style, and especially the popular Cape Cod "salt box" cottage. Since the close of World War II, there has been an increasing number of houses built in the modern or contemporary styles. Each of these styles, traditional or modern, has its particular characteristics and its special kind of beauty. Your preference in house design will depend on whether you are traditional- or modern-minded. Remember that no matter what style you prefer, you should be able to enjoy good design in any form.

THE COLONIAL STYLES. Varying styles of houses were built in different parts of the Colonies during the pre-Revolutionary War period. Many of the people who settled in the Colonies came from England and brought with them English ideas of architecture. During the

Mr. and Mrs. H. G. Ploger

The design of this beautiful modern suburban home was inspired by the type of Southern Colonial architecture seen in Mount Vernon.

eighteenth century they imported parts of houses, mantelpieces, cupboards, and doorways, just as they did fine pieces of furniture. This was during the Georgian period in England, and many American houses reflected the Georgian style.

Northern Colonial. The Craigie-Longfellow house illustrated on page 314 is typical of Colonial architecture in the New England states and is sometimes called Northern Colonial. Notice the formally balanced, symmetrical grouping of windows and doorways and such details as the wooden shutters, hood over the doorway, and the mullioned windows. This type of house has been so pleasing to American home-builders that they have adapted it for today's homes.

The house shown above is a twentieth-century design adapted from the Southern Colonial style. You will see the characteristic arrangement of doorway and windows and, in this case, a covered terrace at the end of the house which provides for the modern love of outdoor living. Some critics object to the shutters on a modern house because they are no longer functional as in the days when they were closed for protection against cold, wind, and storm. Others

Design for a modern house in the Dutch Colonial style.

say that the shutters *can* be functional if we wish to use them and that their decorative value is sufficient reason for putting them on a house.

Pennsylvania Colonial. The upper picture on page 318 shows an adaptation of the Pennsylvania Colonial style. Many homes in eastern Pennsylvania have been designed in this manner. Most of the early houses in this style were fieldstone without the combination of wood siding shown in this modern house.

Dutch Colonial. Another of the pre-Revolutionary styles still popular is the Dutch Colonial. One of its distinguishing characteristics is the gambrel roof with its broken roof line. The architect's drawing above shows how the style has been adapted for contemporary living. In Colonial times there were many of these houses built in the valley of the Hudson River and in New Jersey. It is a style that is easily adapted to the small modern home. Compared with the Northern Colonial style (page 314) or the Southern Colonial (page 324), the Dutch Colonial has a distinctly informal and domestic feeling.

Southern Colonial. The type of house used in the southern colonies differed from that in the North because of the different social

325

Design for a modern house patterned after the Cape Cod cottage.

and climatic conditions. The large plantations of the South were owned by men of great wealth. These men were masters of great estates, and it is natural that their houses should reflect the lives that they lived. Mount Vernon, the home of George Washington, is an example of this type of architecture. If you have visited Mount Vernon you know that it is simple but spacious in effect. Tall square columns extend two stories to support the projecting roof. It is not the type of architecture that is suited to a narrow city lot, but it has been used very successfully as the inspiration for a modern suburban home.

The beautiful home shown on page 324 was built in Kansas City, Missouri. Notice the lovely simplicity of the design. There is a pleasant rhythm in the columns, the chimneys, and the little central turret. There is interesting spacing in the windows, and the doorway makes a good center of interest.

Cape Cod cottage. Another Colonial style, the Cape Cod cottage (see above), is characterized by low walls and a high gable roof with a close cornice. A central doorway and shutters at the windows are also characteristics. Dormer windows are often used, but none are shown in this design. This style, like the Dutch Colonial, is comfortable and informal. Its beauty is based on good proportions and simple lines. There is nothing pretentious or luxurious about it. As you may guess from the name, this style developed on Cape Cod in the early days of our country.

Popular Home Magazine; United States Gypsum Company

A beautiful modern house design with well-planned terrace and reflecting pool.

MODERN STYLES IN HOUSES. Styles in houses change, just as they do in hats and dresses, but new styles in houses do not appear as often as new styles in clothing. Hundreds of years may pass before a completely new style in architecture is invented. The twentieth century in which we are now living has produced a new style which is called the "modern" or contemporary style. Possibly in some future time it will be known as the twentieth-century style.

The house shown above is a nice example of this modern style. Here you can see many of the characteristics which we have already met in our study of modern furniture. The emphasis on long horizontal lines is seen in the flat roof, the wide proportion of the chimney, the picture window at the left with an uninterrupted line running across both door and window, and the long, low stone wall reflected in the pool which adds still another long, horizontal line to the whole design.

Another characteristic of the modern style is plenty of window space to let in air, light, and sunshine. In this house there is a large window and a glass door at the left with two more windows just around the corner, and a window wall extending around three sides of the room at the right.

The wide, projecting roof is another characteristic of the modern style. This provides shade for the room with window walls and protection from sun and rain in the outdoor living space.

Still another characteristic of the modern style is the informal arrangement of architectural features. Formal, bisymmetric arrangement of door and windows, as in the Craigie-Longfellow house and the Cape Cod cottage, is not used in the modern style. Balanced effects are achieved by an informal arrangement of unlike architectural features on either side of the central point in the design.

The most important point in the design of the modern house is functional quality—design for comfortable and convenient living. Architects say that the modern house is planned from the inside out, meaning that the house is planned around the activities of daily living. New and different types of floor plans are typical of contemporary houses, and we will study some of these plans in Chapter 17, "Design Your Home for Better Living."

New use of materials in modern houses

Many modern house designs make use of materials in new ways. The two views of the desert home in Palm Springs, California, on the opposite page, show corrugated aluminum roofing used for walls and roof. The extended wing walls provide wind shelter and reflect heat from the patios. The horizontal corrugations blend with the lines of the roof to give a lower, wider effect. You will observe that the house fits well into the flat desert country with the background of mountains in the distance.

The corrugated aluminum roofing is also used for the living-room ceiling so as to diffuse sound and to carry the attractive exterior corrugation designs inside the house.

New concepts in house design feature the use of new materials for any purpose where they are functional. Consequently, we have new forms and new ideas in house design which at first may seem strange and queer but later may seem highly desirable.

RANCH HOUSES ARE POPULAR. The ranch house is another style which has developed in the twentieth century. Although it is not a completely new style, it has acquired definite characteristics which distinguish it from other styles. It is really a variation of the cottage with long, low lines and informal arrangement of architectural features.

Two views of a desert home with aluminum walls and roof.

In the ranch house shown on the next page you can see the characteristic features of ranch house exteriors. Observe the low-pitched gable roof and broad, flat chimneys; also notice the extended roof which shelters the entry and small porch. These houses generally have

L. F. Garlinghouse Company, Inc.

This comfortable, homey-looking ranch house invites you to come and live there.

a long, rectangular plan or an L shape. They are rambling, one-story buildings requiring large plots, and therefore are particularly suitable for country and suburban homes. High prices for city lots usually prohibit this type of house in the city. You will see that these houses are informal in style with nonsymmetrical arrangement of windows, doors, and other architectural features.

The house shown above has the comfortable, friendly look of most ranch-type homes. Notice the pleasant balanced effect created by the ell which extends forward on the right and the garages and chimney on the left. Interesting variety is secured by the use of vertical siding (board and batten) on the front of the ell and the horizontal siding on the rest of the front elevation.

We will give further study to the ranch-house type in Chapter 17, including special attention to floor plans and their adaptability to daily living.

BEAUTY IN ANY STYLE. In house exteriors as in any article of interior furnishing, good design and functional quality are important.

Important also are good balance, pleasing proportions, rhythmic lines, and a good center of interest. It is interesting to analyze exterior designs for these points. At the same time we should not allow our interest in art principles to make us forget the importance of functional design. Every house should be judged for adaptability to everyday living, and this cannot be done by merely looking at the exterior. The interior must also be considered. Yet there are some features which are evident in the outside design. For example, the Northern Colonial mansion shown on page 314 and the Southern Colonial shown on page 324 are not well suited to the informal kind of life led by most Americans. Houses with high gabled roofs mean waste space in the attic. Doorways with no cover for protection when leaving or entering the house during bad weather are not desirable. Garages with easy access to the house should be protected from stormy weather. Pleasant living requires outdoor living space and this should be provided in the design of the house. These are the things to think of as well as appearance when you judge a house exterior.

SUGGESTIONS FOR FURTHER STUDY. 1. How many different types of domestic architecture can be found in your town? Appoint committees to investigate different parts of the town. Each committee should report to the class the result of its investigations. If you have a camera, take pictures.

2. Choose your favorite style of domestic architecture and read as much about it as you can in other books. Collect pictures from magazines and advertising booklets showing the influence of this type of architecture in modern homes.

3. Study famous historic buildings in your state.

4. Here are some topics for class discussion:

If you are building a new house, why should you consider the neighboring houses in planning the exterior?

What are the special requirements for a house in a warm climate? In a cool climate?

It has been said that we cannot have well-designed houses without a large expenditure of money. Discuss the truth of this statement.

TO TEST YOUR APPRECIATION OF DESIGN IN
HOUSE EXTERIORS

I. Answer the following questions without referring to the discussions in this chapter:

1. How can good rhythmic movement be expressed in the exterior of a house?

2. How can the exterior of a house be made more interesting by the architect when he uses the art principle of proportion? (You might draw a simple diagram to illustrate your meaning.)

3. If you were designing a house, what would you use as a center of interest on the front, rear, and each side elevation? Explain.

4. How can the architect achieve good *informal* balance on the front of a house? Explain with the help of a diagram.

5. How should the house on the side of a hill be fitted to its site?

II. Your teacher will hang at least five pictures of houses on the bulletin board and give each one a number. You should be able to identify the style of each house. Write down the numbers on your paper and the names of the styles opposite the numbers.

III. Which is more important for the person who is choosing the style of the house which he will build: to understand the principles of design as expressed in a house exterior or to know all about the details of each historic style? Give your reasons.

Chapter 15

BEAUTY THAT GROWS IN THE GARDEN

~~~~~~

Our study of beauty in the home has included design problems both inside and outside the house, but they do not end with its exterior appearance. The grounds around the house offer a special kind of art problem—the right kind of planting. The kind of beauty that grows in the garden is extremely important to the outside of your home.

Of the many houses which you have seen, can you not call up mental pictures which fit the following descriptions? One house sits uncomfortably in the middle of bare, surrounding grounds. No trees, shrubs, vines, or flowers relieve the bleak and barren aspect. Often we have the feeling that the house does not belong there but is only temporarily located. There is a lack of unity between the house and its surroundings, and no matter how beautiful the house, it suffers because of its poor setting. The other house is surrounded with a few shrubs and perhaps some vines and trees. It seems to be a part of the ground upon which it stands and may almost seem as if it, too, had grown from the ground. There is a feeling of unity and harmony between the house and its setting.

IMPORTANCE OF FOUNDATION PLANTING. There is particular need for planting around the foundation of a house when the house has been built upon an unsightly foundation of concrete blocks or other material different from the material in the house itself—as, for example, a wood frame house on a brick foundation. The foundation of a house should not show above the ground if the effect is to be

Most attractive foundation planting helps to "tie" this cottage to the ground.

pleasing. When an ugly layer of concrete or other material has been left so that it shows, the only thing we can do is plant shrubbery which will conceal it.

More than mere planting is necessary, however. There must be careful *planning* before the planting. Mere planting may result in a profusion of foliage that is as bad as the cluttering of an interior with too many pieces of furniture or decorative accessories. Or it may result in a placing of shrubs that detracts from rather than adds to the beauty of the house. Let us consider some of these problems in detail.

VARIETY IN SIZE AND SHAPE OF SHRUBS. If all the shrubs planted around the house are the same size and shape, the effect is sure to be monotonous. This is a violation of the principle of proportion. How would you like a privet hedge planted close to the foundation all around a house? The effect would be most uninteresting.

The foundation planting shown in the picture on the opposite page is pleasing because of the variety in shape and size of the shrubs. The tall slender tree at the right, the low clumps of shrubbery beneath the window, and the taller shrub at the left provide excellent foundation planting.

Sometimes in the effort to obtain variety of size and shape, people trim their shrubs severely. An eight-foot shrub may be kept cut down to a four-foot level. Other shrubs are sometimes trimmed down into ball-like shapes. Except in the case of privet or boxwood hedges, this treatment destroys the natural beauty of the shrubs and creates an effect in exceedingly bad taste. Hedges of privet and boxwood can be kept trimmed successfully, however, because the leaves grow in such a way as to produce a solid green mass. These hedges are suitable for the formal garden.

THINK BEFORE YOU PLANT. It is just as easy to plant an interesting arrangement of shrubs, such as that shown on the opposite page, as to plant an uninteresting row of shrubs all the same size. Do your planning first and then plant. The nursery man will help you to choose the kinds of shrubs, and soon you will learn the characteristic shapes and sizes of shrubs native to your locality.

> PLANNING FOR PLANTING. Plan a day when everyone will bring pictures of shrubs and trees. Nursery catalogs are helpful. Learn to recognize at least five shrubs which grow in your district.

PLANTING SHOULD ENHANCE THE HOUSE. Flowers and shrubs should be placed to emphasize the architectural features of a house. The planting in front of the two houses shown on pages 336 and 337 is well designed so as to emphasize structure. In both cases the doorway is accented in a pleasing way. In the house shown on page 336 a climbing rose frames the entrance in a delightful way. On the oppo-

Good foundation planting emphasizes the structural features of this house.

site page, two tall evergreens accent the doorway in pleasing fashion.

Coming back to the first house again, you will see that the windows to the right of the doorway have been enhanced by the clumps of laurel and other plants. The laurel is just high enough to accent the windows but not high enough to obscure the view from inside the house. The windows to the left of the doorway are screened by the shrubs and the small tree. It is sometimes desirable for the sake of privacy to shut off the view from the outside, and in this case it has been done in a very satisfactory way. Naturally, one would not wish to use this kind of planting near all the windows in the house because not enough sunlight and air would be admitted.

In the illustration of the house on the next page, the flowers and shrubs have been well placed with respect to the windows and corners. Notice the tall, graceful juniper tree, which accents the corner of the house to the left of the bay window, and the large shrub which

336

Foundation planting adds beauty to the house.

is placed between the two windows to the left. These contrast nicely with the low, spreading shapes of the shrubs and flowers beneath the windows.

Remember always that planting around the house should do two things: (1) tie the house to the ground, and (2) frame and beautify its structure.

> DECORATION FOR ENJOYMENT. Learn to notice the plantings in front of the houses which you pass and to enjoy those which are well planned.

GARDENS ON HILLY GROUND. Many houses are built on hilly ground, and their garden space slopes away from the house. Some people try to make grassy lawns on these hilly sites and find it very difficult. Even if the grass grows well and does not wash out in rainy seasons,

An interesting house in a beautiful setting of pines and informal garden.

cutting it is a hard job. The above picture shows how one family solved this problem. There is a small area of grass where the slope of the ground is slight. The steep bank on each side of the steps is planted mostly with ground ivy which makes an attractive cover. Natural rock has been used effectively on each side of the steps, at the edges of the foundation planting, and for a rock garden on the slope at the left. Planting among the rocks adds interest to the garden. This treatment of the front garden and the background of pines give this house a very beautiful setting.

A GARDEN TO LIVE IN. The modern way of life includes more and more time outdoors for city and country folk alike. A place to sit in the sun; a shady spot for reading, visiting, and eating; a corner that is protected from wind and rain are all found in the livable garden.

The house and garden shown on the opposite page were planned for outdoor living. A glass door close to the big window gives easy ac-

338

A beautiful house with a livable garden.

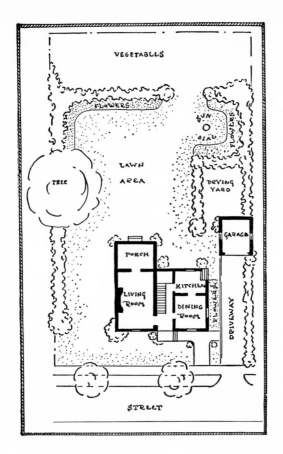

A plan for planting the grounds around a small house.

cess from house to garden. The extended roof provides a shaded area, and the extended wall gives protection from wind. The uncovered terrace furnishes plenty of opportunity for those who wish to lounge in the sun. Notice the recessed lights on the underside of the extended roof for illumination at night.

The ground slopes away from the house, and a stone wall has been built to support the edge of the bank. Steps down from the terrace lead to the stone walk which takes one to the flower garden.

A PLAN FOR THE ENTIRE GROUNDS. It is a good idea to plan our gardens on paper before we start our actual planting. Changes on paper can easily be made, but when we once plant our shrubs and dig our flower beds it is difficult to make any changes. We can make plans for our gardens in the same way that we made plans for placing the furniture in our rooms. The above drawing shows the plan for

340

the grounds surrounding a house on a suburban lot. Notice that the plan includes the whole lot and that the back yard has been made attractive. The living room and porch open directly on the back yard, and the yard is made to serve as an outdoor living room in summer. How many back yards that we know serve only as a resting place for the garbage can and as a place to pile the ashes!

Many people prefer to have the house set near the front of the lot, with more room and the porch at the rear, so as to secure greater privacy. The garage, too, is set as near the street as is feasible. When the garage is set at the extreme rear end of the lot, making a long driveway necessary, space is wasted which might better be used for other purposes. Notice how the vegetable garden and the drying yard have been separated by shrubbery from the part used for other purposes. The open lawn space is larger than it really seems, for the spread of the tree covers part of the lawn.

Imagine yourself living in this house. Can you form a mental picture of the front of the house as seen just before entering it, with its small grass plot and shrubs? Enter the house and pass into the living room. What picture will meet your eyes as you look across the porch? If it is summer, you may pass out into the yard and find a comfortable place to read or work under the tree, where there are some seats and a table.

Every house and yard presents a different problem. The location of the house and trees must generally remain as they are. Although we start with these things which are fixed, by planning thoughtfully we can make our yards attractive.

No space too small for a garden. Even the smallest space can be beautified with some kind of planting.

One city yard, only the size of a large living room, was made into a very livable garden, as shown in the diagram and picture on pages 342 and 343. Even though you are planning a very small garden, it is important to plan well before you start digging. It is easy to try out several plans on paper, but difficult with spade and shovel.

Color in the garden. Color harmony in the garden is just as important as in the house. Flowers which are planted near the house or in window boxes are always seen with the house as a background, and this fact must be taken into consideration. Flowers of themselves are beautiful, but too often we see them as separate units without relation to their surroundings. The same flowers may grow in two different yards. In one yard they blend with the house and surroundings, but in the other yard we must enjoy them in spite of the surroundings.

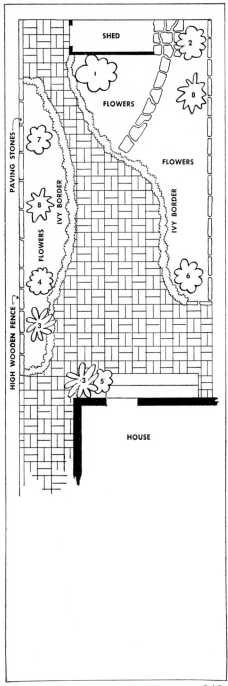

Within the plan image: SHED, FLOWERS, 2, 1, 8, PAVING STONES, 7, FLOWERS, IVY BORDER, 8, IVY BORDER, FLOWERS, 4, 6, 3, HIGH WOODEN FENCE, 3, 5, HOUSE

Woman's Home Companion; Katharine M-P. Cloud

Naturalistic curves lead the eye pleasantly toward the rear gate, while planting of upper right allows space for tall shrubs to act as a screen from neighbors. This gives more feeling of space than if planting had been concentrated along walls and the center left bare.

PLANTING SCHEME

1 Privet	5 Dwarf juni-
2 Rose of	per
Sharon	6 Lilac
3 Rhododen-	7 Mock or-
dron	ange
4 Laurel	8 Forsythia

This garden plan and planting scheme were used for the small city yard shown on the opposite page.

Woman's Home Companion; photograph by F. F. Zimmerman

From the house you look down the yard to the shed at the far end, screened by privet which has been allowed to develop naturally. The back gate is at left of it; city houses are beyond.

The factor which contributes to the harmonious effect in one case and is lacking in the other is color. The flaming scarlet-red of salvias or geraniums is pleasing against a background of white paint or gray stucco, but against a yellow house or a red brick wall the effect is generally inharmonious. Scarlet is aggressive and likely to fight with other colors.

For such a colorful background as a brick wall we must confine the color of our flowers to more neutralized and less aggressive tones. The whites and dull pinks of hollyhocks are far more charming against brick than the emphatic red of cannas. The blues of larkspur and bachelor's-button also blend with the brick wall.

With the white or neutral-colored house as a background, any color in flowers can be displayed attractively, but the more color in the background, the more care we must exercise in choosing the color of our flowers.

Mistakes in planting near the house are frequent. The owner of a big yellow brick house planted a crimson rambler on each side of the doorway. They grew into enormous vines and bloomed magnificently. The effect was most unfortunate. The bright red roses against the strong yellow wall was anything but pleasant to see. The effect would have been splendid had the house been of gray stone or painted white. Of course, the man could not change the wall, but he could have selected a better color for his roses.

Combining the flowers in the flower beds is another color problem in the garden. What flowers combine harmoniously? This depends upon their size, color, texture, and general characteristics. If we plant bright-yellow marigolds near delicately colored sweet peas, we may be sure that the brilliant marigolds will overpower the pastel tints of their neighbors. If we plant scarlet and pink geraniums or tulips together the two will fight. It is a safe general rule that flowers of intense coloring do not combine successfully with flowers of delicate shades. The former must be kept somewhat to themselves, because they overpower the pastels and fight with other bright colors.

If we use our knowledge of color combinations and harmonies, we can plan some charming color harmonies. Blue-purple and purple asters will combine effectively with the small yellow chrysanthemums. This is really a complementary combination. Yellow daffodils and white narcissus with their yellow centers and perhaps some golden tulips make an attractive flower bed in the spring.

There are many flowers in pinks and blues that we think of as belonging to the old-fashioned garden which combine effectively. Larkspur, phlox, pinks, bachelor's-buttons, and cosmos can be used together successfully. Sometimes touches of yellow can be introduced with such flowers as the snapdragon.

The success of such a combination depends partly on the textures and general characteristics of the flowers. The flowers mentioned for the old-fashioned garden have a certain similar fineness of texture which helps them to combine harmoniously. But if we try to combine coreopsis with geraniums the difference in texture and general character spoils the result.

SUGGESTIONS FOR FURTHER STUDY. 1. Draw a plan of the house in which you live and the yard which surrounds it as they are at present. Then draw another plan showing it as you would like to see it. If you live in an apartment building which has no yard, you might make a plan for the grounds surrounding the school building or for the house and yard in which you would like to live.

2. Make a list of the shrubs which grow in your locality. Classify them as to whether they are tall or low and spreading.

3. Draw a diagram showing the front of a tall, narrow house. Your problem is to add shrubs which will make the house look less tall. Then show the kind of shrub or tree that you would use in front of this house to accomplish the desired result.

4. Criticize the house and garden pictures shown on pages 318, 327, and 330 for the following points: Are the house and grounds tied together? Do the shrubs lack variety? Is the yard made to look as spacious as possible? Are the structural features of the house emphasized, and how? Suggest any improvements that you can think of.

5. Make lists of flowers that you think would combine harmoniously in the same flower bed.

To test your ability in garden design

I. Make a list of at least five reasons why "planning before planting" is important.

II. When you plan your own garden, what three mistakes will you try to avoid and what three particular points in design will you try to include?

III. Your teacher will show you the picture of a garden which you have not seen before. Write your comments on it as to good or poor features.

Chapter 16

REMODELING OPERATIONS
—MAJOR AND MINOR

O ften people cannot buy new furniture and new houses to satisfy a desire for beauty in their homes. Frequently we cannot buy what we really need for convenience and comfort. Budgets will not permit the expenditure of large sums of money. Here is where *ideas* plus some homework plus small sums of money will produce good results. Old houses and old furniture can be improved tremendously with only a minimum of money and labor. It is the idea that counts.

This chapter contains some suggestions for remodeling that have been carried out successfully by other people. Some of these remodeling jobs are major operations. Others are minor affairs. All of them have helped to create beauty and convenience for others. Perhaps these same ideas will not fit your own needs, but they may suggest to you other ideas for remodeling that will help you to improve your own home.

WHEN YOU NEED CHESTS OR BEDS. Two essential pieces of furniture for the bedroom are the bed and a chest or dressing table. If your pocketbook will not stand the strain of new ones, you might be able to carry out these suggestions. Secure an old chest or dresser from a secondhand store if you do not have one. The old chest shown on page 347 cost $2.50. Cut off the legs, which are neither useful nor beautiful. Put metal gliders on each post. Gliders are more useful and not so ugly as casters. Next take off the knobs or handles and in their place put strips of molding for handles. Then cut off the protruding

Woman's Day Magazine

*A modern bed unit made from
two old chests, bed springs on
legs, and a mattress. Top:
Chests and bed with panel
headboard. Right: One of the
old chests before remodeling.*

edges all around the top of the chest. With this last operation, you
have a pleasing design in modern style. Both the chests shown were
made from old ones like that shown in the bottom picture. They were
painted white, and with the bed form a nice modern bed unit.

The bed was made from a mattress and a pair of bedsprings on
legs. The headboard was made by attaching a panel of plywood to
the backs of the two chests. The bed fits in between. The whole effect
is harmonious and pleasing.

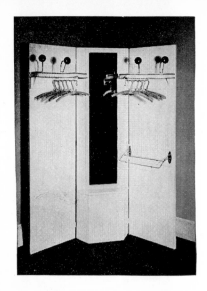

Woman's Day Magazine

An idea for a bedroom with no closet. Left: Cover the outside of the screen with an attractive wallpaper. Right: Fit the other side with closet equipment.

Here is an idea for remodeling an old bed. It was a heavy wooden bed with a high headboard and slightly lower footboard. The headboard and footboard were removed, leaving the four wooden posts at the corners. The posts were cut shorter, making the effect of a low four-poster. This same remodeling operation can be used successfully on old iron and brass beds. The posts can be painted whatever color you choose, and with a pretty bedspread the effect is very good.

Another remodeling operation recommended for bedroom furniture is the amputation of mirrors from old dressers or bureaus. A dresser is generally an awkward looking piece of furniture and when possible should be replaced by a chest and separate mirror. It is quite simple to remove the mirror from most dressers and to hang it on the wall above the dresser, thus making the effect of a chest with a mirror hanging above. This operation is especially desirable when the mirror is round or oval, and when it is held by two arms which extend upward from the dresser.

WHEN THERE IS NO BEDROOM CLOSET. A closet for the bedroom seems like a real necessity, but nevertheless there are many bedrooms in older houses which do not have any. Here is an idea that provides closet space without creating an ugly spot in the bedroom. Secure an old screen from the secondhand store. Paper the outside surface with

348

Two attractive hanging wall cabinets made from an old china cabinet. They are especially useful in a dinette where floor space is limited.

wallpaper of a design and color that are harmonious with the room. (See the opposite page.) Fit the back of the screen with a mirror, hangers, hat stands, shoe rack, and a soiled-clothes hamper, as shown in the illustration.

IDEAS FOR REMODELING OTHER PIECES OF FURNITURE. Almost every piece of ugly, discarded furniture suggests a remodeling operation that will make it into an attractive and useful piece. The two nice little hanging cabinets shown above were made from an old, ugly oak china cabinet, the kind which stands about six feet tall. It was cut in half from top to bottom, thus making two short cabinets which can be hung on the wall in a dinette where floor space is limited. This operation was difficult, so a specialist was employed to cut the curved glass and the frame. The result was worth the trouble and extra expense.

Ugly radio cabinets have been a source of annoyance to many beauty lovers. It has been practically impossible to buy a large radio

Two views of the same wall before and after a small remodeling operation. Top: The built-in bookshelves and better arrangement of decorative accessories produce a much better effect than in the bottom picture. Bottom: The effect is cluttered and ordinary.

Two views of the same living room before and after remodeling. Top: A complete alteration of one wall produces a fine result. Bottom: The ugly fireplace, bookcases, and small windows produce a very poor effect.

351

with an attractive cabinet. Some people have solved the problem by setting the radio inside a built-in cabinet and simply opening the doors of the cabinet when the radio was in use. The lower part of the desk shown on page 218 might be used for such a purpose. One interior decorator placed the radio inside a wall cabinet with coarse wire mesh screen used in the doors instead of glass. These doors do not have to be opened when the radio is played.

Ugly tables frequently can be remodeled to improve their appearance and their usefulness. Tables with long legs can sometimes be improved in appearance and usefulness by cutting the legs down. These tables can then be used as coffee tables in front of davenports. The old-fashioned, long davenport tables can sometimes be cut in two in order to make two end tables. Sideboards can sometimes be improved by cutting off the legs and by removing ugly and unnecessary ornamentation. Chairs are easily transformed with slip covers. Even an ugly Morris chair becomes quite attractive with a pleasing slip cover.

OPERATIONS FOR BEAUTY. Sometimes operations on the house itself are necessary for a more attractive and convenient home. The two pictures on page 350 show one end of a small living room before and after a minor operation for beauty. Bookshelves were built in each side of the fireplace. These shelves, together with other changes, transform the room. The long line across the top of the mantel gives the room an appearance of much greater width. The ivory-colored woodwork blends into the pale green wallpaper, and helps to give the impression of greater space.

The new curtains, which are allowed to hang straight, also blend into the wall and add to the feeling of space. The roller shades were removed. When necessary the drapes can be drawn across the windows.

Notice that the stones around the fireplace were painted a light sand color, and this, too, helps to create an illusion of greater space. A gas heater was placed in the fireplace because it was impossible to turn the fireplace into a real one without an expensive major operation. This was a compromise which the owners did not like, but expense prohibited the real fireplace. At least the gas burner is more suitable than logs in an obviously fake fireplace.

Notice especially the better selection and arrangement of decorative accessories in the remodeled room. In the old room, the general effect is cluttered and restless. Some of the improvement was produced by eliminating certain articles, such as the magazine rack, the basket, and the small bowls. In the final arrangement small articles are grouped to make larger spots of interest. Small accessories on such a large mantel are not effective. Notice also that the picture was lowered so that it seems to belong to the mantel arrangement.

All these changes were very inexpensive. The shelves and paint cost $15.25. Of course, the man of the house contributed the labor. The slip covers, made by the woman of the house, cost $7.50. The window drapes, which were made from a bedspread, cost $1.75. The other windows in the room required three more bedspreads. If you have had experience in buying drapes you know that these bedspreads at $1.75 each were very inexpensive. They are soft green and white, a combination which blends delightfully with the ivory woodwork and pale green walls.

The two pictures on page 351 show the effect before and after a major operation in remodeling. The heavy mantel and clumsy-looking bookcases were torn out and replaced by a fireplace and paneled wall with pleasing proportions. The small windows above the bookcases were walled up, and the bookshelves were extended to the ceiling. The center light and the ugly wall fixtures above the fireplace were eliminated. It was a major operation, but it was a great success!

REMODELING THE EXTERIOR OF A HOUSE. Sometimes it is possible to improve the exterior design of a house with comparatively small alterations. Compare the before and after pictures on page 354. Originally the little cottage was most ordinary in appearance. The little front porch looked "stuck on," and the lines of the roof did not harmonize with the main lines of the house roof. This ugly porch was removed and replaced by an entrance which is much more pleasing. Notice that the lines of the little roof over the entrance harmonize with the house roof. Such details as this are important.

A sun-parlor room was built on to the right-hand side of the house, thus giving the design greater width and better balance. Notice that the slant of the sun-room roof harmonizes with the main lines of the design. The shutters which were added to the window help to give an effect of width.

Several years elapsed between these two pictures. As you can see, there was time for a tree to grow and let its branches hang protectively over the little house. These two pictures illustrate, most emphatically, the importance of planting for beauty around the house.

On page 355 two more before-and-after pictures show the tremendous improvement that can be accomplished by the right kind of remodeling operation. Before remodeling, the house was exceedingly

Better Homes and Gardens Magazine

The same house before and after remodeling and planting the grounds. Top: Greatly improved effect produced by removing front porch and adding room at side. Bottom: Effect here is most unhappy.

drab and dull. Notice what a remarkable change in effect was secured by taking off the ugly, narrow front porch, by adding some small upper windows, adding shutters and small panes of glass to all the windows, and covering the house with shingles. Much of the charming effect is secured through planting, as the trellis over the doorway

Two pictures of the same house before and after remodeling. Top: Pleasing effect after remodeling and landscaping grounds. Bottom: Unfortunate effect before remodeling.

and the planting around the foundation show. The terrace edged with a low stone wall and the stone steps form spots of interest in the grounds.

SUGGESTIONS FOR FURTHER STUDY. 1. From your collection of furniture pictures, select a design which you think could be improved by a little remodeling. Be prepared to tell what the alteration should be.

2. Describe a remodeling operation for the interior of your own home which you think would make your home more beautiful and convenient.

3. Find a picture of a house exterior which you think needs remodeling. Describe the remodeling which you would recommend. If the picture is large enough, trace the house design and show your suggestions for remodeling.

Chapter 17

DESIGN YOUR HOME FOR BETTER LIVING

In the preceding chapters we have studied many problems in the design of a beautiful and livable home. Such homes do not happen by accident; they must be planned, and the planning is fun. Even though you do not expect to have a new home immediately, it is fun to plan your "dream home" of the future. In this chapter you will plan the home you would like to have, the home you may have if you plan well and work hard to accomplish your dream. Of course, you will have the good sense not to plan a home which is an impossibility without a million dollar fortune.

It has been pointed out that the difference between beauty and ugliness is *good design*. You have learned, too, that good design and fine color do not wear price tags. A very livable and beautiful home may cost far less than a millionaire's mansion. Your own good taste and common sense are the most important requirements. At any rate, dreams are free, so you can enjoy this project with no budget at all!

SELECT THE SITE. Let us suppose that you are going to build a new house and that you must find the ground upon which to build it. What are the points that you will consider?

1. Where would you like to live? What is your plan of life for the future? Do you prefer to live in a big city? In the suburbs? In the country?

2. Are utilities available? If you wish to have gas, electricity, water, and telephone for your home, you must consider their cost. For ex-

L. F. Garlinghouse Company, Inc.

*The small ranch house shown above appeals to many people as
suited to simple and comfortable living.*

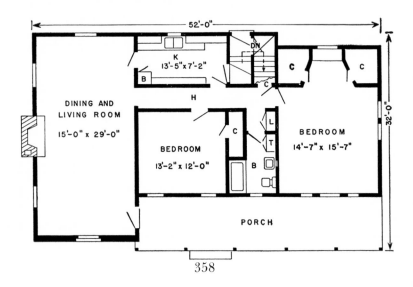

358

Popular Home Magazine; United States Gypsum Company

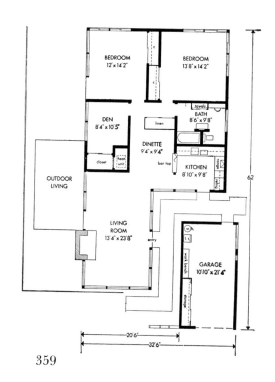

This small modern house, called the "House that's handy to live in," gives privacy to the inhabitants but provides plenty of opportunity for outdoor living.

359

ample, if you are thinking of buying a site in the country, is water available and included in the purchase price, or would you have to pay for digging a well and installing a pump?

3. Are schools within convenient distance? A shopping district? The church which you wish to attend?

4. Is transportation to your work satisfactory?

5. Is the district one where you wish to plan for a permanent home?

> SUGGESTIONS FOR FURTHER STUDY. If you could buy a site for your house at the present time in your locality, where would it be? Obtain prices and particulars about the points discussed in the preceding paragraph.

CHOOSE THE STYLE OF HOUSE. After you have decided on the location of your dream house, you must next decide what style of architecture you prefer. Will it be a traditional or modern type? The illustrations in Chapter 14, "Homes for Today and Tomorrow," suggest different designs in both traditional and modern houses. The pictures on pages 358 and 359 show a small ranch house and a small modern style house. The floor plans are shown with each house.

The little cottage shown on page 358 is a typical ranch-house design. The large porch covered with an extended roof helps to give it a charming, homey atmosphere. The floor plan below the picture shows the front entry at the end of the long porch opening into a large combination living and dining room. A hall leading from this room gives access to all the other rooms in the house and to the basement stairs. A full basement provides space for a laundry, the heating unit, and a recreation room. The exterior walls are finished with a combination of brick veneer and vertical siding (sometimes called board and batten).

Does this delightful little home appeal to you as your ideal home of the future? Certainly it has many features which make it an attractive and livable house.

Now consider the small modern house shown on page 359. The front entrance is reached by a walk between the garage and house. The walk continues around the corner of the garage to the kitchen door. The same roof which covers the house extends over the walk and garage. It also projects from the living-room wall over the outdoor living area.

A study of the floor plan shows that the living room, dinette, and kitchen are arranged in an attractive and convenient way. The location of the garage and the covered passageway to the house provides easy transportation of groceries and other supplies brought home in the family car.

Further study of the plan will show generous storage space. There is a large closet in each bedroom and in the den which could also be used for a bedroom. Storage is also provided in the garage.

This house was designed and built in California, but it is adaptable to moderate climate zones and, with increased insulation, to colder climates. It takes advantage of the opportunity to extend living to the out-of-doors, and a section of the ground is "walled in" with a high board fence which gives that area almost as much privacy as any portion of the house. The street view protects the privacy of the occupants and yet is not forbidding to passers-by.

Do you see why this design has been called the "House that's handy to live in"? Perhaps it will appeal to you for future living.

BUILD YOUR HOUSE TO SUIT THE SITE. It has been pointed out in our previous study that a house built on a hillside should be adapted to the slope of the ground. (See page 319.) It is equally true that a house built on level land should seem to belong to the ground. We know that foundation planting helps to relate a house to its site, but the design of the house is very important in tying it to the ground.

The houses shown on pages 362 and 365 are built on level ground and are designed to fit their sites. The farmhouse on page 362 fits into the landscape very well indeed. The low, wide structure with its spreading roof seems to have grown like the trees which surround it and protect it. The low, horizontal lines blend with the broad, sweeping lines of the prairie. This house in its beautiful setting was built in eastern Iowa, and if you are on a motor trip between Iowa City and West Liberty you can see it from the highway.

The house on page 365 was built in Highland Park, Illinois, a suburban town north of Chicago. Here, too, the house design is harmonious with the flat ground. The trees and foundation planting help to create a pleasing relationship of house and site, but the design of the house itself is the most important factor in producing a unified effect.

Suppose that instead of the houses shown on these two pages, a tall narrow house had been built for the farmhouse and a square brick house like the lower one on page 317 had been built for the suburban house. What sad mistakes these would have been. Unfortunately, many such mistakes have been made. You have only to keep your eyes open as you ride through country and town to see many such mistakes. This is another place where we should think before we plan, and plan well before we build.

This "Design-for-Better-Living Farmhouse" is well suited to its site on a mid-western prairie in eastern Iowa. The floor plan for this attractive home is shown on the opposite page.

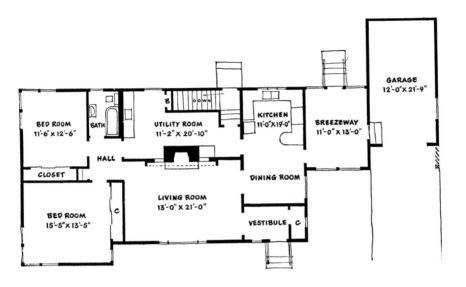

BED ROOM
11'-6" x 12'-6"

BATH

UTILITY ROOM
11'-2" x 20'-10"

KITCHEN
11'-0" x 19'-0"

BREEZEWAY
11'-0" x 13'-0"

GARAGE
12'-0" x 21'-9"

HALL

CLOSET

DINING ROOM

BED ROOM
15'-5" x 13'-5"

C

LIVING ROOM
13'-0" x 21'-0"

VESTIBULE   C

How pleasant life might be in this comfortable and
delightful farmhouse. Set well back from the road, it
is beautifully framed by the great trees on either hand
and by the broad sweep of lawn in front and the expanse of sky behind it. The house with its long, low
lines clings to the ground and seems really to be part
of the ground itself. A study of the floor plan above
shows a thoroughly livable home. The picture window
in the living room looks out upon a fine, far-reaching
view, and the corner windows in the bedrooms provide a maximum of light and leave a maximum of
wall space for placing furniture. The utility room and
the kitchen both have easy access to the outdoors. A
large fireplace in the living room provides for jolly
occasions during the winter months.

363

THE HOUSE THAT GROWS. Many people who want to build a house find that they cannot afford to build as large a one as they would like to have. In many cases, the expansible house is the answer to this problem. Instead of building a dream house complete, a small house can be planned for expansion and growth.

The plan for the complete house is planned first, then the basic unit to be built first is selected. This basic unit must provide all the essentials for a small family, including living room, dining space, kitchen, bedroom, storage space, heating equipment, and laundry facilities. Generally it is necessary for one or more rooms to serve two purposes.

The plan for an expansible house on pages 366 and 367 shows how a small basic unit containing three rooms and bath can be expanded to include six rooms and an alcove suitable for a study or sewing room. In the first stage the house has a large bedroom with an alcove usable as a nursery, dressing space, or study. The kitchen is large enough for a dining area.

In the expanded house, a new living room with fireplace is added, and the old living room becomes the dining room. In the old bedroom, a partition is added which divides the alcove and a small combination guest room and study. The newly added garage helps to create a patio which serves both as an entrance patio and as an outdoor living space for the family.

Many old houses have been enlarged from time to time by building on additions. Generally these additions create the unfortunate effect of a house design that has been patched together without benefit of an over-all plan. If you decide to build an expansible house which will grow with the years, be sure to plan the complete house before you build the basic unit. Only in this way can you be sure of an attractive and livable house at all stages of its development. Study the house that grows, shown on pages 366 and 367, and you will see the advantage of preliminary planning.

THE FLOOR PLAN SHOULD SUIT YOUR NEEDS. The plan of rooms is very important to ease and convenience of living. Think carefully about the arrangement of rooms that will suit you best. Even though you are planning a dream house for the present, you should consider the practical point of view. Think of your house as a place to be lived in, not as a place to show off to your friends. Remember that beauty and utility are partners. (See Chapter 3.)

The plan of the small modern house shown on page 368 has several features which suit the needs of many families. As you study the plan,

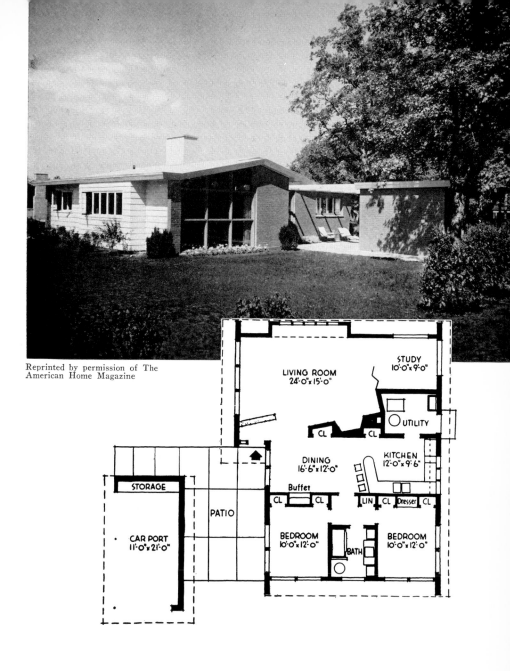

*This delightful suburban house, designed by architect James
Duncan, is beautifully related to its site.*

365

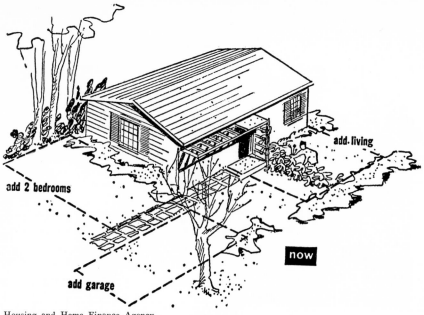

add. living

add 2 bedrooms

now

add garage

Housing and Home Finance Agency

With gable end toward street, this small house expands on a narrow lot. (See opposite page.)

imagine yourself walking along the side of the garage and stepping into the entry. From the entrance hall you can go straight ahead into the living room. As you step into the room you will see the garden through the window wall on the opposite side of the room, the fireplace to your left, and the dining area beyond the fireplace. This gives a pleasant impression to owner and guests alike as they enter the living room.

If this were your own house, you might wish to go immediately to the kitchen and would turn to your left from the entry. Here is a work area including a sewing room, laundry, and kitchen. This unusual combination of units is convenient for the housewife. For instance, it often happens that freshly ironed laundry needs repairs, buttons sewed on, rips sewed, or other mending. Instead of being carried to some other room, the laundry can be mended in the adjoining sewing area before it is put away. Another advantage in having the laundry and sewing areas near is the availability of the ironing board and iron when one is making a garment. Good sewing

later

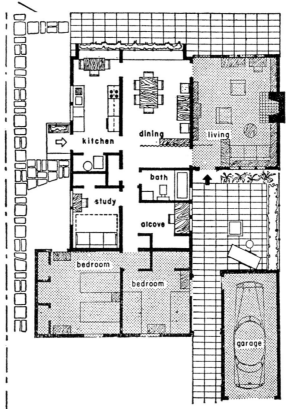

kitchen

dining

living

bath

study

alcove

bedroom

bedroom

garage

Housing and Home
Finance Agency

*The final house
is entered through
the side patio.*

scale 0   5   10   15 FT.

WEST ELEVATION

American Builder; Ann Nicholas

Would you like to live in this house? Try it out by walking into the front entry or by driving into the garage. Then imagine that you go from room to room as you live in the house. Try the garden, too.

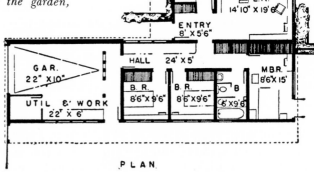

KIT.
15" X 7'

D.R.
10'6" X 7'6

HEAT.

7'6"X 8'
LAUN.

SEW.
7'6" X 7'

L.R.
14'10" X 19'6

ENTRY
8' X 5'6"

GAR.
22" X10"

HALL   24' X 5'

MBR.
8'6'X 15'

UTIL & WORK
22' X 6'

B.R.
8'6"X 9'6"

B.R.
8'6"X 9'6"

B
8'X 9'6'

PLAN

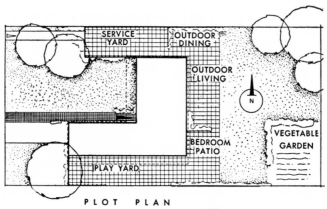

SERVICE YARD

OUTDOOR DINING

OUTDOOR LIVING

N

BEDROOM PATIO

VEGETABLE GARDEN

PLAY YARD

PLOT PLAN

368

requires frequent pressing. The sewing area in this plan has a built-in cutting table which folds away when not in use. This table is also useful for piling the freshly ironed sheets and other laundry as it comes from the ironer.

Starting again in the entry hall, let us suppose that you wish to go to a bedroom. You can turn to the right directly from the hall without passing through another room. This arrangement where any room can be reached from a central point without going through another room is a feature which many people like because it cuts down the traffic through the rooms, thus saving wear and tear on floors and carpets and preventing annoyance to those who do not wish to be disturbed.

Notice the unusual location of the garage in this plan and the entrance through the hall in the bedroom section. Generally the integral garage is located so that the entry is through the kitchen. Some people object to this arrangement because they say it causes unnecessary traffic through the kitchen and the convenience of depositing the groceries in the kitchen is not the chief consideration. The car is not always used to bring home supplies. There are many more times when it is more desirable to go from the garage directly to the bedrooms for putting away coats and wraps.

The plot plan at the bottom of the page shows the location of the service yard near the kitchen door, dining and living terraces on the garden side of the house, and a play yard which is reached through the garage door.

JUDGE A HOUSE PLAN BY "USING" THE HOUSE. The best way to decide whether you would like to live in a house from a plan on paper is to imagine yourself walking through the rooms and carrying on your regular daily activities. The plan should include the outside or plot plan. If you like outdoor living, you will wish to choose a house that allows easy access to the outdoors. The picture on page 370 shows the corner of an L-shaped house which provides a delightful terrace for leisure hours.

PLAN FOR YOUR DREAM HOUSE. During the study of houses you have probably found a style of house which you want for your dream house. You should also have decided upon the kind of plan which suits you best.

Collect pictures of houses and plans which appeal to you. These are available in current magazines, newspapers, and advertising booklets.

It is now time for you to start your permanent collection of pic-

A delightful spot for outdoor living in the corner between the two wings of an L-shaped house.

tures and drawings for your portfolio called "My House." A large manila envelope makes a good portfolio.

1. Prepare a short, neat statement about the site which you have selected. Give particulars about cost, available utilities, and zoning ordinances. Also the facilities for transportation, church, and schools. If possible get a snapshot of the site.

2. Select the house styles and plans which are most nearly like the house you would like to build, and mount them nicely on colored construction paper. Put a brief comment on each sheet telling why you like the house and plan.

BUILT-IN STORAGE SPACE IS ESSENTIAL. Every house plan should include plenty of built-in storage space. Every part of the house from basement to garret, and from front door to back, needs storage space. There is not a room in the house which does not need convenient

370

places for keeping some kind of equipment, such as clothing, household supplies, card tables, game equipment, musical instruments, dishes, or some other necessity for daily living.

In older houses not much thought was given to storage space. Houses were built without coat closets near the entry and with bedrooms that had no closets. People were expected to hang their coats on a coatrack near the front door and to buy big, cumbersome pieces of furniture known as wardrobes for their bedrooms. In more recent times, architects have paid more attention to requirements for the truly livable house. All kinds of storage space are now planned for the modern house.

STORAGE SPACE IN THE MODERN KITCHEN. Kitchen furnishing includes more pieces of equipment of various sizes, shapes, and descriptions than for any other room in the house. Architects and industrial designers have created many kinds of cabinets which are fitted with shelves and drawers for convenient storage. The cabinet sizes are standardized so that they fit together, making a wall of cupboards as seen in the modern kitchens shown on pages 194 and 397.

The pictures on page 372 show four of the convenient storage arrangements found in modern kitchen cabinets. The upper left-hand picture shows a drawer which is divided into compartments for convenient storage of knives and forks. This simple arrangement is a great timesaver for the cook who is in a hurry. Here it is very simple to pick up the utensil you want instead of scrambling through a mixed-up pile of equipment thrown together in the same drawer.

Another great convenience is the rotating shelf, as shown in the upper right-hand picture. Instead of requiring you to reach into the back of the cabinet for something you cannot see, the shelf swings out into the open and the pots and pans are ready for you. This kind of shelf is especially helpful in a corner cabinet where it is difficult if not impossible to reach the farthest spot.

The cabinet shown in the lower left-hand corner has an arrangement for storing trays and cookie sheets. Instead of storing the trays in a deep pile, making it difficult to get the bottom ones, they are filed in vertical compartments. The dividers are chrome-plated rods. Vertical compartments also provide convenient storage for cake and pie tins.

The towel rack and drier shown in the lower right picture is a great convenience. It provides a handy, out-of-sight place for hanging tea towels. The chromium racks slide out into the room when towels are needed and then slide back into the cupboard. A blower at the

371

A St. Charles Kitchen

Adequate storage space in the kitchen helps to make a livable house. Top left: A divided cutlery drawer. Top right: A swing shelf in a corner cabinet. Bottom left: Convenient tray storage. Bottom right: Sliding towel racks with blower for drying.

The Business of Farming Magazine; United States Gypsum Company

This is a convenient storage cupboard for dishes used every day when located near the sink.

bottom blows warm air into the cabinet for drying wet towels quickly.

The picture above shows a convenient dish cupboard which saves numberless steps when it is hung above the dish-drying rack. In this cupboard the shelves are just far enough apart to allow room for a stack of two teacups or a sherbet glass, and stacks of six or eight plates. This is much better than shelves which are farther apart, allowing deep stacks of plates with the small plates on top of the large ones, thus making it difficult to get the bottom plates in a hurry.

Industrial designers have created many other useful cabinets which you can obtain for the modern kitchen. The plan for your dream house should include adequate storage space for kitchen equipment.

STORAGE SPACE IN THE BEDROOMS. Storage space in the bedroom of the modern house is far different from the days when it consisted of an old-fashioned wardrobe or a small closet with a few hooks. Modern storage for your wardrobe has become a storage wall extending across one side of the bedroom. The pictures on pages 374 and 375 show two storage walls containing drawers, cupboards, and shelves extending from floor to ceiling. In the storage wall on page 374 the drawers are built beneath a high window, and the cupboard to the right is divided into three sections. The top section is intended for storing

This section of bedroom storage wall provides ample space for clothing and bedding.

Ponderosa Pine Woodwork

This storage wall provides adequate storage space, takes the place of a separate chest of drawers, and creates an attractive background wall for the bedroom.

blankets and other articles which are needed only when the season changes. The middle section is fitted with slanted shelves for shoes, and the lowest section has a rod for hanging blouses or shirts. Hooks on the inside of the door provide places for hanging belts.

The storage wall shown in the above picture was planned for books and an old clock as well as for clothing storage. In this wall the doors slide back and forth, thus eliminating the nuisance of a door which swings out into the room and obstructs movement from one part of the wall to another.

LIVING ROOMS NEED STORAGE WALLS. Living rooms, too, need storage space for the numerous articles required for daily living. Books, newspapers, magazines, game equipment, photograph books, maps, electric fans, card tables, and records are some of the things which must be kept somewhere, and the storage wall seems to be the answer

The attractive storage wall shown here adds interest to the living room.

Here is a storage wall that includes a radio cabinet, a desk, bookcases, and an interesting background wall.

Popular Home Magazine; United States Gypsum Company

Clever built-in cabinet for an entrance with a small cupboard for storing car keys and gloves and an open shelf for incoming mail.

to the problem. The storage wall on page 376 is pleasing in effect and offers generous storage space. Again beauty and utility go together.

In the storage wall shown on page 377, a panel pulls down to open the radio cabinet. When the leaf is down it forms a table surface for magazines and other articles. The panel to the right of the radio forms a desk when open. The panels above the radio are equipped with sliding doors which may be left open if desired to reveal an attractive arrangement of books and decorative accessories.

Most storage walls are made from plywood, which is available in a variety of woods ranging from the cheaper soft woods suitable for painting to the more expensive woods with beautiful grains that can be finished with stain or left the natural color. The walls shown on page 376 are finished with birch, which has a pleasing grain and takes a nice finish. The walls on page 377 are a beautiful walnut plywood. Very nice effects can be secured by painting the plywood as shown in the bedroom storage walls on pages 374 and 375.

BUILT-IN STORAGE SPACE FOR ANY ROOM. Built-in storage space is especially welcome in the dining room, where there is seldom enough room for the china, silver, and table linens.

Even the front entry can be made more livable by the addition of a small built-in cabinet like that shown above. It is a wedge-shaped fixture wider at one end than the other with a tall mirror above the wider end. There is a small cupboard for gloves and car keys and an open shelf for the daily mail.

STORAGE WALLS ARE ECONOMICAL. The built-in storage wall is one of the characteristic features of the modern house. Anyone who is planning to build a house or to remodel one should consider the advisability of including storage walls. They serve several purposes. First, they provide more storage space than is possible in any other way; second, they can take the place of one or more pieces of furniture, such as book cases, a desk, buffet, china closet, or radio cabinet; and third, they create interesting and pleasing backgrounds which help to give a unified and harmonious effect to the room.

The storage wall which reaches from floor to ceiling and from wall to wall provides more storage than several pieces of furniture standing against the same wall and costs no more or probably less than the furniture.

PLAN THE BUILT-IN STORAGE SPACE FOR YOUR DREAM HOUSE. After you have decided on the plan and style of your house, consider the storage problem. Examine the plan which you have selected to see whether enough storage is included for each room.

If you feel that the space planned for storage is not adequate, add it to your plan. Place tracing paper over the plan and add the new storage space to the plan which you have traced.

FURNISHING THE LIVABLE HOUSE. The most important objective in planning an ideal home, inside and outside, upstairs and down, is livable quality. As we have said many times, this includes comfort, convenience, and beauty. Now that you have reached the point for planning the furnishing of your dream house of the future, remind yourself of this never-to-be-forgotten aim in all house furnishing— *livability.*

There is no standard pattern to follow in choosing furnishings for the livable house; each room is a new problem to be solved. In the following pages we shall consider the convenience, comfort, and beauty of several rooms. After this study you will be better prepared to furnish your own rooms successfully.

THE ENTRY HALL. Older houses usually had "front halls" sometimes of considerable size. Many houses more recently built have no halls, and the front door opens directly into the living room. Other modern houses have small vestibules.

Whatever the size of the entry, it should be made as pleasant and

Mr. and Mrs. Harold G. Taylor

A pleasant and interesting hall which invites us to enter the beautiful living room shown on page 381.

inviting as possible. Even though it is a room which we use only as a passageway, it should give the impression that one is about to enter a comfortable, friendly home. Too often the hall is neglected and bare. Even in the smallest entry, there can be something to de-

A pleasant living room furnished in comfortable Colonial style.

note hospitality and friendliness. A gay rug on the floor or a pleasing picture on the wall suggests warmth and happiness within.

The hall shown on the opposite page is the entrance to a house furnished in Colonial style. The interesting lighting fixtures and the beautiful Oriental rugs create a pleasant effect. This hall leads directly into the delightful living room shown above.

THE LIVING ROOM. The very name *living room* suggests the quality that we seek to achieve in all rooms—livability. It is here that the family gathers for their hours together, and it is here that they entertain their friends. A living room should be convenient and pleasant for hours of visiting, playing games, reading, listening to the radio and watching television, and resting. For these activities we require comfortable chairs, good lighting both by day and at night, tables and shelves for books and magazines, and a pleasant, restful effect throughout the room.

The living room shown on this page has a delightful, friendly atmosphere which invites us to tarry awhile. We feel at once that here

A typical living room in the Victorian period.

is a place one could read, rest, or visit with pleasure. The combination of white woodwork, bookshelves, cretonne, Oriental rugs, brass and copper fireplace accessories, and mullioned windows has been skillfully used to create a lovely room.

Now compare the two living rooms shown on these two pages. The first is a reproduction of a living room furnished in the Victorian style and during the 1890's would have been considered a very beautiful and elegant room. Judged by modern standards it does not seem so satisfactory. First of all, the windows with their disturbing curtain arrangement demand our attention. Next, the ostentatious gingerbread decoration on the furniture, the conspicuous pattern of the rug, and the figured wallpaper compete for our consideration. The only sources of artificial light in the room are the center chandelier and the lamp on the center table. This is hardly suggestive of comfort in the living room as we know it! The whole room reflects foolish and fussy ostentation which does not provide for visual comfort. The type of furniture is not conducive to physical comfort, nor is its arrangement convenient for the activities carried on in a living room.

Compare the effect in the Victorian room with that in the modern room shown on the opposite page. Notice the severity of line and the absence of decoration in all the furnishings. Notice, too, the

A living room furnished in the modern style.

group of windows admitting plenty of sunshine and daylight with only fish-net curtains to soften the glare. Modern furnishing is sometimes described as having dominant horizontal lines. This is evident in the shape of the window, the chairs and table, and the lamp shade.

> AN EXPERIMENT TO TRY. Look at the Victorian room shown on the opposite page for one minute and try to imagine yourself living in this room. Then try to express in words the feeling which this room arouses in you. Repeat this experiment with the modern room shown in the above illustration.

The two living rooms shown on pages 384 and 385 are both charming and very livable, but they differ in character. Either one may suggest to you the type of room that you would like to have for your own; either is a good choice. The room on the left-hand page is modern in design although the furniture is traditional in style. Here we see several of the characteristics of the modern house: plywood-wall finish, built-in shelves and cabinets, cove lighting, and extensive use of mirrored glass above the mantel shelf. The fireplace is modern in design. Altogether the effect has charming simplicity which suggests informal living in the twentieth century.

The living room shown on the right-hand page is completely tradi-

United States Plywood Corporation

In this living room a modern-style background is combined pleasantly with traditional-style furniture.

tional in character. The Colonial fireplace with a family portrait above, the chintz draperies, slip covers with flounces, and traditional furniture make an unusually pleasing combination. The forceful patterns of the drapes and slip covers do not "fight" nor do they compete with other furnishings for attention. The whole effect is elegant and luxurious.

> PLAN YOUR LIVING ROOM. 1. Collect pictures of rooms, furniture, samples of drapery, and slip-cover fabrics, and other pictures which will show the type of living room you would like to have.
>
> 2. Draw a large floor plan showing how you would place the furniture. Remember that you should use the floor plan for the living room in the house plan which you selected.
>
> 3. Add two or more sheets of drawings, samples, and pictures to your portfolio.

THE DINING ROOM. The dining room should express the same quiet, livable atmosphere which we find essential in the living room. Some authorities hold that since we spend a short time each day in the dining room, we can use stronger color and more exciting patterns with-

A spacious living room with an effect of luxury and elegance but with a decidedly livable quality.

out becoming bored. Others feel that three times a day for several years is sufficient time in which to become weary of wall paper with a strong figured pattern or a too brightly colored rug.

The dining rooms shown on pages 386 and 387 have a happy, pleasant atmosphere, yet they differ in character. The dining room on page 386 is informal, simple, and comfortable. The people who use it prefer the charm of simplicity. The dining room on page 387 is much more elegant and luxurious. The people who use this room prefer a more formal and "dressed-up" kind of effect.

Both rooms are in good taste. The first room depends for its beauty on furniture with simple, straight lines, chintz drapes, and walls with board paneling. The second room depends on the rather elaborate Chippendale chairs, Oriental rug, paneled walls, a Chinese table runner, and silk brocade drapes. There is no ostentatious display of silver or china in either of these rooms. The few pieces of china in the wall cabinet shown on page 386 add a pleasant decorative touch. A few good pieces of design and color can be used successfully on a sideboard or table. It is a good idea to remember that the dining room is a room to live in, not a display room in a china shop!

California Furniture Shops, Ltd.; C. R. Kayser and Co.

A dining room furnished in simple, informal style.

In many small homes today, the traditional dining room has been omitted as a separate room, and one end of the living room is used for serving meals. The picture on page 388 shows the dining-room end of a combination living room and dining room. This room is

A dining room furnished with more luxurious and formal furnishings than the room on the opposite page.

pleasingly furnished in modern-style furniture. The table, chairs, and sideboard shows a particularly nice harmony of rectangular shapes.

ONE'S OWN ROOM. Most of us have only a bedroom which we can speak of as our own room. Of course, we use the room for sleeping, but since it is the only room where we may secure privacy, many of us choose to use the room also for other activities, such as writing, reading, sewing, and similar occupations. The furnishings depend on how the room is used.

It hardly seems necessary to state that the primary function of the bedroom is to provide rest, yet we see so many bedrooms furnished in an unrestful manner that it seems necessary to emphasize this point. Again, we find it necessary to provide for visual as well as physical comfort. It is exasperating to lie in bed and find one's eyes compelled to travel ceaselessly back and forth over the diagonals or stripes of a patterned wallpaper. There is a real sense of discomfort and unrest in a bedroom where the furniture is too large for the room. It seems to crowd in upon one.

Modern-style furniture used in the end of a combination dining–living room.

Compare the bedrooms shown on the opposite page. The second bedroom illustrates nearly every possible mistake, increasing the feeling of unrest. The wallpaper has a brightly colored red-and-green pattern which forces our unwilling attention. The "Modern Colonial" dresser is clumsy and heavy. All the furniture is set askew, and the curtains are tied back in a fashion that adds to the general disorganization. Now look at the first bedroom and feel the contrast. The plain walls, and the furniture set straight and in scale with the size of the room, help to give a tranquil feeling. How much more joy and satisfaction we would get from this beautiful chest of drawers than from the ugly dresser in the other room.

These two rooms afford an interesting comparison in another respect. Can you imagine what type of person would live in each of these rooms? In which would you expect to find the person of refinement, culture, and good taste? In what way does the first room fail to express these qualities? We can scarcely fail to understand how a room expresses individuality as we compare these two rooms. The very selection and arrangement of things in a room are an outward

W. F. Whitney Co., Inc.

Two bedrooms which differ greatly in character and art quality. Top: A pleasing bedroom with Colonial-style maple furniture. Bottom: An ugly bedroom which expresses a most uninteresting personality.

expression of personality. The first room is ordinary and common-place, and the same description might be applied to its owner. It lacks that quality which we speak of as individuality.

Your choice of a furniture style will depend upon your personal preferences. If you like period styles you may choose Colonial furniture like that in the upper picture on the opposite page. If you like the modern style you may choose furniture like that in the lower picture. Either choice is a good one. When it is time for you to choose your furniture, you must decide what type gives you the most pleasure. This is one way in which you express your own individuality.

> PLAN THE DINING ROOM. 1. Collect pictures and samples of materials which you would use in furnishing the dining room of your dream house.
>
> 2. Prepare two or more sheets showing your decorating scheme.

GOOD TASTE AND PLANNING PRODUCE BEAUTY. The pictures on pages 392 and 393 show what happened in a small, dreary city apartment. A home economics class in Hunter College was asked to decorate an apartment on a limited budget. The bedroom had a tile floor, plain walls of uninteresting color, and an ugly steam radiator under the window with exposed steam pipes running to the floor above beside the window. The pictures show what careful planning and imagination can do.

The picture on page 392 shows a sleeping and reading corner designed with a bookshelf headboard and small chests at either side of the bed. An interesting print above the headboard and modern lights at either side give a delightful effect. The floral pattern of the chintz bedspread is repeated in the window draperies, as shown in the picture on page 393. This picture shows the beauty treatment that was given to the ugly radiator and pipes. Built-in units across the length of the wall give a feeling of width and space to the modest-sized room. The kneehole dressing table and storage cabinet have a twofold purpose: They save space and conceal the radiator and part of the pipes.

The picture on page 394 shows another room in the same apartment planned for the two children. The furniture was painted bright blue-green. A play–work table was made by placing a wooden plank on top of an old barrel. The double-hung curtains were made of unbleached muslin with bands of orange and blue-green. The beds have dark brown spreads.

Montgomery Ward; Hallmark Furniture

Modernage Furniture Corp.; Man-Low

Two bedrooms of contrasting styles. Top: Quaint charm revealed by Colonial style. Bottom: Simple severity expressed by modern style.

391

Tom Leonard; reprinted from Living for Young Homemakers

A sleeping–reading corner in an attractive bedroom.

The picture on page 395 shows a little girl's room equipped for play and sleep. Little folk as well as grownups like to have their own rooms furnished to suit their needs and interests.

The bedroom on page 396 is a modern style with a fine harmony of rectangular shapes. Rectangular form is emphasized in the furniture design and in the rubber-tile floor. The whole effect is one that is likely to appeal more to men than to women, probably because of the geometric motif.

> PLAN THE BEDROOMS. Collect pictures and samples of the materials you would use in your imaginary house. Make a separate plan for a bedroom, and write a description of the person who will occupy each room.

THE KITCHEN. Kitchens come last but are not least in our discussion of room furnishings. Everyone knows that the kitchen has an extremely important utilitarian value, but we sometimes forget that it can be a very beautiful room. The smooth, gleaming surfaces of

Tom Leonard; reprinted from Living for Young Homemakers

Another view of the bedroom on the opposite page, showing a useful built-in cabinet which hides an ugly radiator.

modern kitchen equipment, the lovely colors of linoleum and tile floors, and the modern, streamlined design of the furniture all contribute to the beauty and usefulness of the kitchen.

The two kitchens on page 397 have the same arrangement of sink, corner cabinet, and range, but other details of the furnishing are different.

The upper kitchen was designed as a jolly country kitchen. The colors are ironstone white and barn red. The floor is a brick pattern in red, and the walls are painted in a matching tone. The dead white of the cabinets, sink, range, and dishes contrasts sharply with the red background. A sawbuck table set with milk-glass goblets and blue-and-white dishes blends with the country theme. The double-hung curtains are made from red-and-white dotted Swiss.

The lower picture shows still another treatment of the same basic kitchen. Blue cabinets with blue-and-white chintz curtains and matching wallpaper create a tidy, New England atmosphere. The floor is blue plastic, and the base cabinets are white. A maple table,

A delightful room for sleeping, playing, and working when you are very young.

a wooden rocker, and rush-bottom chairs add to the quaint effect.

The two treatments of the same basic kitchen show the effects which are possible. Each of them creates a homey, comfortable atmosphere through the use of color and various accessories. It sometimes happens that the modern kitchen is left white and bare-looking because we are afraid to use anything that is colorful and interesting.

PLAN THE KITCHEN. 1. Collect pictures and samples of materials which you would like to use in your dream kitchen.

2. Add your kitchen plan to your portfolio.

A gay, livable room for a very young lady.

American Tile and Rubber Company

Perhaps the men in your family would like this bedroom.

DREAMERS CAN BE PRACTICAL. Dreams are worth working for and waiting for, but in the meantime we must deal with the realities of the present. Your dream house of the future is probably years away, and your home for the present may offer a real problem to be solved. You should not be discouraged because you cannot have everything you want at once, but be happy to work at making your present home more livable. You have learned much that should help you to tackle a decorating problem with success. You might begin by doing over your own room or with the consent of your parents refurnishing some other room in the house. Perhaps before many years you will establish your own home though you are not able to build the house of your dreams.

The following story of a young couple who were forced to live in a one-room apartment tells how they made it a very livable home.

ONE-ROOM APARTMENT—CONVENIENT, COMFORTABLE, AND BEAUTIFUL. The young couple who rented a one-room apartment despaired

(*Text continued on page 400*)

396

Two charming styles of furnishing for the same kitchen.

Reprinted by courtesy of Woman's Day
Magazine, copyright, 1951

*Top: Built-to-fit bookshelves and
desk make fullest use of space.
Left: "Before" photograph of
room's work end.*

Simplicity and interesting colors create this pleasant room.

The bed–sofa unit is shown closed for daytime use; also (bottom) pulled out to full size, with arms, cushions, and slipcover removed. Convenient storage bins hold extra bedding.

(Continued from page 396)

of ever being able to squeeze into it all the things that they would need. Besides the usual equipment of chairs, table, bed, and chests, they would need ample desk space, for the husband, a writer, worked at home.

Two built-to-fit pieces, one at each end of the long, narrow room, took care of two major necessities and at the same time made the room appear wider. Across the window end of the room, a desk was constructed in free flowing form from wall to wall, surrounding the radiator at one end, as shown in the picture on page 398, and tapering to a point at the other end, as shown in the color illustration opposite page 398. The radiator was concealed with a metal box cover. All available wall space between the fireplace and window and above the desk was used for bookshelves. Below the desk at the right a small chest of drawers to hold paper and supplies was made part of the supporting structure.

At the other end of the room a bed–sofa unit was built, with bookshelves across the top and a slanted support for the sofa cushions during the daytime. The bottom part of the cabinet allowed the bed to slide underneath so that only half of the bed is used as a daytime davenport. Convenient storage bins hold extra bedding, as shown in the lower picture on page 399.

A most pleasing color scheme of green walls, ivory woodwork, black furniture, and cretonne draperies and slip cover in tones of green-blue, yellow, and black make a handsome color effect. Accents of Chinese red in the mane and tail of the ceramic horse and in the zinnias add spice to the harmony.

This project in creating a livable home proves once more that ingenuity, imagination, and good taste are more important than an unlimited budget.

References for Further Study

GENERAL DESIGN AND
COLOR HARMONY

Cheney, Sheldon and Martha. *Art and the Machine*. McGraw-Hill Book Company, 1936.

Downer, Marion. *Discovering Design*. Reinhold Publishing Corporation, 1950.

Goldstein, Harriet and Vetta. *Art in Everyday Life*. The Macmillan Company, 1940.

Graves, Maitland. *Art of Color and Design*. McGraw-Hill Book Company, 1941.

Lee, Kathryn Dean. *Adventuring in Art*. Appleton-Century-Crofts, 1939.

Payant, Felix. *Create Something*. Design Publishing Company, 1939.

Smith, Janet K. *A Manual of Design*. Reinhold Publishing Corporation, 1950.

Van Doren, Harold. *Industrial Design*. McGraw-Hill Book Company, 1940.

INTERIOR DESIGN

Agan, Tessie. *The House: Its Plan and Use*. J. B. Lippincott Company, 1948.

Austin, Ruth E., and Parvis, Jeannette O. *Furnishing Your Home*. Houghton Mifflin Company, 1952.

Brown, Effa. *Designs for Living*. Halcyon House, 1942.

Burris-Meyer, Elizabeth. *Decorating Livable Homes*. Prentice-Hall, 1937.

Cobb, Hubbard H. *Make Your House a Home*. Houghton Mifflin Company, 1952.

Cooper, Dan. *Inside Your Home*. Farrar, Straus and Company, 1946.

Craig, Hazel Thompson, and Rush, Ola Day. *Homes with Character*. D. C. Heath and Company, 1952.

Davis, Mary Allen. *Principles of Window Curtaining*. U. S. Department of Agriculture, Farmer's Bulletin No. 1516.

Devieux, Mary, and Stevenson, Isabelle. *The Complete Book of Interior Decorating*. Greystone Press, 1948.

Erickson, Emanuel E., and Soules, Roy. *Planning Your Home*. Charles A. Bennett Company, 1938.

Genauer, Emily. *Modern Interiors —Today and Tomorrow*. Illustrated Editions Company, 1939.

Gillies, Mary Davis. *Popular Home Decoration*. William H. Wise and Company, 1940.

Goldstein, Harriet and Vetta. *Art in Everyday Life*. The Macmillan Company, 1940.

Hardy, Kay. *How to Make Your House a Home*. Funk and Wagnalls Company, 1947.

Lewis, Ethel. *Decorating the Home*. The Macmillan Company, 1942.

Judson, Jeanne. *What Every Woman Should Know about Furniture*. Frederick A. Stokes Company, 1940 (J. B. Lippincott Company).

Knauff, Carl G. B. *Refurnishing the Home*. McGraw-Hill Book Company, 1938.

Koues, Helen. *How to Be Your Own Decorator*. Tudor Publishing Company, 1938.

Merivale, Margaret. *Furnishing the Small House*. Studio Publications, 1940.

Miller, Duncan. *Interior Decorating*. Studio Publications, 1937.

Miller, Duncan. *More Color Schemes for the Modern Home*. Studio Publications, 1938.

Miller, Gladys. *Decoratively Speaking*. Doubleday and Company, 1939.

Miller, Gladys. *Furniture for Your Home*. M. Barrows and Company, 1946.

Murray, Walter. *Interior Decoration for Today and Tomorrow*. Murray and Gee, 1946.

National Board of the Young Women's Christian Association of America. *Decorating the Small Apartment*. Bradford Press, 1949.

Ogg, Elizabeth. *Decorating the Small Apartment*. Woman's Press, 1949.

Ornstein, J. A. *Paintbrush Fun for Home Decoration*. Greenberg: Publisher, 1944.

Patmore, Derek. *Modern Furnishing and Decoration*. Studio Publications, 1936.

Rutt, Anna H. *Home Furnishing*. John Wiley and Sons, 1935.

Schultz, Hazel. *Housing and the Home*. Appleton-Century-Crofts, 1939.

Storey, Walter Rendell. *Furnishing with Color*. Plantin Press, 1945.

Terhune, Florence B. *Decorating for You*. M. Barrows and Company, 1944.

Waugh, Alice. *Planning the Little House*. McGraw-Hill Book Company, 1939.

Wenham, Edward. *Old Furniture for Modern Rooms*. G. Bell and Sons, 1939.

Whiton, Sherrill. *Elements of Interior Design and Decoration*. J. B. Lippincott Company, 1951.

Wright, Mary and Russel. *Guide to Easier Living*. Simon and Schuster, 1951.

HISTORIC STYLES IN FURNISHING

Miller, Gladys. *Decoratively Speaking*. Doubleday and Company, 1939.

Pratt, Richard. *A Treasury of Early American Homes*. McGraw-Hill Book Company, 1949.

Whiton, Sherrill. *Elements of Interior Design and Decoration*. J. B. Lippincott Company, 1951.

EXTERIOR DESIGN

Erickson, Emanuel E., and Soules, Roy. *Planning Your Home*. Charles A. Bennett Company, 1938.

Gray, Greta. *House and Home*. J. B. Lippincott Company, 1935.

Newcomb, Rexford, and Foster, William A. *Home Architecture*. John Wiley and Sons, 1935.

Schultz, Hazel. *Housing and the Home*. Appleton-Century-Crofts, 1939.

Waugh, Alice. *Planning the Little House*. McGraw-Hill Book Company, 1939.

DESIGN AND COLOR IN GARDENS

Abbott, Daisy T. *The Indoor Gardener*. The University of Minnesota Press, 1939.

Better Homes and Gardens Garden Book. Meredith Publishing Company, 1951.

Bissland, James H. *The Rock Garden*. Hale, Cushman, and Flint.

Hottes, Alfred Carl. *Climbers and Ground Covers*. A. T. De La Mare Company, 1947.

Ortloff, H. Stuart, and Raymore, Henry B. *Garden Planning and Building*. Whittlesey House, McGraw-Hill Book Company, 1939.

Robertson, Florence Bell. *Planting Design*. McGraw-Hill Book Company, 1940.

Storm, Katharine and Arthur. *The Small Garden*. Frederick A. Stokes Company, 1939 (J. B. Lippincott Company).

FLOWER ARRANGEMENT

Arms, John Taylor, and Noyes, Dorothy. *Design in Flower Arrangement*. The Macmillan Company, 1937.

Biddle, Dorothy, and Blum, Dorothea. *Flower Arrangements for Everyone*. M. Barrows and Company, 1949.

Cary, Katharine T., and Merrell, Nellie D. *Arranging Flowers Throughout the Year*. Dodd, Mead and Company, 1938.

Conway, Gregory. *Flowers—Their Arrangement*. Alfred A. Knopf.

Dunlop, Hazel Peckinpaugh. *Let's Arrange Flowers*. Harper and Brothers, 1943.

Ferguson, Donita, and Sheldon, Roy. *Fun with Flowers*. Houghton Mifflin Company, 1939.

Gannon, Ruth. *Winter Bouquets with Color*. Studio Publications, 1949.

Hine, Mrs. Walter R. *New Flower Arrangements*. Charles Scribner's Sons, 1936.

Roberts, Patricia Easterbrook. *Flower Craft*. Crown Publishers, 1949.

Rockwell, F. F., and Grayson, E. C. *Flower Arrangement*. The American Guild and Doubleday and Company, 1948.

Rockwell, F. F., and Grayson, E. C. *Flower Arrangement in Color*. William H. Wise and Company, 1940.

Taber, Gladys, and Kistner, Ruth. *Flower Arranging for the American Home*. Macrae-Smith Company, 1947.

Watson, Margaret. *Arranging Flowers*. Studio Publications, 1941.

Prints of famous pictures can be secured from:

Art Aid Corporation, 40 East 49th Street, New York City.

Art Appreciation Publishing Company, Akron, Ohio.

Art Extension Press, Westport, Connecticut.

Art Institute of Chicago, Chicago, Illinois.

Associated American Artists, 711 Fifth Avenue, New York 22, N. Y.

Brown Robertson Company, 35 West 34th Street, New York City.

Colonial Art Company, Oklahoma City, Oklahoma.

Curtis and Cameron, Boston, Massachusetts.

Detroit Publishing Company, Detroit, Michigan.

Elson Art Publishing Company, Belmont, Massachusetts.

Living American Art, 315 Fourth Avenue, New York City.

Medici Society of America, 759 Boylston Street, Boston, Massachusetts.

Metropolitan Museum of Art, New York City.

Museum of Modern Art, New York City.

National Committee for Art Appreciation, Jersey City, New Jersey.

New York Graphic Society, 10 West 33rd Street, New York City.

Raymond and Raymond, 40 East 52nd Street, New York City.

Rudolph Lesch, Fine Arts, Inc., 225 Fifth Avenue, New York City.

Small casts of famous sculpture (suitable for home decoration) can be secured from:

Associated American Artists. 711 Fifth Avenue, New York 22, N. Y.

Boston Sculpture Company, Sudbury Street, Boston, Massachusetts.

P. P. Caproni and Brothers, 1914 Washington Street, Boston, Massachusetts.

Good art pottery for the home can be secured from:

Associated American Artists, 711 Fifth Avenue, New York 22, N. Y.

The Cowan Pottery, Rocky River, Ohio.

Frankoma Pottery, Sapulpa, Oklahoma.

The Hager Pottery, Dundee, Illinois.

Newcomb Pottery, Sophie Newcomb College, New Orleans, Louisiana.

Pewabic Pottery, Detroit, Michigan.

The Rookwood Pottery, Cincinnati, Ohio.

The Van Briggle Pottery, Colorado Springs, Colorado.

Index

405

407

35626

INVENTORY '80